Scandinavian Values

Religion and Morality in the Nordic Countries

EDITED BY

Thorleif Pettersson and Ole Riis

UPPSALA 1994

ACTA UNIVERSITATIS UPSALIENSIS
Psychologia et Sociologia Religionum
10

Printed with support from NOS-S

Abstract

Pettersson, T. & Riis, O. (editors). 1994. Scandinavian Values: Religion and Morality in the Nordic Countries. Acta Universitatis Upsaliensis. *Psychologia et Sociologia Religionum* 10. 212 pp. Uppsala. ISBN 91-554-3411-8.

The nine studies included in this collection focus on religious and moral values in the Nordic countries. As a general background to the subsequent studies, the first study investigates religious change in the Nordic countries during the period 1930–1980.

The following eight studies present empirical investigations of value systems among the Nordic people. These studies are based on data from the European Value Systems Survey. The first of these studies compares Scandinavian value systems to value systems from other cultural regions within Western Europe. The differences between Scandinavians and other West Europeans are found to be most noticeable in the case of religious and moral values. In the following studies, work values among Catholics and Protestants are compared, Scandinavian patterns of secularization and religious individualization are described, and religious differences between the Nordic countries are related to national identities and views on gender values. A study of Iceland shows Icelanders to be more religious than the other Nordic peoples.

This volume further includes a study of the effects of religious individualism on bio-ethical values and a study of secularization and value change, where qualitative interview data are used as as a complement to the EVSSG quantitative data. A final study focuses on value change and demonstrates a differentiated impact of generational population replacement on various value dimensions.

Key words: Religious values, Moral values, Work values, Secularization, Individualization, Value change, The EVS study, Scandinavia, Nordic countries.

Thorleif Pettersson, Department of Theology, Uppsala University, Box 1604, S–751 46 Uppsala, Sweden.

ISSN 0283–149X
ISBN 91–554–3411–8

Printed in Sweden 1994 by Gotab, Stockholm

Contents

Preface

The subject of this book is value systems among the Nordic people. These people belong to five independent countries, e.g. Denmark, Finland, Iceland, Norway, and Sweden, respectively, and are scattered over a large area. The Nordic people have common historical roots, and most of them are Scandinavians in linguistic and ethnic terms. Outsiders often regard the Nordic people as culturally homogeneous, whereas the Nordic people themselves tend to stress the differences among them in values and moods. At the same time, they often feel closer to each other than to people outside Scandinavia. Against this background, the main theme of this book is to present empirical studies of the similarities and differences in value systems among the Nordic people.

Values may be investigated in many ways. This study is based on the European Value Systems Study (the EVSSG study), one of the largest comparative survey studies ever carried out. In 1978, an international group of European academics formed a research group in order to make a comparative study of values in Western Europe. In 1981, the group succeeded in doing surveys in all the EEC countries. This comparative survey of values was a success and the study was taken up in many other countries, including the Nordic ones. In the late eighties, the research group endeavoured a new round, based on a slightly modified questionnaire, and in 1990 a second wave of the European Value Systems Study was carried out in almost all the countries of Europe, as well as in several non-European countries. Preparing the second round, the Nordic sociologists involved in the project formed a research group, which aimed at improved coordination of the Nordic value surveys and better integration of the Nordic data into the general European comparative analyses. The group was funded by the Nordic Foundation for Comparative Social Studies, NOS-S.

The European Value Systems Study covers an exceptionally wide range of subjects such as religion, morality, family, work, politics, etc. The choice of these issues was based on in-depth interviews concerning what people considered most important in their lives. The scope of the questionnaire reflects the broadness of the responses. Of course, the final questionnaire was not designed particularly for studying values among the Nordic people, and some of the questions are of less relevance to them. It is also possible that some topics which may be more relevant to Scandinavians have been left out. Nevertheless, the questionnaire provides a broad range of values, seldom found in a single survey study. The EVSSG data thus opens a broad range of comparisons, both between the various Nordic countries and between Scandinavians and other Europeans.

The studies included in this volume focus on religious and moral values. One reason for this choice is that these values seem to distinguish the value systems of the Nordic people. Nordic countries seem to be among the most secularized in the modern world. Also, Nordic countries tend to demonstrate a specific profile in moral values, i.e. strictness on social morality and permissiveness on private. Therefore, a focus on religious and moral values highlights some of the most characteristic features of Scandinavian value systems.

The EVSSG questionnaire reveals how people present their values and views to outsiders. The answers do not necessarily correspond with people's actual behaviour. This is, however, a minor problem, as the theme of this study is people's values, their ideals and wishes, rather than their daily-life acts. The EVSSG data obviously yields quantitative data on individuals' value systems. In order to shed additional light on the EVSSG results, one of the studies included in this volume uses qualitative value data as a correlate to the EVSSG data.

Most of the chapters of this book were originally presented as papers at a NOS-S-sponsored conference at Skalholt in Iceland. The papers supplemented each other so well that it was agreed to collect them into a publication. Pettersson and Riis were appointed as editors. That task has been light. We have only suggested some minor modifications, especially in order to avoid overlaps and to secure some unity of approach. The English texts have been subject to a critical revision by Dr. Simon Coleman, Cambridge. Otherwise, the authors were free to present their findings as they thought most appropriate.

Some understanding of the general Scandinavian religious context is necessary in order to read the findings correctly. Therefore, the first chapter summarizes a large project, which analyzed religious changes in the Nordic countries during the period 1930–1980. The results from this project, which was sponsored by NOS-S, were published in a two-volume report in the Scandinavian languages. Göran Gustafsson, who headed the project, has summarized the findings and brought them up-to-date in order to give a proper background to the findings of the EVSSG study.

The following chapter by Halman focuses on the peculiarities of value systems of the Nordic people. It covers the whole range of themes which are included in the survey. Thereby, it provides an important background to the following more detailed studies, which in various ways relate religious values to other value dimensions. Lindseth and Listhaug focus on the relation between religion and work values. Sundback pinpoints gender and national identity. Pétursson and Jonsson take up family values. Riis describes the patterns of secularization in Scandinavia, and Straarup analyzes the possible impact of secularization on the views of life and death. Combining the Swedish EVSSG data with qualitative value data, Hamberg discusses the relation between secularization and changes in various value dimensions. Pettersson rounds up the presentation with an analysis of the processes of value change in the Scandinavian countries. In all these studies, the relation between religion, social values, and morality, is illustrated in many important aspects.

Comparisons between the Nordic countries may be undertaken from different angles. The Nordic countries may be compared to other European cultural regions. This is the angle chosen by Halman and by Lindseth and Listhaug. One may also focus on the similarities in religious values among the Nordic people, as Riis does, or one may underline the differences, as Sundback does. To notice both similarities and differences does not necessarily reveal a contradiction. Comparing national distributions of responses, one commentator may stress that the averages are significantly different, whereas another may underline that to a large extent the distributions are overlapping. Furthermore, one may focus on a specific case and compare it with the other Nordic countries, as do Pétursson and Jonsson in their study of Iceland and Hamberg in her study of Sweden. One may also look for common European and/or specific Nordic processes of value change, as Pettersson does.

It is the hope of the editors that the set of studies presented in this volume may provide a better understanding of the identities of the Nordic people, both among themselves and among outsiders. In an era of globalization, it is vital to study the processes by which national and regional identities are maintained and/or changed. The Nordic countries are all subject to influence from outside, especially from Anglo-American culture. Still, some characteristic national and regional values seem to remain.

The authors represent all the Nordic countries. Norway is represented by Lindseth and Listhaug, who are at the University of Trondheim. Iceland is represented by Jonsson and Pétursson, who are at Haskoli Islands, Reykjavik. Finland is represented by Sundback, who is at Åbo Akademi. Denmark is represented by Riis, who is at the University of Aarhus, and also by Straarup, though at Uppsala University. Sweden is further represented by Hamberg and Gustafsson, at the University of Lund, and Pettersson, at Uppsala University. The only non-Scandinavian among the contributors is Halman, who is at the Catholic University of Tilburg, the Netherlands. As one of the leading EVSSG researchers, Halman was asked to participate in the work of the Nordic research group. We would therefore like to address a special note of thanks to him for his friendly advice during this project. A further note of thanks is directed to the NOS-S, which supported the Nordic research group, the Islandic data collection, the meeting which prepared this book, and the book's ultimate publication.

Uppsala and Århus, September, 1994
Thorleif Pettersson and Ole Riis
editors

GÖRAN GUSTAFSSON

Religious Change in the Five Scandinavian Countries, 1930–1980[1]

1. Introduction

A distinctive characteristic of religious conditions in the five Nordic countries is the large degree of similarity which exists. It is no doubt exceptional to find five adjoining countries in which religion has such similar levels of significance and where patterns of religious organization have been so alike as in Denmark, Finland, Iceland, Norway, and Sweden.

The similarities in religious life in the Nordic countries are visible primarily in the presence of a dominant state or folk-church in all five countries. These state churches also carry on some functions of a nonreligious character which afford them certain privileges not held by other churches and denominations present in the countries. In each of the five countries, about 90 percent of the population are members of the state church. The parishes, of which the churches are comprised, are territorial in nature with the result that every square inch of land in the Nordic countries is covered by a parish, and each individual person is tied to a particular parish dependent upon where one lives. Theologically, the Nordic state churches are Evangelical Lutheran and trace their position as state churches back to the Reformation which, itself, was rather parallel in the two state configurations – Denmark/Norway/Iceland and Sweden/Finland – which comprised the North at that time.

Furthermore, the Nordic countries have in common the appearance of various religious lay-movements during the nineteenth century. These movements met strong resistance from the worldly authorities, from the official churches and from the clergy. Much of the more intensive religious engagement present today in the Nordic countries stems from the organizations which emerged out of the nineteenth- and early twentieth-century spiritual revivals. These organizations vary in their relations to their particular state church. On the one hand, they can be characterized as free churches, originally in strong opposition to the state church,

[1] An article under the same title and principally with the same content as that in the first four sections of this article has been published by the author in *Comparative Social Research*, Vol. 10, pp. 145–181 (1987). The JAI Press Inc. has kindly given its permission for the publication of a revised and enlarged version of the original article.

as in Sweden. Or they might have developed into movements for foreign and domestic mission activities with certain ties to the state church, as in Denmark and Norway. Furthermore, these organizations might have become movements for spiritual revival within the state church as in the case of Finland and Iceland.

Against this background, it is not surprising that outside observers often view the five Nordic countries as unified with respect to religion and the five state churches as similar entities. In his *A General Theory of Secularization*, David Martin (1978) discusses what he refers to as a particular Scandinavian pattern of religious change. The outcome of this pattern is that the Nordic countries now have (Martin 1978, 59) a low degree of religious pluralism, little anticlericalism, high status for the clergy, low church attendance, a distinctive religious conservatism, and a clear intellectualization of religion. Further characteristics of the Scandinavian pattern, according to Martin, are the preservation of the state church system, the secularization of the educational system, and the insignificant role of religious political parties. Martin's Scandinavian pattern is a variation of the pattern which, according to him, characterizes Great Britain. The difference between the main example and its variation is in part that religious pluralism in Great Britain is greater than in the Nordic countries, and that British society does not as clearly differentiate between the church's social functions and religious functions as is the case for the Scandinavian societies. Furthermore, in the Nordic countries, Martin finds an example of what he calls "the beneficent circle" of religious change, and which he places in opposition to "the vicious circle" he observes, for instance, in France. The former is characterized as "where mutual fears do not accelerate and conflicts are not superimposed one to the other to the point where religion is part of one 'package' and irreligion is part of the other, there the beneficent circle is established" (Martin 1978, 17).

A more penetrating analysis of the Nordic countries reveals that the variations between the religious systems are as evident as are the issues of the general position of religion within the countries, and of the theological self-interpretation common to the state churches in Scandinavia.

A situation of structural similarities on the religious level is an ideal subject matter for comparative studies in the sociology of religion. There are, however, only a few studies of religion and religiosity which adopt an inter-Nordic approach. Apart from studies in church history of movements arising in the spiritual revivals (Thyssen 1969), and of the churches in the crisis- and war-situations of 1930–1945 (Larsen & Montgomery 1982), there is only one study (Lundby 1977) with a comparative sociology of religion perspective. It examines the amounts of time allotted by the Nordic national radio companies for religiously oriented radio and television programmes.

Despite the shortage of literature comparing religious conditions in the Nordic countries, there are, nonetheless, strong opinions about differences and the directions in which they point. One such common opinion is voiced in a textbook analysis of social conditions in the Nordic countries: "Secularization, that is to say, the successive dissolution of Christian beliefs and church activity, has progressed quite far in Denmark and Sweden, and to a lesser degree in Norway and Finland. This is related to the progress of secularization in the footsteps of urbanization" (Lindblad *et al.* 1972, 87).

2. A Cooperative Nordic Research Programme

When the Committee for Comparative Nordic Social Research (*Nordisk samarbeidsnemnd for samfunnsforskning,* NOS-S) made funds available in 1980 for a comparative sociology of religion research programme, the research group[2] that was constituted discussed whether any specific aspect of Nordic religion should be given priority for study above others. As in almost all research in the sociology of religion, the discussion focused on the concept of secularization. In particular, the ambiguity of the concept (see for instance Shiner 1967; Dobbelaere 1981) was challenging. Given the diffuse nature of the concept, secularization can variously be used to describe how religious institutions lose their nonreligious functions, how there occurs a general retreat from religion on a social or individual level, and how there occurs a shift within the religious sphere to values and means which are prevalent in secular society. However, given this diffuse nature, it is not always clear whether the various processes of change referred to as secularization are simultaneous or whether they point in the same direction. Against this background, the focus of the research group became clear: *The research programme was to cover a broad array of religious conditions and to study these conditions at different points in time.*

One advantage of the model chosen was that new, costly individual data did not need to be collected. It was not satisfactory, however, to work merely with official documents and collective data on the national level in order to clarify the legal and practical aspects of religion in the Nordic countries. In order to more clearly examine the conditions of religion as experienced by the people themselves, it was determined that the research programme should consider not only the *national aspect* and the *time aspect,* but also a *level aspect.* This would be carried out by looking at conditions on the national level as well as conditions within a local area in each of the countries. The local studies were to be concentrated on a moderately large town which had not undergone great changes during the period studied.

Despite the diffuse and ambiguous nature of the concept of secularization, its general usage points to a decline in religious belief and practice and a weakening

[2] In addition to the author, the research group consisted of one representative from each of the Scandinavian countries: Curt Dahlgren, Lund, Sweden; Knut Lundby, Oslo, Norway; Pétur Pétursson, Lund, Sweden (representative for Iceland); Ole Riis, Århus, Denmark; and Susan Sundback, Åbo, Finland.

of religious institutions within society. As a key concept, it was decided to use *"religious change"* instead of "secularization". The expression is more neutral than secularization and does not presuppose a given direction for all religious change, i.e. that religion and religious institutions are weakened.

As with "secularization", "religious change" occurs in various areas. It would have been possible in this comparative study to examine one or several limited focuses and do parallel studies in each of the five countries. The research group chose another strategy: *To study extensively different phenomena in each of the countries at three points of time in order to determine changes in the relevance of religion for society and culture, and also to consider changes in how, and to what degree, the individual encounters religion.*

The years 1938, 1958, and 1978 were chosen as the points of time for the comparisons. The choice of 1938 was made with thought to it being prior to the Second World War, yet somewhat removed from the economic crisis of the early 1930s. Twenty year intervals led to the years 1958 and 1978. It was desirable that one year (1958) should be included when the immediate effects of the war were no longer felt in the countries directly involved (Denmark, Finland, and Norway). The years chosen served more as markers than absolute points in the comparative study; the availability of data and material have necessitated adjustments by one or more years in some cases. Furthermore, it appeared unjustified to exclude relevant information of events after 1978 when it was clear that important changes had occurred later.

Whereas the choice of years for the comparisons was unanimous, the choice of variables with which to study religious stability and change led to lengthy discussions. From the outset there was consensus that both qualitative and quantitative variables would be included. However, the term "variables" was replaced by "indices". Entirely new material relative to certain conditions is used only in exceptional cases. Instead, the objective has been to present conditions and relationships which have already been documented to serve as indices of the position of religion at the given points in time. By means of grouping together a large number of such indices, it is possible to obtain an indirect measure of religious change. Viewed independently, each of the indices is perhaps somewhat imprecise. When viewed together – with several pointing in the same direction – they serve to indicate the presence of stability or change. More than 75 indices of religious change were discussed and initially compressed into five different groups. The groups were:

I. Indices of the official position of religion in society;
II. Indices of organizational change within religious institutions;
III. Indices of popular attitudes to, and participation in, religious activities;
IV. Indices of folk-religious conceptions and behaviours;
V. Indices of the relationship between religion and the cultural system in society.

Demerath's extensive article on "Trends and Anti-Trends in Religious Change" (1968), often neglected within the sociology of religion, which discusses a large number of possible measurements of religious change, was not available to the research group during the discussions of indices. The group later discerned that its own approach in many aspects was consonant with his ideas about appropriate indices of religious change.

Overview of the Indices of Religious Change

The initial categorization of the indices proved difficult to maintain, primarily because it was impossible to clearly distinguish between indices of type IV and V; the folk-religious conceptualizations are an integral part of the cultural system of society. The final version of indices comprised four groups with somewhat altered definitions. These are discussed rather extensively as an introduction to the presentation of the results of the comparisons.

Group I: The official position of religion and the relationship between religion and other institutions. This first group of indices focuses on the position of the folk-church as preserver and participant in a "civil religion" system, that is, the degree to which it represents the official religious ideology of society and the degree to which Christianity – as manifested by the folk-churches – provides a real or rhetorical legitimization of the functions of other social institutions. The position afforded the church and its representatives at national celebrations provides an indication of integration between religion and secularsociety. The same is true with reference to the relation between the Royal house or the presidency and the church as is the degree to which the opening of parliament is enjoined with religious elements.

Another aspect of the integration between church/religion and society centres on the legal protection given religious symbols and actions. This official protection can be exemplified by laws which concern the sacredness of Sunday and which grant holidays a special status by forbidding certain forms of entertainment. In this group of indices are included possible laws against blasphemy as well as the outreach of such religious protection: does it benefit only the official religion or does it apply as well to other denominations and faiths?

The Lutheran state churches have often played a role within institutions which are not primarily religious. The separation of these nonreligious duties is an example of functional specialization. Changes within three social institutions illustrate this process of differentiation and serve as indices of religious change. First, judicial institutions: is there an oath on the Bible and do court proceedings have any religious elements? Second, military institutions: what is the role of religion and the clergy within them? Finally, and perhaps most important, educational institutions: do religion and the church have a place therein not solely motivated by the dissemination of knowledge? Examples here are the presence of obligatory services in the school and the right of the clergy to control any school activities. The content of religious/Christian education was determined to belong to Group IV indices.

Religion and church can also maintain a position not mandated by law in the official life of society. This is especially true of the relation between religion and politics as evidenced by several indices. Are church and religion dealt with in the opening debates in the parliaments?; these debates are of great significance in all the Nordic countries. Another indicator is the extent to which religious leaders are elected to parliament. Finally, the appearance of special Christian groups within the political sphere as well as how the political parties – especially the Social Democratic parties so politically influential in all the five countries – treat church and religion in their party platforms are relevant indices of how religion and politics are interrelated.

The churches and denominations interact variously with different institutions. Furthermore, they are also a part (if small) of the social economy. As an indication of change in their relevance, one might consider their portion of the public economy. Related to this is that the administrative routines differ greatly among the Nordic countries and it is difficult to locate true comparisons. For this index, and for several others, especially Group II, the participants in the project focused primarily on information which could shed light on the development in their own countries. Of special interest are the trends of the individual countries which are then compared with trends in the other countries.

An indicator of the position religion maintains in society is also the proportion of all university students who are students of theology and/or the proportion of all degrees that are theology degrees. Another indicator of the value placed by society on the religious sector is obtained through a comparison of the relative salaries of clergymen.

Group II. The organizational development of the folk-churches. The heading of this group of indices embodies restrictions imposed rather late in the research. It would have been of interest to also examine the organizational development of the mission societies and the free churches in the different countries. However, a comparison of the organizational development is possible only to the extent one concentrates on the folk-churches. The other organizations have unique national characteristics and a separate research programme would be needed to study their comparative development.

A quantitative measure of the organizational development of the folk-churches can be observed in the territorial structuring process; has the number of parishes and dioceses increased or decreased? Has attention been given the movements of population from rural to metropolitan areas, and has the division in parishes been altered to be in accordance with the secular administrative division of the state?

Further questions, with reference to organizational development, focus on the appearance of new central organs with more or less specialized functions, whether or not new professional categories have appeared within the churches, and numerical changes within the different groups of the church-employed, priests, lay-workers, and administrative personnel.

Other, more qualitative indices concern aspects which, from an organization theory perspective, have to do with the folk-churches. Has the influence of lay-people increased through a process of democratization? Further, has there occurred a bureaucratization through increased control functions of the superior organs, and has there been a process of professionalization of occupations within the church such that special positions have been created for special goals? Integral to this question is the presence of increased or decreased stratification within the clergy. The development within these areas cannot be satisfactorily covered by series of statistics from the various countries. Within the research group, each participant has treated the issues raised here against the background of the special conditions of each of the countries in an attempt to present an overview of the organizational structure and change of the particular church. Ecumenical advances are treated in similar fashion as these, too, comprise measures of organizational change in the area of religion.

Under the heading "The organizational development of the folk-churches", two issues vital to most of the Nordic churches being studied are examined. One involves the relations between church and state, as indicated by the conditions surrounding the debate over the issue at different times, and if there have been governmental committees investigating the relations. This issue can easily be treated under the topic "The organizational development..." as well as under "The official position of religion...". Given this choice of classification, an ideologically loaded question has been somewhat diffused by treating it as a practical problem. In similar fashion, but with lesser reason, the issue of women priests – one raising much debate in several of the Nordic countries – is treated. Again, the presentation focuses on whether the issue was given attention at different points in time and if so, whether it was an issue of debate or of practical importance. While the categorization might be questioned, it can hardly be denied that it points to a form of religious change.

Group III: Participation in religious activities. It is in this group of indices that quantitative measures have been used to the greatest degree. Data on the national level were sought. Lacking this, regular time-series with information about a diocese or larger metropolis were substituted as acceptable sources as they reveal trends which are probably relevant for the entire country.

The most sought after indicators of religious activity are data covering church attendance and communion participation as well as baptisms, confirmations, and funerals within the folk-churches. An additional measure of attitudes toward religion, both within the folk-church and in other denominations, is the celebration of matrimony. The state of relations between the church and the general public can also be measured by the proportion of the population not being members of the folk-churches and the number who, during a given year, have left these churches.

In the Nordic countries, there are people who do not belong to the folk-churches but who are still religiously active, and people who, although they are members of the dominant churches, have the bulk of their religious activities in other churches and denominations. Therefore, the proportions of the population belonging to revival groups, free denominations and sects, and immigrant churches also provide important measures of the occurrence of religious participation.

Group IV: Religion in the sociocultural system. The fourth group of indices is intended to shed light on the ways in which the individual encounters, or at least might encounter, religion in daily life or on special occasions. Several of these indicators touch upon religious socialization and might easily have been included under a heading "The transmission of the religious tradition". The contents of the study plans for Christian/religious education on the mandatory school level are important sources of information for this category. In the transmission of religious tradition is included the educational activities carried on by the churches themselves; the objectives of the plans of study for confirmation classes have been treated as a separate indicator.

A mixture of both quantitative and qualitative measures sheds light on the position of religion in the press. The presence of and circulation rates for daily newspapers and periodicals published by churches and religious organizations are measures of the position held by the churches and denominations in cultural life. Also included in this group of indices – in a negative sense – is criticism of religion: have there been general discussions of religion or Christianity as such, or have any antireligious rallies taken place? Also, to what extent do antireligious organizations exist?

An easily accessible indicator of the position of religion in the sociocultural system is the space allotted to Christian evangelization by the state-controlled radio and television companies in the five countries. Since the occurrence of these programmes is highly repetitive, it was determined that a study covering two weeks of air time for each of the years covered by the study was sufficient.

The collection of material for use in this research project which proved to be most demanding was an examination of the daily and weekly printed media for the purpose of studying how religion is treated in media not related to religious institutions. The object was to determine both how much and which news material with religious/Christian connections was presented at different times, and whether and how religion was presented in material of an entertaining and informative nature. This was to give an indication of the extent to which matters concerning institutional religion were presented to the general public. However, examination of the daily and weekly press also revealed the extent to which these media, which vie in a highly competitive market, considered it within their purview to include themes of a folk-religious nature.

The weekly press material chosen for each country was two publications with broad family appeal. The study included all issues for the years concerned. The attempt was to register all material in which religion comprised a major part of the presentation and to use the following categorizations: (1) Christianity; (2) Other world religions; and (3) Supernatural beliefs. The material on Christianity was also divided according to whether it treated institutional religion or private religiosity. All fictional material and advertisements were excluded from the analysis.

The material from the daily press was analyzed following the same criteria as applied to the weekly press material. Included from each of the countries were: one Social Democratic newspaper, one newspaper with a conservative emphasis, and one newspaper generally accepted as liberal or culturally radical. For each of the three years of study two periods were chosen: the month of December and Easter week. The reason for these choices was to include, besides the general material, material from the two most celebrated Christian holidays, and to determine the extent to which changes occurred in the number of Christian symbols the publications contained.

Yet another form of material was collected from the daily press. This included the death announcements and necrologies which were carefully analyzed to determine the extent to which they gave expression to traditional Christian concepts (reference to God, Jesus, the Bible, or hymn book verses), folk-religious concepts of a life after death, or purely secular conceptions.

The Local Community Studies

A general idea behind the studies in the local communities was that the same indicators of religious change that had been used in the studies on the national level should also be used on the local level, and that the main years for the comparison should be the same at both levels. The indicator groups were transposed to take account of local conditions instead of national conditions; the new headings were:

Group I. The official position of religion in the local community and the relationship between religion and other institutions;

Group II. The organizational development of the parishes;

Group III. The supply of and the participation in religious activities;

Group IV. Religion in the sociocultural system of the local community.

A main problem with this part of the study was to decide which towns should be chosen for the comparisons. The directing principles for the choices were that the towns should have about 20 000 inhabitants at the beginning of the 1980s, that they should be dominant local centres and that they should have at least one newspaper of their own for the whole period under study. The selection processes ended up with Silkeborg on Jutland in Denmark, Vasa at the Gulf of Bothnia in Finland, Akureyri in the north of Iceland, Kongsberg, west of Oslo in Norway and Vänersborg in the western part of Sweden. Vasa has a far greater population than the ideal for the study but the opportunity to take account of the religious life among both the Finnish-speaking and the Swedish-speaking population in Finland in one and the same town was seen as a great advantage.

The Reports from the Research Programme

With the national indices reviewed above serving as a basis, the members of the research team each compiled accounts for their own countries of approximately 50 pages which were then published conjointly (Gustafsson 1985). These reports cannot be summarized here for various reasons, including the fact that they are already strongly condensed in their present form. The results contained in the separate chapters on religious change in the Nordic countries have, in part, been published elsewhere and in English. Many of the findings concerning the official position of religion in Finland (Sundback 1984), Iceland (Pétursson 1984), and Sweden (Gustafsson 1984), are collected in a volume entitled *The Church and Civil Religion in the Nordic Countries in Europe.* At the 1985 CISR (Conference Internationale de Sociologie des Religions) conference, results of studies from within the inter-Nordic research programme were presented concerning the religious mass media contents in Denmark (Riis 1985) and in Finland (Sundback 1987). The results from the studies of religious life on the local level have also been compiled in accounts of about 50 pages each and those reports were published in a special volume (Gustafsson 1987).

Sections 1–4 of this article have been published in volume 10 (1987) of *Comparative Social Research*. The original text took account of the principal changes concerning the laws with an impact on the religious system and concerning the organizational development within the churches taking place up to 1985. Vital changes after that year have here been inserted in the form of footnotes.

3. Results and Comparisons: The National Studies

The task at hand is to attempt to determine, from the descriptions of religious change in the five Nordic countries, if the countries are and have been as similar to each other as appearance would have it, and if the similarities have increased or decreased; also to determine if the changes in the different areas dealt with by the four groups of indices are parallel within and among the countries.

First, comparisons are presented which deal with conditions and changes related to Group II-indices, i.e. those describing "The organizational development of the folk-churches". This is followed by a discussion of the results of Group I-indices, those having to do with changes in "The official position of religion and the relationship between religion and other institutions". Group I- and Group IV-indices are to some extent similar, and it seems natural to follow the comparison of "The official position of religion" with the group of indices dealing with "Religion in the sociocultural system". The similarities between the two groups are seen primarily in how the Group I-indices consider the place of religious socialization in society, and how the Group IV-indices look at the contents of (formal) religious socialization. Finally, the countries are compared on the basis of the findings of Group III-indices: "Participation in religious activities". It is in reference to this group of indices that most of the quantitative data are found, and it is here that one most closely approaches individual religious behaviour.

The differences in "Participation in religious activities" can in part be viewed as contingent upon differences in structural conditions which were reviewed in the groups of indices covered earlier. However, this does not deny that, given a broader time perspective, "The official position of religion" and "Religion in the sociocultural system" are dependent upon the status of religion among the wider populace.

State and Church

As has already been observed, the dominant Evangelical Lutheran churches in all the Nordic countries are state churches, but with differing degrees of autonomy in relation to the state. This denotes that there exists an historically determined connection between church and state and, earlier on, that citizenship implied church membership. The system with a state church means to this day that the state authorities, through various political or administrative institutions, carry out a greater or lesser part of the decisions concerning church matters such as appointments of bishops and the determination of liturgical forms. During the twentieth century, the churches themselves have increasingly attempted to play-down their being state churches and instead emphasize their status as folk-churches, i.e. churches who construct their identity on the fact that almost all citizens in the actual nation are members. As folk-churches, they mean that they have to render religious services to all people, both the religiously active minority and the dominant portion for whom church-membership is basically a formality.

The most stable relationship between state and church is observed in Denmark, where no changes in relations have occurred during the past 50 years. To be sure, state-authorized commissions have on two occasions studied questions concerning the organizational structure of the Folk-church, but without questioning the state church system. With the exception of some far-right and far-left parties, the Danish political system is in agreement that the Folk-church should remain a state church. It is vital in connection here to note that the Social Democratic Party presently supports the preservation of the Folk-church/state union and, furthermore, that the Danish parliament must have the final responsibility in determining the framework for the church's activity.

The question about the relations between church and state has not received any comprehensive treatment in Iceland yet. The situation is such, however, that there appeared to be stronger political support of the church as a state church toward the end of the period of study than was evident earlier in the period. Furthermore, the Church of Iceland has become more autonomous in internal matters following the introduction of a Church Assembly late in the 1950s.

Norway was the first of the Nordic countries to appoint a commission to study self-government by the Church, albeit within the framework of the state church system. In part, against the background of the open strife between the church and the occupying forces during the war, the commission proposed in 1948 the formation of a representative church council (*kirkeråd*) with certain governing functions. The proposal was defeated following opposition by the Social Democratic Party. Toward the end of the period being studied, the Social Democrats – then in the position of power – arranged for changes in the organization of the Church of Norway. Among other things, the proposal called for an annual Church Assembly within the framework of a preserved state church system. This even reflects a change in attitude of Norway's largest political party toward church and religion. The development culminates in the association of the fundamentals of the welfare state with Christian ideals, the responsibility of the state for the conditions in the church, and that freedom of religion should include practical possibilities for everyone to have access to services.

In Sweden, the state church issue has been more persistent than in the other Nordic countries. Several state commissions were appointed between 1958 and 1981 to deal with the problem. Following a compromise involving the major political parties, parliament passed a law in 1982 called "The Church of Sweden Law", which can only be altered by an act of parliament. It calls for, among other things, the governmental appointment of bishops, but it also prescribes that the elected Church Assembly, in which the government has no representation, has the exclusive right to decide on matters of faith and ritual. Through this 1982 law, the Church of Sweden has become more independent of the state but not necessarily further removed from the political system since the political parties increasingly engage themselves in the elections for the Church Assembly. The Swedish Social Democratic Party has expressed less concern in recent party programs with religious questions than its Nordic counterparts; however, it is important to note that the demand for the separation of church and state was eliminated from the platform in 1960.

Finland is unique among the Nordic countries with relation to the church and state relations issue. The country has two state churches: a small Orthodox Church in addition to the Lutheran Church. But, more important, the Finnish Evangelical

Lutheran Church has long enjoyed a broad autonomy from the state particularly in the decision-making functions granted the Church Assembly of which all the bishops are members. Also particular to Finland is that the Finnish folk-church maintains the population records only for its own members and not, as the churches in the other countries, for members and nonmembers alike.[3] The question of church and state relations arose late in Finland with the initiative coming from within the church. A recent proposal grants the church an even greater degree of autonomy within a preserved state church system through a demarcation of church and state functions and by limiting the areas in which parliament and Church Assembly decide jointly. The political parties in Finland, including the Social Democratic Party, have displayed less interest in stating where they stand, principally vis-à-vis the state church, than is seen in the other Nordic countries, and the demand to abolish the state church system has disappeared from the Social Democratic Party platform.

In summary, the differences between the statuses of the state churches in the various countries have increased rather than decreased. In the countries where the churches early on enjoyed a greater (Finland) or lesser (Sweden) degree of autonomy they have evolved toward increased self-determination whereas very little has happened in Denmark where the Folk-church remains closely bound to the state. Initially, Norway's situation resembled that of Denmark, but it is becoming more like Sweden, as is Iceland, particularly in reference to the autonomy of the folk-church within the preserved state church system. There is a tendency toward increased political party engagement in the churches to the degree that state organs disengage their influence on certain levels. The political parties exert themselves through the adoption of church policy programs and/or through engagement in general elections for the decisive bodies of the parishes. Due to the Church Assemblies themselves being wholly or partially chosen through indirect elections where the representative bodies of the parishes have voting rights, the Church Assemblies attain, in part, a political party composition. Tendencies in this direction are clearer in Sweden than in Finland.

The Ordination of Women

The development of a further measure of religious change, that of women priests and the attention the issue has received, appears to be connected to the evolution of church and state relations. The two countries in which the state church system is least challenged, Denmark and Iceland, got their first women priests in 1948 and 1974, respectively. The resistance to ordaining women to priesthood was short-lived in these countries. Norway was, in fact, first (1938) to give women the right to

[3] After 1991 all the population registers in Sweden have been administered by the local tax authorities.

serve as priests, but not until 1961 were women ordained and, no doubt due to continuing resistance from within the church, the number of women priests remains small.[4]

In Sweden, where the Church Assembly might express the opinion of the church but where parliament served as decision-maker, women were granted the right to be ordained priests in 1958 following a partial breakdown of resistance within the Church Assembly. The issue of woman priests, who at present represent a significant proportion of the clergy, is still a controversial issue within the Church of Sweden. In Finland, the question of the ordination of women is strictly a Church Assembly question, but the majority necessary for change was not reached before 1986. The issue in Finland has not grown to the dimensions that it has in the Church of Sweden. The in-between position with church representatives who could express an opinion concerning the ordination of women, but who lacked decision-making powers, appears to have been the structure which generated the most opposition to the kind of religious change that the ordination of women represents.

The Number of Parishes and Priests

Among the issues over which the state has maintained a decisive influence in all five Nordic countries, is the division of the countries into dioceses and parishes; how many of each there should be and, except for Finland, how many and which positions there should be for the clergy. Between 1938 and 1978, the Nordic countries experienced extensive population growth and a general concentration of the increases was in the capital city regions and other heavily urbanized areas. As a result of these increases, Norway, Finland, and Denmark each gained one or more new dioceses. However, no such divisions have taken place in Iceland or Sweden. The number of parishes has increased due to the division of heavily populated parishes in Iceland as well as in Sweden, Norway, and Denmark, while the number has decreased in Finland. In all the countries the changes are small, and the efforts made in preserving the territorial division into parishes, which in rural areas was often determined in the Middle Ages, is a phenomenon common to the Nordic countries.

The average population per parish has increased in all five countries (see Table 1). The average parish in Finland is now ten times larger than in Iceland, whereas the differences between the other countries are minimal. Between the years 1938 and 1978, there occurred a turnover in parishes; small parishes were combined and new ones have appeared in urban areas. The most radical reform took place in Reykjavík which in 1930 was one large state church parish but which has since been apportioned into 10 parishes. As seen in Table 1, parishes in Finland have considerably larger populations than those in the other countries.

[4] In 1993 Norway became the first of the Nordic countries to appoint a woman as bishop.

Table 1. Inhabitants per parish and per parish priest 1938 and 1978.

	Per parish		Per parish priest	
	1938	1978	1938	1978
Denmark	1 850	2 500	2 300	2 700
Finland	6 100	7 300	3 450	3 500
Iceland	700	750	1 200	2 000
Norway	2 900	3 700	4 000	3 850
Sweden	2 700	3 100	2 250	3 350

There is no doubt a connection between the size of the parishes in Finland and the fact that the parishes have developed organizationally much more there than in the other countries.

Also directly comparable are the data on the number of inhabitants per parish priest in the different countries (see Table 1). In common for Denmark, Iceland, and Sweden, is that the concentration of priests has lessened; this is particularly true of Sweden and Iceland. Iceland, however, still distinguishes itself as the country where priests have the smallest average number of parishioners, although the concentration of priests has increased in Norway. At present there is a division into groupings; on the one side Denmark and Iceland, and on the other Sweden, Finland, and Norway. It should be noted, however that the voluntary Christian organizations in Norway, which work in conjunction with the folk-church, employ as many priests as there are priests with parishes. The low concentration of clergy in Finland is at least partly compensated for by the large number of theologically educated, but not ordained, employees in the church who carry out social and educational services. It would thus appear that the Church of Sweden is the one with the smallest number of qualified personnel and the one, relatively speaking, with the smallest workforce for services to parishioners.

Tendencies in the Organizational Development of the Churches

The fundamental structure of the folk-churches of all the Nordic countries has remained unaltered. However, between the highest level (the church board and/or a department in the government office) and the grass-roots level (the parish) there has occurred an extension of both the legal and the voluntary organizational structure during the period examined in this study. Denmark is the exception in this case in that the largest organizational change concerns a semi-representative institution (*provstiudvalg*) on the level between the diocese and the parish; it has been given increased economic duties. In Norway, the organizational development until the early 1980s was mainly concentrated in the establishment of a body where the leaders of the diocese councils could meet. During the 1980s, the Church of Norway has undergone vast organizational changes.[5] The most important change for the Church of Iceland concerns the establishment of the Church Assembly mentioned earlier, and the founding of a central economic institution to be instrumental in a further organizational development.

During the period under study, the establishment of several legally nonregulated cooperative bodies comprised the most important aspect of church development in Sweden. In addition, the bureaus within the Church of Sweden responsible for mission, evangelization, lay-work, and so forth, received further duties and additional personnel. A service institution was established for the parishes in each of the dioceses on the diocese level; legally nonregulated representative councils were instigated. More important, however, was the pressure-group type organization to which the parishes bound themselves and which had become a real power structure within the church at the end of the period studied. Also in Sweden, the 1980s brought about considerable organizational change for the Church on the national level resulting from the adjustments in the church and state relations.[6]

Within the Evangelical Lutheran Church of Finland, organizational development began early in the period being examined. During the first half of the period, a Board of Directors for the church was appointed and a general budget department was instigated. In addition, the truly powerful Convention of Bishops, strengthened with some lay-representatives, came into being. As the result of an early 1970s reform, the Church Assembly meets on an annual basis, the Board of Directors has become still more powerful, and there has been an expansion of the organization of special institutions. On the diocese level, representative bodies have been established.

The conclusion of this description is that the organizational differences between the folk-churches of Denmark/Norway and Sweden/Finland remained unchanged until the 1980s and have increased since then. Insofar as church organization is concerned, Iceland now more nearly approximates Sweden than Denmark which, until 1918, heavily influenced Iceland's administrative development.

A comparison of the degree of democratization of the Nordic church organizations is difficult due to the various meanings often attributed to the term democratization. The concept may imply the extension of voting privileges in elections to various church institutions, that representative bodies are implemented, that existing institutions are given a more representative composition, and that the parish priest does not automatically serve as chairman of certain committees. If there is a parliamentary democracy and the government departments have a strong influence over the church, as has occurred in Denmark and Norway and, in part, in Iceland,

[5] The changes of the organizational structure has ended up with the creation of a representative body on the national level (*Kirkemøtet*) as well as of a central administrative board (*Kirkerådet/Mellomkirkelig råd*) with many staff members.

[6] An overview of the changes is given in Gustafsson 1990.

there is one kind of influence of members over the church. Sweden and Finland enjoy a different form of member influence through the elected Church Assembly and through the specially elected representative bodies in the parishes. Both the aforementioned forms entail limited influence from the clergy. Against this background, it would be difficult indeed to compare the process of democratization within the five folk-churches of the Nordic countries.

The establishment of the Church Assembly in Iceland (1957) and the increase in the proportion of lay-representatives in Church Assemblies in Finland (1973) and in Sweden (1951)[7] at the cost of clergy representation has led to increased lay influence over the decision-making structure of these churches. An obvious example of the democratization process in Finland is also the discontinuation in 1954 of graduated voting rights in the parish elections. In Sweden, the 1961 law regulating the organizational structure within the parishes clearly limited the influence of the priest in the local church council. In common for both Sweden and Finland is the parish representation at the diocese conferences which came into being following the Second World War. Little has occurred in Denmark which can be described as a democratization of the local and regional church institutions.

To speak of tendencies in the direction of increased bureaucracy during the period under study is also contingent upon choice of definitions. The older structure characterized by its departmental control (Denmark/Norway), or by influential cathedral chapters is not far removed in the handling of church affairs from what is often associated with classical definitions of bureaucracy. The development of a comprehensive church organization with specialized institutions, such as has occurred in Finland and as is presently happening in Sweden and Iceland, may also imply bureaucratization tendencies. The 1971 decentralization of various decision-making functions in Denmark no doubt entailed a debureaucratization of the handling of church matters. A form of bureaucratization not dealt with here but one which is perhaps more meaningful than the "sociological" bureaucratization tendencies to those seeking help from the church, is the extent to which the priests' time and availability have been regulated.

Different forms of job-differentiation might be seen as an aspect of a broad conceptualization of bureaucratization. Differentiation of the offices of the clergy, i.e., the institution of specialized pastoral functions, is on the increase in all the countries. This tendency appears more clearly in Norway and Finland than in Iceland and Sweden where, as in Denmark, most priests with special ministerial functions, such as prison and hospital chaplaincies, carry on these functions as a part of their ordinary parish pastoral duties.

Yet a further form of differentiation appears when the original diffuse role of the priest is limited by other functionaries within the parish who assume some of

[7] The Church Assembly in Sweden has no seats reserved either for the bishops or for the rest of the clergy since 1983.

the traditional duties of clergymen. These tendencies are least prevalent in Denmark and Iceland (with their higher concentrations of clergy), observable in Norway and Sweden, and very manifest in Finland. This differentiation can lead to the formation of a hierarchy among the employees of the parish.

The "old" church exhibited an obvious economic hierarchy among priests. Attempts in all the countries to even out salaries should have decreased the differences in economic status between the higher and lower echelons of the clergy. However, the organizational development may have led to new forms of hierarchy within the clergy. In all the countries, the deanery, the level between diocese and parish, has become a more significant being, in some of the countries also associated with various representative bodies. In this manner, the deans have gained a more clearly defined position between the bishops and the ordinary parish priests.

The increased number of board positions at the national level in the churches in most of the countries has resulted in a situation where some priests have several assignments of this type while others have no assignments at all. Therefore, priests who share the same formal level within the church hierarchy often find themselves on different levels related to the centre of power within the church. The outcome of this development should have given the bishops greater significance. The "old" bishop maintained an unchallenged position in his own diocese but had little influence in the national church as such. The "new" bishop, on the other hand, enjoys a more rationally, rather than traditionally, legitimated authority in the diocese while also maintaining a certain amount of influence on the national level in different institutions of both a formal and voluntary nature.

One might also point to a countertrend in the process of differentiation and hierarchicalization. In several of the Nordic countries a revision of the liturgy is taking place. In the proposed new orders of worship services, laymen are given a more active role, for example in scripture reading, than was allowed them in the old orders. The once clearly marked difference between priest and layman within the church has thus become less clear.

In sum, one can see obvious changes in the Nordic folk-church organizational structure except within the Danish Folk-church. The majority of the indicators reveal the greatest changes in Finland. The changes have been somewhat less in Iceland and Sweden and even less[8] in Norway. It might be concluded that the organizational differences between the Nordic folk-churches, already large at the beginning of the period under study, increased during the period. During the 1980s, however, there were certain tendencies toward convergence.

[8] This only holds true up to 1985.

The Economic Resources of the Churches

A factor, significant for the churches' internal organizational development and of importance for changes in types of activities, is the economic framework within which the churches exist. Attention has not been given to that portion of church economy arising from real-estate ownership or voluntary contributions; only the resources attained through parish taxes or its counterparts are considered here. The information in the national reports shows how the folk-church portion of the public domain has developed and how the resources have changed when inflation is controlled.

Compared with the differences between the Nordic countries examined in the previous section, the parallels for changes in the economic position of the churches are large. For each of the countries, the folk-church portion of the national budget or of the municipal tax funds has largely decreased. In other words, the activities of the churches have not increased in line with other public-sector activities. The general economic expansion in the Nordic countries, which took place during most of the period studied, meant, however, greater resources for the churches even with allowances for inflation. The growth was especially strong from 1960 to 1980.[9]

The increased resources, neither reflecting increase in population nor increased employment to carry out the churches' religious activities, might also have aided the churches' non-religious activities, such as planning and caring for cemeteries and maintaining population records. The resources might also have been used for the churches' extensive building projects, for increases in salaries, to recompense those who earlier worked on a voluntary basis, or to buy announcements in newspapers. Irrespective of how the resources were used, it might be assumed that the economies of the churches have become increasingly integrated with the national economies of the respective countries and that they more than ever have been influenced by circumstances outside their own area of control.

The salary development might also be considered a part of the church economy. Already, at the beginning of the period under study, there was a movement away from the older system whereby the priest was recompensed through the products from a farm. Residency in special parsonages was, and still is, a survival of this old system. The development of salaries for the priesthood is characterized by a levelling-out of the differences in pay for low- and medium-level positions. There is a clear tendency toward an improved economic position for the priesthood in Denmark. In Sweden, no change has occurred when comparing bishops to higher civil servants and vicars to other civil servants with an academic training. Much of the same is true for Iceland as well. In comparison, salaries for the priesthood have fallen behind those of other civil servants in Norway, and in

[9] The integration of the economy of the folk-churches with the general public economy has been clearly demonstrated in the 1990s when at least the churches in Finland and Sweden are facing real economic problems.

Finland, one can also detect somewhat of a decrease in the financial status of the priesthood. Thus, the development is in different directions, and there does not appear to be any correlation between salaries and the internal organizational development of the churches or with available resources. Perhaps the reason is that salaries for the priesthood in most of the countries are determined by national bodies in which the churches have little or no influence.

Ecumenical Activities

Changes relative to ecumenical activity have received little attention among the indices of religious change in the research project. As for Sweden, it is difficult to refer to any significant development of organized ecumenical strides for the period under study. Yet, it is believed that attitudes toward ecumenical activity have changed. By 1938, ecumenical relations involving the Church of Sweden and cooperative ventures among various free-church denominations had taken shape. Since then more churches and denominations have been participating in ecumenical work in Sweden. Finland's Ecumenical Council, clearly dominated by the Evangelical Lutheran Church, began in 1972; at about the same time a similar council was initiated in Iceland. Norwegian ecumenical contacts have mainly been on an informal level and have never involved all churches and denominations. The Catholic Church, for example, was not invited to participate when the discussions about a Norwegian Christian Council started in the 1970s.[10] The problem in Denmark has been the lack of a definite organizational level in the Folk-church from which it can establish contacts with other churches and denominations.[11]

It appears that both the denominational structure and the relations of the folk-churches to the state have influenced the development of ecumenical activity in the Nordic countries. In comparison with other organizational indices, there is a difference insofar as Sweden has both charted the course and gone further than Finland in the area of ecumenical relations. On the domestic level, it might be concluded that the developments are in the same direction in all the Nordic countries. This is even more the case in their relations at the international level.

Religion in Official Contexts

It is difficult to conceive of a country with a state church where the church and state powers do not interact and support each other in the official realm. From an historical perspective, one could point to many examples of such reciprocal legitimation. The historical examples, however, are more convincing than are the recent

[10] The Norwegian Christian Council was organized as late as in 1992. The Church of Norway, the Catholic Church and several of the free churches were among the constituents but the second largest religious organization in Norway, The Pentecostal Movement, is not a member of this council.

[11] In 1989 an ecumenical council was established in Denmark.

examples from the Nordic countries. The external changes in the religious legitimation of the power structure and the nation during the period being studied were not extensive, and, to the extent such changes occurred, they have doubtless been understood as changes in an obsolete rhetoric. An illustration of this is the exclusion of the phrase "by the grace of God, Sweden's King" from the Swedish constitution of 1974.

There is an observable difference between the three monarchies (Denmark, Norway, and Sweden) and the two republics (Finland and Iceland). As for the former, the constitution stipulates that the Head of the State shall be a member of the respective state church, which is not the case for the latter. This does not hinder the President of Iceland from being the formal head of the folk-church nor does it keep the President of Finland from using his personal influence in appointing persons to church offices.[12] The connection between state and religion is demonstrated by the special worship service held at the opening of parliament in each of the five countries. In Norway the opening service was the responsibility of the church and not parliament; it was discontinued during the 1980s.

Glimpses of a religious legitimation of the nation are caught in the Christmas and New Year talks given by the Heads of States or Prime Ministers in most of the countries, and even more so on national holidays. The celebrations vary from country to country but religion retains a prominent role. The National Day celebrations are most sacred in Finland, least in Denmark. The newly established National Day in Sweden appears to have assumed the same voluntary semireligious character as the observation of National Days in Norway and Iceland. In conclusion, there is an observable connection between church and state/nation in the North, but in all five countries the coupling is unassuming.

The state can both respect and protect religious values by, among other things, legally forbidding gatherings on Sundays and sacred holidays and by suppressing aggressive speech and writing against religion and religious conceptions. Except for Iceland, there is a tendency toward more liberal regulations regarding entertainment on Sundays and religious holidays. In Sweden, and particularly in Finland, the calendar has been secularized through the realignment of certain holidays to always fall on Saturdays or Sundays.[13] While the laws against blasphemy in Sweden have been repealed, no comparable changes have occurred in the other Nordic countries.[14] However, laws against blasphemy are apparently rarely enforced in any of the countries.

During the period being studied, religious freedom has been expanded and codified in Norway and Sweden. Denominations and churches other than the

[12] The position of the President in relation to the Evangelical-Lutheran Church will be weakened in a new Church Law under discussion in the 1990s.

[13] From 1992 the Epiphany and and Ascension Day have resumed their traditional days in the calendar and are celebrated as public holidays.

[14] In the 1990s the laws against blasphemy have been abolished in Finland.

folk-churches have been granted semiofficial status particularly by giving them the right to perform marriages. A tendency toward expanding freedom of belief to include churches and denominations other than the state church and religions other than Christianity, is visible in legislation in Norway, Denmark, and Iceland, all of which have laws against discrimination on the basis of faith. A change in the same direction has occurred in the press laws in Sweden. From this it might be concluded that state protection of Christianity and the regard granted to specifically Christian conceptions has decreased in the North, and particularly in Sweden.

Religion in the Judicial and Military Systems

Changes in religious legitimation within the judicial and military defence institutions have been given special attention. The role of religion in the judicial systems of the different countries varies sharply. The Swedish legal code still includes advice to judges concerning the connection between religion and law from the Reformation. Special religious services are held every year for court members[15] and until 1975, the oath taken by witnesses could have a religious content. Finland is similar to Sweden, but has retained the religious oath and has made the court services optional. Denmark and Iceland no longer have counterparts to these traditions in Sweden and Finland, and in Norway, the religious aspect of the witness oath was recently discontinued. Despite these differences, some similarities exist. Paradoxically, it is in Finland and Sweden, the two countries which exhibit the greatest degree of freedom between the church and state, where religion, at least rhetorically, continues to give its legitimation to the judicial system.

The formalization of freedom of religion in Sweden, Norway and, in part, Finland, has been given concrete expression in the discontinuation of the requirement to participate in worship services while serving in the military. At the same time, however, in those countries with a military defence, there has been an expansion of the office of chaplain. With the exception of Denmark, the countries parallel each other in this area, though Finland has gone further in developing the role of the military chaplain. This development might be seen in the light of what was discussed earlier concerning the differentiation of the role of the clergy. These changes may also be considered in view of a general change in attitude toward religion. From being an integral part of the collective, religion has become something for which many people feel a need and for which society has taken on the responsibility, even though it belongs more to the private than to the public sphere.

[15] These services have ceased to be obligatory but they are still arranged for many of the courts.

Religion in Public Education

Public education in the Nordic countries was originally a confessional education. Church and school were administratively intertwined and Christian education was dominant in the schools. Prior to the period of time being studied here, there existed a large degree of conformity between the countries. Throughout the decades, however, the relationship church and school has gradually been dissolved and the religious educational material has changed.

The process of change began first in Sweden where the catechetical-dominated education was formally replaced in 1919 by a plan of study which placed the Bible in the centre of teaching and with an emphasis on the ethical teachings of Jesus. Two hours per week were devoted to the study of Christianity. Somewhat later, in 1930, and lasting to the 1950s, action was taken which resulted in the termination of all administrative relations between the church and the schools. The 1919 plan of study was, in principle, in effect until 1969 when Christian education was replaced by religious education, including also the study of religions other than Christianity. The hours formally allotted to religious education have remained unchanged although the amount of religious education for the pupils has increased, along with the increase in the number of years spent in education on the whole. The latest plan of study (from 1980) integrates religious education with other socially-oriented subjects, which allows for a more experience-focussed education than did the earlier plan of study, which emphasized existential questions and which prescribed an objective approach by the teacher.[16]

A development, somewhat parallel to that occurring in Sweden, took place in Iceland where the changes occurred in an atmosphere of broader understanding between the church and the schools than was the case in Sweden. The local parishes' responsibility for education ceased in 1926. The same year saw the emergence of a plan of study with an emphasis on the Bible and church history. Since then, involvement of the clergy has further decreased. The number of hours allotted to religious education has remained unchanged since 1926, even following the school reform of 1974. Presently, even with the attention given to other world religions, the significance of Christian education has increased given the new objectives set for the schools.

In Denmark, the public school responsibilities of the clergy were limited in 1933 and discontinued entirely in 1975. A plan of study from 1937, which in essence prescribed an evangelical education "on the foundations of the folk-church", remained in effect until 1975, when a plan of study was adopted to provide pupils with knowledge of Christian existential questions and to prepare them for reaching independent decisions on religious issues. The number of hours allotted for religious education has decreased to where it is lowest in the Nordic countries.

[16] Several studies have documented that the religious education does not get the number of lessons in the schools that it should have according to the plan of study.

Changes in the status of religious education in Finland did not begin until after the Second World War. The Catechism was the text most used until the end of the 1930s, and as many as four hours per week were allotted to Christian education. The hours were decreased by half during the 1950s and have further decreased since. Parallel to these developments might be noticed the decreased influence of the national church over the contents of the texts used and, on the local level, the disappearance of clergy control over the education. The teaching has in principle remained confessionally Lutheran despite the emphasis on orientation rather than indoctrination. The study of other religions has been included in later plans of study so as to "create an environment in which other world religions might be experienced as holy".

In Norway, the time allotted for religious education remained at two hours per week from 1939 to 1980. As for Sweden and Iceland, religious education has retained its number of hours in the schools; but, the time spent in school has increased. The influence of the church and clergy over education has had a development similar to that in the other countries, the difference being that the separation of church and school has not gone as far as in Sweden. This becomes apparent in the retention of the subject-title "Christian education" and in the duty of the teachers to present the subject in a manner consonant with the doctrines of Evangelical Lutheranism. Most important, however, is that the objectives, set forth in 1936, to "give a Christian and moral up-bringing" remain unchanged. Other religions and existential issues are offered as part of social studies for Norwegian children.

Religious education in the schools in the Nordic countries has changed at the pace of other reforms in education. From 1955 to 1975, changes occurred in all the countries involving decreased influence of the church over the school and/or the deconfessionalization of the curriculum. After 1979 the subjects of Christian/religious education have not undergone any greater alterations, and those which have occurred have entailed equally increased and decreased possibilities of mediating Christian beliefs in the schools. An attempt to summarize the changes which have occurred following the 1919 plan of study in Sweden might be that three countries – Sweden, Iceland, and Denmark – are much alike, having transformed from a normative Christian education emphasis to an orientation of religious education character. Christian education has been retained in Finland and Norway, but Finland tends more toward the other three countries in terms of the content of religious education than does Norway.

Preparation for Confirmation

The dissemination of Christian knowledge and tradition has never taken place exclusively nor principally through the public schools. The instruction prior to confirmation served to complement home and school training, and was initially aimed at teaching the principles of Christian dogmatics by means of catechetical instruction. Since the school's religious education is no longer primarily directed towards a Christian upbringing, it might be expected that the churches' own confirmation instruction has assumed a more important role than ever. At the same time, however, this instruction has become more difficult to carry on since it can no longer be connected to the Christian education offered by the schools. Within the Nordic folk-churches, there have been many attempts to meet this problem by providing instruction prior to confirmation and to provide plans of study for this instruction.

In Finland and Sweden, three plans of study for confirmation instruction have been in effect since the 1930s. The first plan of study was adopted in Norway in 1978, and in Iceland the issue has been discussed in the 1980s. In Denmark, the lack of a formal plan for youth instruction has not been seen by the Church as problematic.[17] These differences appear to reflect more the various organizational structures of the churches than the different levels of deconfessionalization found in the schools.

The earlier plans of study in Sweden and Finland comprised a codification of the given forms of cathechetical instructions at the time. The study plans of 1978 and 1980 reflect both the non-active Christian backgrounds of the pupils involved and the pedagogy practised in the schools. The Norwegian study plans are similar to the others with an orientation against existential issues and with the objective of allowing youth to participate actively in various parts of the Christian life of the parish during confirmation preparation.

The altered position of the church in society is apparent in the changes in its youth instruction. The situation has changed from where the church dictated both the contents (catechism) and the form (recitation) of the school's Christian education, to where the churches presently adopt both the contents (existential issues-orientation) and the forms (groupwork and "practice" in the everyday life of the parish) from the study plans of the public schools in their attempts to make confirmation instruction attractive to the youth.

Religious Radio and Television Programmes

At the beginning of the period covered by this study, national radio networks had been established in all the Nordic countries; religious broadcasting (worship services and morning prayers) from the beginning has been a regular part of the broadcast schedules. At the time of the second reference year (1958) television had just begun. For the entire period under study, all five countries had state-owned broadcasting companies which enjoyed monopolies over radio and TV diffusion.

[17] The Danish Folk-church has only given some recommendations about the confirmation instruction.

In general, the public could choose from between one and three radio stations and one or two television channels.[18]

Public broadcasting has radically altered the possibility for people to hear the Christian message, but has also given the possibility for many of hearing different messages. And, though religious radio and television programmes are mainly heard and seen by active Christian people, they also reach some of those who seldom participate in religious services. For many active Christians, the public broadcasts bring them into contact with Christian traditions other than those they are accustomed to and with forms of worship not experienced in their own denominations. In these ways, and in countless other ways, broadcasting has made its imprint on religious culture.

The number of hours allotted to religious radio programmes has increased in four of the countries during the period under study, Denmark being the exception. In proportion to the total number of programmes, however, the religious share has generally decreased. It would seem likely that there exists a level of saturation among even the most interested for how much religious broadcasting there can be.

Perhaps more important than the lesser share of broadcast time is the change in the contents of the religious programmes. While worship services and morning prayers comprised almost exclusively the types of programmes broadcast during the 1930s, contemporary programmes are often a mixture of monologue and song, news, and debate shows with material concerning Christian and non-Christian religion alike. This altered repertoire is clearly observed in all the Nordic countries and applies to television as well. There are many more religious television programmes now than in 1960. The Finnish audience enjoys the greatest possibilities of tuning in to religious programmes, but these are also the most tradition-bound programmes. Denmark and Iceland offer least in the area of broadcast time for religious programmes. As to the amount of religious material available on radio and television, the differences among the Nordic countries are, however, surprisingly small.

Religion in the Daily and Weekly Press

It is difficult to determine trends in religion in the daily press. Definite results are seen in relation to Denmark and might be summarized in terms of increase, broadening, and convergence. The daily press in Denmark printed more about religion in 1958 than in 1938, and more in 1978 than in 1958. The increase and

[18] The changes with regard to the supply of broadcasted and televised religious programmes are more obvious than the changes according to any other of the indices after the research programme was completed. The satellite channels give the Nordic peoples religious television programmes, radically different from the supply offered by the state-owned channels. The establishment of numerous local religious radio transmitters has also changed the situation. So today Norway alone has about one hundered radio transmitters operated by different local religious organizations.

broadening of religious materials in the daily press are related. These newspapers, which at the onset of the period under study mostly contained items about preaching, have maintained these and have also included material of an informative and discursive nature. The latter material deals not only with the church and with Christianity, but also with individual religiosity and other religions. The tendency toward convergence refers to how publications with different political colours have become similar in their presentation of the folk-church of the country. This latter tendency is largely observed in all the Nordic countries, perhaps with the exception of Finland. The Social Democratic publications increasingly select material related to Christianity and the church in much the same fashion as do other publications.

The increase in religious material between 1938 and 1958 applied to all the countries, whereas the observed increase after 1958 differed from country to country. The broadening in the selection of religious material is characteristic of all the Nordic countries in that more attention is given to religion as an individual phenomenon, and greater space is given religions other than Protestant Christianity, as seen in news items concerning the Pope or related to the Islamic world. The amount of purely preaching material has not decreased. On the other hand, there appear fewer reviews of Christian literature and more general information on religion. A true comparison of the amount of religious material in the daily press for the various Nordic countries is not possible; however, it would appear that material of a preaching nature is presented most in the Finnish (non-socialist) papers, and that the presentation of religious news items is most comprehensive in Denmark and Norway.

A survey of several weekly publications does not reveal similar changes occurring in the religious content, nor does it point to linear changes in the Nordic countries. In the Icelandic publication reviewed, there was an increase in the religiously oriented material between the years singled out for comparison; this applies to both Norwegian publications as well. Of the two sources chosen from Denmark, Sweden, and Finland, the amount of religious material increased in the one and decreased in the other. A general trend visible in all the countries is the replacement of the treatment of institutional Christianity with material relative to private religiosity and particularly exotic religions. More apparent, however, is the tendency that articles about belief in the supernatural, such as spirit beliefs and telepathy, have become more common. In line with this development is the increasing publication of horoscopes and the substitution of Christian Christmas and Easter symbols by profane or folk-belief oriented symbols.

The results from the studies of radio and television media and the press reveal the distribution of religious material to vast numbers of people. The material is increasingly of an informative or entertaining nature. The religious media contents have received limited prior attention in the Nordic countries, and even less attention has been given to changes in the contents. However, the changes which have been noted point in the direction of a secularization process. Religion in the mass-media, particularly as presented in the weekly publications, is not characterized as *ganz Anderes*, rather it is intermixed and presented with other types of information and entertainment. The appearance of religious material in the various media might produce the dual result of (1) providing increased knowledge of a wide religious field including both cultural Christianity and other religions, and (2) leading to a vulgarization of opinions of religion as it is presented in conjunction with material about the secular popular culture.

The survey of the daily and weekly publications gives an indication of the type of religious material available to the reader in general. The survey does not, however, give any indication of how the material is comprehended. A special study was made in four of the countries of a limited number of death announcements and necrologies in an attempt not only to see what is done by the editors, but also to observe the general public's understanding of religion. The announcements and necrologies are written with broad public and religious references and are assumed to reflect a religious consciousness among those behind the publishing.

The tendencies, as they are deciphered from the material, do not point in the same direction in the four countries. Stability is most specific to Norway (one of the publications analyzed here was, however, from Norway's most religious area) where there is no change apparent in the content of the announcements. For Iceland, Christian references have increased in the lengthy necrologies so characteristic of that country. Religious references have also increased in the Swedish material, but the increase is more of a folk or general religious character than on an expressly Christian level. In Finland, it is more the general religious phrases than the specifically Christian connotations that have decreased.

A comparison of trends in the various countries cannot reasonably be based on the small amount of material for each of the countries, but the information in general suggests that the messages in the death announcements and necrologies do not reveal any diminution of ties to religion and Christian faith at the end of the 1970s compared to forty years earlier.

The Religious Debate

The general attitude toward religion in a country is naturally influenced by both positive and negative voices. This study has mainly examined the activities having positive influences such as Christian education and confirmation instruction. The powers which negatively influence religion are not as easily spelled out in indices. The religious debates which occurred during the years of this study have been analyzed, but the years 1938–1958–1978 do not capture changes in the general discussions about religion and Christianity.

Around 1950, debates on religion raged in several of the countries. In these debates either the entire Christian faith was put into question, as in Sweden, or parts of it, as in Norway. During the latter half of the 1960s, religious issues again were at stake in several countries but in a different way than earlier. Several Christian groups saw their religious values being threatened by various political decisions, particularly with reference to the public schools, to liberalized abortion laws and certain spectacular aspects of the secular culture. While, earlier, Christianity was attacked in the debate, later the Christians counter-attacked. In Finland, the debates took a different path than in the other countries as a consequence of the moderating participation of some prominent church leaders. The outcome was constructive proposals as to the churches' organization and role in Finnish society.

A characteristic of the Nordic countries, and perhaps a manifestation of David Martin's "beneficent circle", is that antireligious organizations have always been weak. Movements of this kind crop up now and then and disappear. In Finland, the Free-Thinkers have had a sort of continuity, and in Sweden, Denmark, and Norway, new leagues in support of freedom of religion and human-ethical issues were organized during the 1950s. In addition, Norway has its recently organized heathen association and Iceland its Asa association devoted to worship of the Old Norse gods; both of them have only a few adherents and there is no reasonable relation between their strength and the attention they are given in the media. It appears that anti-Christian organizations are stronger in Finland and Norway than in the other countries. This is perhaps not unrelated to the fact that it is in these two countries that Christianity has its strongest official status.

Sacraments

In most of the Nordic countries nation-wide statistics on participation in the sacraments of the folk-church appeared late.[19] The absence of statistics on baptism, confirmation, marriage, and funerals is an indication that the participation in these rites was at such a high level that it was not considered of interest to show the few deviations. The data available (see Tables 2–5) suggest that the sacraments were most widely observed in Finland and Iceland at the close of the 1970s, least so in Denmark and Sweden; Norway more nearly resembled the former two countries than the latter two.

In Denmark, the rate of baptism within the Folk-church was still above the 80 percent mark as compared to over 75 percent in Sweden (see Table 2). It should be observed here that membership in the Church of Sweden is not conditional upon baptism; whether or not the parents are members determines whether their children are also members. The countries are ranked about the same with reference to the frequency of confirmation as with the frequency of baptism, while the differences in percentages are somewhat greater (see Table 3). In Norway and

[19] In a theological sense, only baptism and communion are regarded as sacraments in the Nordic Lutheran Churches.

Table 2. Baptized within the Nordic folk-churches of all newborn (percentages).

	1938	1958	1978
Denmark	–	–	85
Finland	–	96	93
Iceland	–	–	93
Norway	96	97	91
Sweden	–	86	76

Table 3. Confirmed in the Nordic folk-churches of youth aged fifteen (percentages).

	1938	1958	1978
Denmark	–	–	91*
Finland	–	–	92
Iceland	–	–	96
Norway	97	91	87
Sweden	–	87	71

* 1974

Denmark confirmations have fallen to 85–90 percent, and in Sweden by the end of the 1970s, two-thirds of the youth participated in confirmation instruction.

Marriage statistics have for many years been more complete than those for the other sacraments. This is related to the existence of the civil marriage alternative practised in several of the countries during the period under study, but without being mandatory in any of the countries. Church marriage figures for Finland and Iceland for 1978 were over 80 percent, in Norway around 66 percent. In Sweden 60 percent were married within the Church of Sweden, to which may be added the 5 percent married in some other church or denomination. Denmark is clearly the country which distinguishes itself as having the lowest percentage of marriages legitimated through church ceremonies; the phenomenon is not new since Denmark has had more civil marriages since the 1930s (see Table 4).

Denmark is also the Nordic country with the highest rate of civil funerals (see Table 5). Civil funerals are in principle impossible in Iceland and rarely occur in Sweden. In Sweden funerals not held within the folk-church most often take place with priests or pastors from other churches and denominations as officiants.

Table 4. Marriages within the Nordic folk-churches of all marriages (percentages).

	1938	1958	1978
Denmark	64	74*	56
Finland	96	91	87
Iceland	–	93	87
Norway	90	85	68
Sweden	91	90	60

* 1967

Table 5. Funerals within the Nordic folk-churches of all funerals (percentages).

	1938	1958	1978
Denmark	–	–	96*
Finland	–	–	95**
Iceland	–	–	100
Norway	97	97	96
Sweden	–	96	95

* 1974 ** Estimated figure.

The proportion of the population baptized and confirmed says something about the relation of parents with children and of youth to the folk-church. The churches and denominations, however, desire not only "sacramental relations" to the growing generation, but also attempt to foster the growing generation through different forms of child and youth activities. During the latter part of the period under study, this work has changed in some of the countries where a transition from the traditional Sunday school to the arrangement of child activities on weekdays has occurred. These changes make it difficult to describe trends and to compare the countries. It is evident, however, that religious work among children is strongest in Norway, where one-third of children come into contact with Sunday school, and in Finland, where one-fifth of the children are involved in Sunday school and half of the pre-school children participate in weekday activities of the parishes. Sweden maintains a position behind Norway and Finland, but ahead of Denmark and Iceland, in the proportion of children participating in different kinds of church activities. As for Iceland, it should be noted that the YMCA and YWCA carry on active religious youth work.

Table 6. Average mass attendance on Sundays and Sacred Holidays of folk-church members (percentages).

	1938	1958	1978
Finland	3.4	3.1	2.5
Sverige	–	2.9	2.0

Church Attendance

Lengthy time-series are available for worship service attendance for Finland and Sweden. Attendance at mass is recorded for all parishes and the number of participants during a year is then divided by the number of Sundays and sacred holidays. The average number of participants arrived at by this method is related to the number of members in the folk-church without consideration of age structure or other variables. Mass attendance for the two countries is presented in Table 6.

In Finland mass attendance has declined by almost a third over a forty-year period, and a similar decline is observed for Sweden between 1958 and 1978. These figures, as well as a similar trend in Norway, suggest that participation decreased less from 1938 to 1958 than from 1958 to 1978. Behind this rather recent decline might be hidden a change of mass attendance to participation in other forms of worship services. It should be observed that the aggregate figures give no indication as to what proportion of the population regularly participates in the worship services of the folk-churches. Information from interview questions asked in Denmark and Sweden suggests that monthly church attenders have become fewer toward the end of the period of study as compared to the mid-1960s and the mid-1950s. The decrease in the number of church attendances and the proportion of church attenders within the population during the forty-year period appear to be general Nordic trends.

In all the countries there has been an observable increase in the number of communion participants in the folk-church. Finland had the highest communion participation at the end of the 1970s, showing about one act of participation per two adults per year, while Sweden and Norway averaged one per three adults. Communion participation was noticeably lower for Iceland than for the other countries. The increase in participation at communion cannot, for any of the countries, be assumed to stem from a larger number of persons involved. Instead, the increase most probably is related to a higher frequency of participation of the relatively small group which is active in different parts of the parish life.

Membership in Religious Organizations

In the Nordic countries the term "religious organization" covers a large variety of alliances and groups. The term might refer to different movements within the folk-churches which are loosely organized and are bound more by a particular interpretation of Christianity than by formal institutional ties. Furthermore, the term might refer to denominations outside the folk-churches, to new sects, or to non-Christian groups. In all the Nordic countries except Sweden, there are strong lay movements within the folk-church. In Norway, such movements are estimated to include one-twentieth of the population and in Denmark the (nonorganized) followers of Grundtvigianism[20] and the members of the Inner Mission comprise about six percent of the population according to interview results. Some four percent of the Finnish population belong to the revivalist movements within the folk-church, and in Iceland a similar proportion belong to the Evangelical Lutheran free-congregations which maintain a more organizational than ideological profile in relation to the folk-church. The organized low-church movements in Sweden comprise less than one percent of the population. In Norway and Sweden, at least, the low-church movements have experienced decreases in membership numbers during the period covered by this study.

The proportion of the Swedish population belonging to churches and denominations other than the Church of Sweden increased from three to about four percent between the 1930s and the 1970s. Included in these figures are the national denominations, the Orthodox and Roman Catholic Churches, and sects such as the Jehovah's Witnesses. In Finland and Norway similar heterogeneous groups comprise about three percent, and in Denmark and Iceland about two percent of the population. Several observations might be made concerning the relative strength of the religious groups: there are at least as many Orthodox in Sweden as in Finland, where the Orthodox Church comprises a second state church; the Roman Catholic Church in Sweden and Denmark is second in size only to the folk-church; the Jehovah's Witnesses are relatively strongest in Denmark and Finland; Muslim minorities are significant groups in both Sweden and Norway; and the esoteric movements in Iceland have a unique position.

In summary, it is worth noting that the Lutheran organizations, with their pietistic-oriented revivalist piety, have diminished in strength except in Iceland and Finland. Finland is, furthermore, an exception to the trend toward increased religious pluralism brought in by various immigrant groups through their own religious traditions. In addition, pluralism has been more the outcome of increased international migration than of internal recruitment.

[20] Grundtvigianism is a national and cultural movement within the Danish Folk-church, named after the priest, philosopher and hymn-writer N. F. S. Grundtvig (1773–1872).

Membership in the Folk-Churches

The members of several of the religious organizations mentioned in the above section are not members of the folk-churches. The proportion of those not members of the dominant churches has increased in all the countries. This increase is also attributable to the increasing number of persons who elect to remain outside of any religious organization. The proportion of those without any religious affiliation has increased since the 1930s in those countries with reliable statistics on denominational membership, namely Norway, Iceland, and Finland. The proportion without religious affiliation is largest in Finland with 7.5 percent. About 10 percent of the Finns are not members of the Lutheran folk-church, and the figures for Norway and Iceland are about 7 percent. Approximatcly 4 percent of Swedes do not belong to the Church of Sweden, and even fewer Danes do not belong to the Danish Folk-church.[21]

4. Conclusions from the National Studies

The results presented in the previous section might seem somewhat paradoxical against the background of the examination of religious change in the third category of indices, that referred to as "Participation in religious activities". It was shown in reference to this group that Sweden and Denmark exhibit lower participation in the sacraments, less church-sponsored work among children, and lower attendances at worship services than in the other three countries. Yet, it is Sweden and Denmark whose citizens to the greatest extent are members of the folk-church. This surprising result is not, however, unique to this study. It is often the case that findings both within and between the groups of indices have countered each other. Countries often cannot be rank-ordered whether in reference to present conditions according to different indicators, or in the magnitude of the changes which have occurred in the area of religion in the Nordic countries.

The object of this study was earlier stated as an attempt "to determine [...] whether or not the countries are, and have been, as similar as appearance would have it and if the similarities have increased or decreased". There have always been differences in the organization of the folk-churches between Denmark/Norway/Iceland on the one hand, and Sweden/Finland on the other. These differences have become more marked in recent years with the increase in autonomy in relation to the state for the churches in Sweden and Finland, and through the organizational development of the churches in these two countries in the direction of democratization and bureaucratization. At the same time, little has happened at

[21] The percentages of non-members in the folk-churches of the total population have increased in all the countries during the 1980s.

the level of church and state relations and church organization in Norway[22] and, most particularly, in Denmark. The Church of Iceland, on the other hand, has widened the gap with the Danish tradition and has begun to resemble the Church of Sweden organizationally. The conclusion is that the Nordic folk-churches organizationally do not have much more in common than the principle of territorial parishes, nor are there any strong indications that the resemblances have increased in recent years.

The official position of Christianity and of the folk-churches in the Nordic countries is constitutionally much the same, but the different traditions represented allow for various church functions to be emphasized in varying degrees. For example, in one country the regulations against entertainment events on Sundays might be overlooked while in another country corresponding laws are removed. This situation renders it difficult to point to definitive trends about changes with reference to the first group of indices. Norway emerges as the country which, officially, is most clearly Christian through the emphasis on the role of public schools in Christian education offered as an aid to parents who are formally required to raise their children in the teachings of the state-religion. Also, in relation to Finland and Iceland, objectives are set forth for school education in religion which, in conjunction with other circumstances, might lead to the suggestion that religion in these countries maintains a stronger official status than in Denmark and Sweden. With reference to the first group of indices, we conclude that religion and church are still present in the official sphere in all the Nordic countries and that this presence is tending to become less important with time.

If religion is only marginally present in the official arena of society, it is present to a much greater degree in the public arena through the mass-media. Religion is present in the cultural system of all the countries, not only by way of formal education in the public schools, but also by way of radio, television, and the daily and weekly press. In all five countries, religion occupied a larger place in these media at the end of the period of study than at the beginning. A transitional trend shared by all five countries alike is that the mass-media no longer deal primarily with the Christian message, but also provide general information concerning church and religion as well as material on world religions, private religiosity, and folk and transcendental beliefs. In weighting the effects on the sociocultural system of such entities as formal education in religion and Christianity, confirmation instruction, and the time allotted religion by the mass-media, it is concluded that the overall attention given religion is more limited in Denmark, and more generous in Norway and Finland, than in the other countries.

Internationally, the Nordic countries, as mentioned earlier, are considered similar in the area of "Participation in religious activities". This judgement has generally been based on a high level of participation in the sacraments, but

[22] This only holds true up to 1985.

low-level church activity otherwise. The results presented here hardly negate these generally accepted conceptualizations. The relatively few data from the 1930s indicate that nearly all children were baptized, that nearly all youth attended confirmation classes, and that nearly all burials took place in the folk-churches. Sparse information suggests that church attendance was low even before the Second World War. Subsequent changes are parallel in the five countries. Fewer members participate in the sacraments and attendance rates have fallen. Sweden was comparatively lower than the other countries as regards nearly all figures at the beginning of the period of study, and continues to be so, but the similarities among the countries were greater toward the end of the 1970s than earlier.

Thus the Nordic countries are similar in reference to religion, and the changes that have occurred since before the Second World War have, in effect, increased the similarity. With the exception of "The organizational development of the folk-churches", it becomes apparent that religion has best maintained its official status, experienced greatest participation, and held on to its position in the sociocultural system in Norway and Finland, and that religion's regression, according to these three groups of indices, is clearest in Denmark and Sweden. Iceland holds an intermediate position and, quite unexpectedly for its isolated location, has rapidly followed the mainstreams of transitions seen in the other countries.

Perhaps more interesting than to offer a necessarily schematic conclusive description of the situation, is to speculate over the interrelations between the different groups of indices. The differences among the countries in the first and fourth group of indices are not so great that one cannot speak of a common religious culture in the five Nordic countries. The folk-churches function within this shared religious culture with somewhat varied resources and with different forms of organization according to the Group II-indices. That the churches vary and have developed differently, according to this group of indices, would not appear to have much affected their success in Christian outreach, nor the extent to which the public utilizes the services of the churches, i.e., the circumstances described with the help of Group III-indices.

Comparable individual data on the central form of participation in religious activities, i.e., church attendance, have not been presented in the earlier material. It is, therefore, reasonable to present some such data including the folk-churches as well as well as other churches and denominations for the five countries. According to Demerath (1968, 367), church attendance figures are among the most reliable indicators of interest in religion. Through an international study of life values including Denmark, Iceland, Norway, and Sweden (Listhaug 1983, 7; Pétursson and Björnsson 1986, 20), and with the help of a Finnish Gallup study (Lotti 1983, 5), comparable and simultaneous (1981–1982) figures are available on the percentage of the adult population which attended worship services at least once a month:

Denmark	12 percent
Finland	12 percent
Iceland	11 percent
Norway	14 percent
Sweden	13 percent

The differences in this behaviour variable are insignificant in comparing the Nordic countries (as compared to differences in belief and attitude variables), and it might be questioned whether factors external to the religious culture and the churches' organizational forms are not most important in determining religious activity. The parallels which emerge between the countries, with reference to the behaviour variable, are more like the position of religion in the mass-media in the five countries than to any other of the indices.

5. Some Tendencies from the Local Community Studies

When the research programme about religious changes in the Nordic countries during a time period of fifty years ended it was evident that the local community studies had got a double function. First, in many ways they gave a tangible form to the results from the national studies and illustrations of the impact of the formal policies in the daily and seasonal life of the parishes and congregations. Second, they could demonstrate that the religious course of events in the daily life of individuals, groups and communities has a lot of facets that not are caught with the help of documents and collective data describing greater entities such as nations or churches. The aim of this section is to give some glimpses of the religious life in the five local communities under study; it can be repeated that these local communities were Akureyri in Iceland, Kongsberg in Norway, Silkeborg in Denmark, Vasa in Finland and Vänersborg in Sweden.

The Significance of the Revival Movements and the Denominations

All the reports on the national level give information on the numeric strength of the revival organizations working within the folk-churches and of the varied group of immigrant churches, free churches and sects which are active within each of the five countries. The percentages of the populations registered as members in those different associations are rather small, and looking at the specific groups they might be seen as tiny. The studies on the local level present a different picture. Although these organizations and denominations do not in all the cases have greater percentages of the populations in the five towns than they have of the population of the actual country, the inventory of what the organizations and denominations have and what they do in the five towns gives an impression of the very real presence they are seen to have not only for members but also for non-members.

"Presence" in this context implies that it can be thought that the common man in these towns does not reflect in terms like "The Baptists, that is the group that comprise one half of a percent of the population in the town and who are in favour of adult baptism" but in terms like "The Baptists, that is the group that have their meetings in the brick church near the square and who are running the Sunday school that the children of my neighbour are so eager to attend". The activities of the organizations of low-church or inner missions character as well as of the free churches have been and at least partly still are of quite another scale than the numbers of members indicate.

The comparisons are in favour of the organizations and the free churches also if they are done in relation to the number of active groups within the actual state church parish. At the beginning of the period under study the activities in not only relative but also absolute numbers were often more comprehensive within the free church congregations and the low-church and inner mission associations than they were within the parishes of the folk-church in the same town. So the congregations of the free churches in Vänersborg had more children in their Sunday schools in 1938 than the parish of the folk-church had the same year. In several of the towns the associations or the free congregations have arranged a greater number of meetings and worship services than the number of services arranged by the folk-church parishes, which have an overwhelming majority of the population as their members.

However, the presence of the low-church associations, the revival movements and the free churches has been restricted to a non-official sphere in the life of the towns. Mostly the movements and the denominations have had all their activities confined to within the walls of their own localities and they have not in the same way as the parishes of the folk-churches also had a prescribed presence within the life of other sectors, especially the institutions of public education, of the local communities.

Nearly all the children and the youth in the five towns have been in contact with the folk-church and the clergy a few times a year and these contacts have taken place independent from the religious interest in their homes. For a substantial part of the children and the youth, the pastor or the preacher and the chapel has been something they have been close to and that has been important for them during some period of the adolescence.

Taking its modest number of members in consideration, the Salvation Army appears to be a most visible part of the religious life of all the Nordic "normal" towns, except Akureyri. In spite of the anonymousness of the Army Temples, the Salvationists are highly visible with their singing and preaching in the market places and their fund-raising and colporteuring. Another kind of visible presence is presented by the Jehovah's Witnesses. There is some kind of a Kingdom Hall in all the five towns; however, it is not through their places of worship that "the Witnesses" are observed but through their active canvassing all over the towns.

The active visibility of small groups like Jehovah's Witnesses can be compared to the more anonymous presence of two of the world-wide established churches. Vasa has an Orthodox congregation and its offical status as the place for worship services of one of the two state churches in Finland is demonstrated by the site of the church building. In other ways it seems to be hard to observe the presence of an Orthodox community in the town. All of the towns, except Vasa, have Catholic parishes and in Akureyri and Silkeborg the Catholic presence has a long tradition. This Catholic presence is clearly visible only in Silkeborg; in Kongsberg the Mass is celebrated in a private home and in Vänersborg the Catholics meet in a building outside the town.

The Decline of the Revival Movements and the Free Churches

The local community studies not only give a new perspective on the significance of the free congregations and the revival movements in the totality of local religious life, they also give a concrete form to the weakening, i. e. the decreasing proportions of the population who are registered as members, that the revival movements and most of the free churches have gone through. The development of the congregations belonging to the Methodist church gives an illustration of what a decrease a few per mille on the national level implies on the local community level. Vänersborg does not have a Methodist congregation of its own any more; in Kongsberg the number of Methodists has been halved since the 1930s and in Silkeborg and Vasa the congregations have stagnated although there have been general increases of the populations.

A pan-Nordic tendency that is very clear on the local level is that the Salvation Army – in spite of the common goodwill it enjoys – has great problems in maintaining its activities. There are also clear tendencies in the local data that the low-church organizations within the folk-churches are on the decline; that can be seen both for the YMCA and YWCA in Akureyri and for the Inner Mission association in Kongsberg.

It is not only the retrogression of the older free religious organizations that can be observed in the reports from the local community studies; the winds of Pentecostalism that have blown, the result of which being that the Pentecostal movement has grown in all the five countries, are also evident in the reports from the five towns. Even very late phenomena within the field of religion can be observed in the descriptions. Different expressions that can be traced to the charismatic wave can be seen in Vasa, Silkeborg and Kongsberg. The reports from the two last-mentioned towns also give evidences that the new religious movements are on the offensive in the Scandinavian periphery: In the accounts of the total religious supply one can see names like Ananda Marga, Rajneesh Foundation and Guru

Marahaj Ji. When it is added that there are descriptions of the establishment of the Catholic Church in Kongsberg and Vänersborg as a result of recent immigration from southern Europe it becomes clear that the studies of the local communities give distinct pictures of tendencies, not always caught by the indices of religious change used in the national studies.

The Folk-Churches on the Offensive

The national reports give clear evidence that church-going within the folk-churches has decreased and still more clear evidence that the use of the sacraments has become less common. Equivalences of these national tendencies are also clearly documented in the reports from the local communities. However, these reports also give indications that there are other tendencies of development within the parishes of the folk-churches. In some ways it could be said that there has been an offensive of the folk-churches.

One of the signs of this offensive is the erection of new churches. In four of the towns new churches have been erected or it has in other ways been arranged that the parishes have adequate localities for their activities in the districts of the town where most of the population have their dwellings. However, it is clear that the church buildings in the centre of the towns, in spite of the fact that they constitute "the adjacent church" for only a small part of the populations, still have an unquestioned position within the totality of worship services of the parishes of the folk-churches.

It is not surprising that the increase of the numbers of church buildings has also involved a greater number of worship services in the actual towns. Only considering the church building in the centre of the town, Akureyri, Kongsberg and Vänersborg had a greater number of worship services at the end than they had at the beginning of the period under study. It seems that this increase is especially marked during the principal Christian holidays and the result has been that the church buildings in the centre of the towns are often the churches for the festivals.

However, the supply of the worship services of the folk-church parishes has not only increased, it has also been differentiated through the arrangement of special worship services for families and for youth and also through the arrangement of new types of worship services, especially those arranged in connection with the great Christian holidays. The occasions of presentation of "religious" music have been more frequent in all the five towns. Those occasions that are mostly arranged in the church buildings in the centre of the towns can be seen as another component in the same differentiation process.

One of the outcomes of the tendencies just mentioned seems to be that the parishes of the folk-churches are in charge of a substantially greater part of the total supply of worship services in the five towns at the end of the period under study than they were at the beginning of that period. In the same way these parishes are now responsible for a greater proportion of the Christian work among children and youth than they were in the 1930s, irrespective of the fact that the total extent of these activities has decreased.

Adjustment to New Situations

The activities of the parishes of the folk-churches are in many ways dependent upon decisions taken on the national level and many changes seen in the reports from the local community studies are connected with such decisions; for instance that is true for the relations between the church and the educational institutions. It should be noted that well-established relations of this kind can be maintained or take on new forms even when they have lost obligatory status. The reports from the studies of the local communities also give much more tangible evidence about how the parishes and congregations manage to adjust their activities to the changes going on in society than can be seen in the national reports.

The activities for the children and the youth have in many ways been particularly adapted to maintain relations with substantial parts of the populations. The Sunday school of the parish of Vänersborg has been closed down and this is illustrative of the development within the Church of Sweden because there is now a concentration of the parish acitivities for the children to the weekdays. A parallel change can be seen in Vasa where both the Finnish-speaking and the Swedish-speaking parish now manage "day-clubs" of a substantial extent. In both the towns there have been problems in reaching the children for the traditional activities of Sunday morning. The reason seems to be that the families have acquired new leisure time habits.

The free congregations have also to adapt to the changed conditions within society and to find new ways to reach children. The Inner Mission association in Vasa has opened its premises during the afternoons for school age children whose parents are at work. The Pentecostal congregation in Akureyri has started a day nursery with financial means from the local municipality. This may be an example of the fact that the changes within society can bring about quite new conditions for the parishes and congregations.

Other forms of adjustment have to do with the fact that people nowadays are much more mobile during their leisure time than they used to be. In Kongsberg, the parish of the folk-church arranges Sunday school and worship services in a newly-erected mountain chapel during the Easter holidays. In Akureyri, there are open-air worship services at the skiing hotel. However, it is not a new phenomenon for the denominations to have arrangements related to common needs of recreation. The Covenant Church congregation in Vänersborg has for a long time had a locality open during the summer just outside the town. The activities there seem mainly to have been arranged in order to offer the members of the congregation an alternative for the spending of leisure time within the context of the separated religious group. The "new" leisure activities of the parishes in Kongsberg and Akureyri are not "closed" in any way but outward-looking and evangelizing.

An example of a totally different form of how religious groups can link up with new values and new needs is found in Silkeborg where Christian groups have opened second hand shops and arranged a contact centre.

The Growth of the Folk-Church Organization

One result from the studies on the national level was that the folk-churches in all the Nordic countries, except in Denmark, had acquired a more complicated organization and that new governing bodies had been established. This development can as well be seen on the level of the parishes, except in Silkeborg. The number of clergy and of other top-level positions has grown, especially during the most recent part of the period under study, to adjust to the growth of the population. However, the most obvious development is not the increase of the number of persons engaged in the teaching, the caring work and the spiritual guidance of the parishes, but the growth of the administrative staff.

Kongsberg has got new boards for the administration of caring work and church music. The number of meetings with the parish council has grown and the number of matters that the council has to consider has increased tenfold. A parallel development can be seen in Vasa where not only the parish council meets at least monthly but where it has also been necessary to establish a working committee within the parish council to take current economic decisions. In Akureyri, the formal organization has not grown obviously but the establishment of a facultative coordinating board, with representatives of the employees of the parish, representatives of the free organizations for Christian work and representatives of the parish council, indicates that the structure of decision-taking has become more complicated.

The growth of the religious organizational apparatus in Vänersborg is demonstrated both through the fact that the expenditures of the parish have grown nearly twenty-fold in fixed prices although the population has merely been doubled and through the fact that it is the number of employees working with administration and caretaking that has increased. The just-mentioned categories of employees are now more numerous than the categories of clergy, deaconal workers, church musicians and employees working with children and youth; this change of numbers has taken place mainly after 1958.

The impacts of these organizational changes for the parishes, for the persons working within different spheres of the parishes and for those people who are "the customers" of the parishes cannot be seen in the data. However, it is evident that the organizational development of the parishes has been parallel to the development of the non-religious sectors of society. The governing organization has become more complicated and to be engaged in the governing of a parish seems to take more and more time both from those who are engaged as elected representatives and from those who are employed by the church or the parish.

Church Tendencies among the Denominations

An interesting tendency not seen in the national reports but at least indicated in the reports from the local community studies is that different activities take on a more "churchly" character both within the religiously-active nucleus of the lay-organizations related to the folk-church and within the broad circles mostly interested in the ceremonies of the folk-church.

The revival movements and the Inner Mission organizations and also the Salvation Army have restricted their supply of religious meetings in some situations or even tried to bring it in line with the supply of worship services of the parishes of the folk-churches. These restrictions and adjustments not only seem to depend on a policy of avoiding competition but at least as much are aimed at avoiding putting the members of the organizations in "cross-pressure"-situations implying that they should make a choice between attending the meetings of their own organization and attending the services of the folk-church. The revival movements and the Inner Mission organizations cannot on the whole offer celebrations of the Holy Communion and this is a problem as the Eucharist has acquired a clearly strengthened position in the general religious consciousness in the Nordic countries during the period under study.

An example of the other type of a more "churchly" orientation is found in the description of Akureyri, where nowadays nearly all the baptisms and the wedding ceremonies take place in the church building; at the beginning of the period under study they often took place either in the home of the clergyman or in the home of the parents of the child.

So, the position of the folk-church and the church building as the centre for religious life have been strengthened in two different ways and at least in the latter-mentioned example the tendency seems to be the result of a deliberate policy. An unintended result from the processes mentioned may have been that what could be labelled "the nucleus of religious life" has become more concentrated on the special setting constituted by the church building and coincidently has become more isolated from everyday life.

Cooperation and the Toning Down of Conflicts

In nearly all the Nordic countries there has been a development of ecumenism since the 1930s and this development is concretized very clearly in the reports from the local community studies. These reports give an understanding that ecumenism is not only something to be seen in personal contacts and statements on the top-level of the churches and denominations but that it also implies cooperation and the organization of joined activities on the local level; this is true especially for the latter part of the period under study. Besides, the reports demonstrate that local ecumenical operations do not take place without tensions between the parts involved. The relations between associations related to the folk-church and the free congregations often seem to be particularly complicated, and the reasons are both the different views of theological questions and the consciousness that inter-denominational contacts can be an incitement for some members to change their religious affiliation.

Another trait clearly seen in the reports from the local community studies is that the conflicts within the religious area have been toned down during the fifty-year period. That is evident in Silkeborg where the antagonism between the Grundtvigians and the adherents of the Inner Mission has been reduced. The relations between the Finnish-speaking and the Swedish-speaking parishes within the folk-church in Vasa have steadily improved. A parallel improvement is seen in Akureyri where the relations between the theologically liberal folk-church parish on the one hand and the more pietistic-oriented Inner Mission association and the YMCA and the YWCA on the other hand have changed since the 1930s.

There are many indications that the Christian front now stands united in quite another way than it used to do. This also implies that the cooperating churches and denominations have a watchfulness so that controversial persons or phenomena are not given any kind of legimitation from any part of the local Christian establishment. Examples are given through the treatment of a Pentecostal preacher with the gifts of healing in Kongsberg and the obstacles the new charismatic movement met in Silkeborg.

The Anchoring in Middle-Class Values

The programmatic attitudes of the political parties and especially the Social Democratic parties related to churches and religion in general are described in the national reports. The reports from the local community studies give another view on the contacts between the political system and the religious system in presenting the different ways in which the clergy and other representatives of the parishes and congregations have been active in local political life. From four of the towns there is information pointing in the same direction: The leading personages of the parishes and the congregations have often been active within the bourgeois political parties or they have in some other way been tied to dominant bourgeois circles.

These tendencies are seen most clearly in Vasa. Several of the clergy and of the employees of the parishes have for some time been members of the Finnish parliament. These categories have also been represented in the town council for a long time. Besides, the free congregations in Vasa, especially the Baptists, have provided a recruiting-ground for both parliamentary members and town councillors. In Kongsberg, the clergy, the preachers and prominent lay-persons within both the parish of the folk-church and the Inner Mission association as well as the Methodist congregation have held positions within the local administration. Mostly, they have been tied to the Christian People's Party and in a few cases to other bourgeois parties.

The middle-class colour of the political attitudes of the clergy in Vänersborg is seen in the fact that they have accepted being elected to the parish council with the help of a "non-political" ballot contesting the Social Democratic ballot. Some of them have also held positions of trust within the communal boards but this has been as much a sign of public confidence as of political activity. An indication of the social circles the clergy in Vänersborg has frequented is found in the fact that many of them have been active within the local masonic lodge. Some leading lay-members but no preachers of the free church congregations have been active within local political life and these activities have mainly been within the bourgeois parties. The clergy in Akureyri have not been involved in active political work but some of them have been members of the main bourgeois party in Iceland. They have also in different ways demonstrated their sympathies with the local commercial chamber which in many ways exerts an influence in local affairs.

Some of the clergy in Silkeborg have also been active within the bourgeois parties but there are at least as many of them that have been elected to public offices for the Social Democrats. Silkeborg is also a deviant case compared to the other four towns because its examples of a politically active clergy are late in time while at least the "strong" cases from the other towns are found during the first years of the period under study. One common trait for the four first-mentioned towns seems to be that the phenomenon of "clergymen active in local political life" is becoming successively rarer. This fact may result either from the unwillingness of the clergy to take on public responsibilities in local civic life or from the reluctance of the political parties to present them as their candidates for public offices.

The Local Newspapers as an Aid of Religion and the Churches

The national reports gave clear evidence that the space or the time that the media assign to issues of religious or Christian interest had nearly without exception increased since the 1930s. Careful examination of the contents of the local newspapers published in the five towns gives support for the results from the national studies; the space given to news and comments about church life and religion was at least the same in 1978 as it was in 1938 and in two of the towns there was a clear increase of this kind of newspaper content. Mostly, the generous space is used for presentations that are positive for the parishes and the congregations or for (Christian) religion in general. The parishes and the congregations have the privilege of having the news-items about their activities they give the editorial offices published uncut. The local church and denominational life is mostly presented for readers without critical evaluations of their real news-value. It is not uncommon with elements of preaching, and the local clergy and preachers are in this way given the opportunity to reach more numerous audiences than those reached from their pulpits. Even if the discourses are read by only a small minority of the general public, they may still be observed by the majority and the identity of the local clergy is, in this way, kept alive for the population in the towns.

Critical views on religion and church are rare items in the local newspapers. Such ideas can be seen in the letters to the editor but mostly they do not go unchallenged. The number of letters concerning religion in these columns seems to have grown with time and the number of the letters indicates that the editors of the columns have found that the views on religion and church are observed by many of the readers. It can also be observed that the space given to religious books and to the general religious culture nowadays is very sparse.

For the local newspapers the activities of the parishes and the congregations are a vital part of the life of the local community they are working in. What is going on in the churches and in the chapels is in many ways an integrated part of the local culture and for the newspapers mainly serving locally-oriented readers the publication of news-items describing this sector of the local community life is a natural part of their mission. One of the main results from the local community studies is that the newspapers are vital agents for the religious presence demonstrated through so many of the indices used in the latter part of the research programme. A very short summary of the results from the local community studies within the research programme about religious change in the Scandinavian countries is that religion is still present in many ways in the everyday life of the people of these countries.

References

Demerath, N. J., 1968

"Trends and Anti-Trends in Religious Change". Pp. 349–445 in: Eleanor Bernert Sheldon & Wilbert E. Moore (eds.), *Indicators of Social Change.* New York: Russel Sage Foundation.

Dobbelaere, Karel, 1981

"Secularization: A Multi-Dimensional Concept". *Current Sociology* XXIX:2.

Gustafsson, Göran, 1984

"Civil Religion in Sweden: Some Notes on its Contents and Local Expressions". Pp. 90–99 in: *The Church and Civil Religion in The Nordic Countries of Europe.* Geneva: LWF Studies.

Gustafsson, Göran (ed.), 1985

Religiös förändring i Norden 1930–1980. Malmö: Liber Förlag.

Gustafsson, Göran (ed.), 1987.
Religion och kyrka i fem nordiska städer. Malmö: Liber Förlag.
Gustafsson, Göran, 1990
"Sweden: A Folk Church under Political Influence". *Studia Theologica: Scandinavian Journal of Theology* 44:3–16.
Larsen, Stein Ugelvik & Ingun Montgomery (eds.), 1982
Kirken krisen og krigen. Bergen: Universitetsforlaget.
Lindblad, Ingmar *et al.*, 1972
Politik i Norden. Stockholm: Aldus.
Listhaug, Ola, 1983
Norske verdier i et komparativt perspektiv. Trondheim: Institutt for sosiologi og samfunnskunskap.
Lotti, Leila, 1983
Some Aspects of The Religiosity of the Finns 1951 and 1982. Helsinki: Delfoi Oy.
Lundby, Knut, 1977
"Kringkasting og avkristning". Pp. 215–244 in Pål Repstad (ed.), *Det religiöse Norge.* Oslo: Gyldendal Norsk Forlag.
Martin, David, 1978
A *General Theory of Secularization.* London: Basil Blackwell.
Pétursson, Pétur, 1984
"Civil Religion in Iceland". Pp. 155–165 in *The Church and Civil Religion in the Nordic Countries of Europe.* Geneva: LWF Studies.
Pétursson, Pétur & Björn Björnsson, 1986
"Um truarlif Islendinga". *Kirkjuritid* 52:6–30.
Riis, Ole, 1985
"Religion in The Danish Mass-Media 1930–1980". Paper presented at the XVIII International Conference for the Sociology of Religion, Louvaine, Belgium.
Shiner, Larry, 1967
"The Concept of Secularization in Empirical Research". *Journal for The Scientific Study of Religion* 6:207–220.
Sundback, Susan, 1984
"Folk Church Religion — A Kind of Civil Religion?". Pp. 35–40 in *The Church and Civil Religion in the Nordic Countries of Europe.* Geneva: LWF Studies.
Sundback, Susan, 1987
"Religion and Mass Communication in Finland in the 1980s". *Temenos* 23:109–120.
Thyssen, Anders Pontoppidan (ed.), 1969
Väckelse och kyrka i nordiskt perspektiv. Copenhagen: G. E. C. Gad.

LOEK HALMAN

Scandinavian Values: How Special are They?

Introduction

The purpose of this article is to describe the distinctive characteristics of the Scandinavian countries regarding values and attitudes. When the peculiarities of a country or a few countries are to be detected it is obvious that these countries have to be compared with other countries. These may be single countries or geographical areas, consisting of more than one country, and in this particular case the aim is to compare Scandinavia with the rest of Europe.

Comparisons can be related to a large number of features. In the following article we limit ourselves to a comparison of the Scandinavian countries with the rest of (Western) Europe. This implies that we are not interested in differences and similarities concerning all kinds of structural characteristics, such as income distributions and income inequalities, Gross National Products, population statistics, unemployment rates, and so on. The comparisons we aim at have to do with basic social values and behaviours in some important domains of life, such as religion and morality, politics, work, family, marriage and sexuality.[1]

The Scandinavian countries are often viewed as a separate part of Europe, internally homogeneous and very different from the rest of Europe. Peabody (1985) for instance argued that the influence of Protestantism will be particularly responsible for this peculiar position of the Scandinavian countries within Europe. However, the assumed differences and similarities are often based on mere speculations, stereotypical images and common sense knowledge of Scandinavia. A firm empirical verification of these images is hardly ever given. Apart from Denmark, the Scandinavian countries are not yet members of the EC, but eager to become members. An unanswered question is whether these countries share the same values as other European countries and if not how special these values are? In what respect are they special and to what degree?

In this article we want to investigate what is true about the assumed particularity of the Scandinavian countries. Do the Scandinavians share common values which have to be distinguished from the values which are shared by other Europeans? Are Scandinavians indeed special, or do these populations resemble the rest of Europe in such a way that speaking of a separate part of Europe is useless?

[1] The author is grateful to Prof. Dr. R. A. de Moor (Tilburg University) for his comments on an earlier version of this article.

If there indeed exists a typical Scandinavian value pattern, this would imply that there are values which appear only in these countries and not in others, or that Scandinavian people have value preferences different from other people in Europe.

European Values

The specificity of Scandinavian values is explored using data from the 1990 European Values Survey (EVS). This survey was carried out as a follow up of a similar survey in 1981 in all countries of the EC (except Greece), the Nordic countries, United States, Canada and many countries in Eastern Europe (for more information see Halman & de Moor 1991). Sample sizes ranged from 1 000 to 2 800 and the way these samples were drawn enables us to generalize the research findings to the whole population of the various countries. After these data have been weighted, they may be used to generalize to Europe and Scandinavia. The questionnaire covered topics like religion and morality, politics, primary relations and work. In all these domains several basic orientations or values have been distinguished,[2] and some of them will be discussed in this article.

One of the main purposes of the European Values project is to get at a better understanding of the common features of the European countries. The initiators of the project were convinced that, despite many and often large differences between the various populations of the European countries, Europeans share a set of basic values which distinguishes them from other great cultures in the world. In a recent paper one of the initiators of the project formulated the main purposes as follows:

> The "Founding Fathers" of the European Values Study were [...] aware of the fact that Europe, notwithstanding its search for closer unification, remains and intends to remain a richly varied part of the world, not only by its main languages but by old, regional subcultures, value scales, religious and ideological traditions, political and educational systems. Nevertheless, the original teams [...], believed that deciphering that which is common in the collective conscience of the men and women of Europe and those aspects which they share to a lesser extent or not at all could be an important contribution not only to a better mutual understanding but also for peace-keeping (Kerkhofs 1992, 1f).

[2] Using various latent structure models (factor analysis, latent trait analysis) latent variables are constructed which indicate values. The scores on these latent variables (values) indicate individuals' value preferences or value orientation. By calculating a mean score for the inhabitants of a certain country the position or value orientation of the countries can be compared (for more information see Halman *et al.* 1987; Ester & Halman 1990; Halman 1991; Halman & Vloet 1992). By comparing these scores between countries it becomes clear what values are highly preferred in some countries and which values are rejected in some countries. The specificity of countries in terms of values appears in these kind of comparisons.

And indeed Europeans appeared to share many things in common, which does not imply that Europe is homogeneous in its values. Dogan (1988) argues that European countries mainly differ in the degree of value preferences, but not in the kind of values. A further unification of Europe in which nation states cooperate is thus not so much hampered by the fact that countries have different values as by the fact that they have different value preferences. However, there is an increased quest for recognition of national and particularly regional identity. The many cultures in Europe refuse to be levelled down by economic and monetary laws. "Marketing, profit-making, and a common currency, although necessary, will not guarantee people's happiness" (Kerkhofs 1992). The various cultures want to safeguard their own identities and instead of speaking about a Europe of the nations it will be better to talk about a Europe of the local or regional cultures.

The cultural-historical developments in the European countries, Scandinavia as well as the rest of Europe, resemble each other to a large extent. This makes it very unlikely that the specificity of Scandinavia manifests itself in values occurring in these countries only. If a typical Scandinavian value pattern indeed existed, it would imply that the Scandinavian countries shared certain values not found in other European countries. As Dogan has already concluded, the main difference in values within Europe is not that the values as such are specific to a country or region, but that there are (large) differences in value preferences between countries (Dogan 1988). The question to be answered in this article is therefore limited to a question of differences and similarities in value preferences. In case the Scandinavian countries have common value preferences clearly distinctive from other European value preferences, it is to be concluded that Scandinavian countries are special. In technical terms the within (Scandinavian countries) variation is small, whereas the in-between variation (Scandinavia versus Europe) is large.

However, the rest of Europe is far from homogeneous, but consists of a multitude of countries which resemble each other in some respects and which are very different on others. Within the EC a rough division of Europe is often used, in which the northern countries are distinguished from countries in Southern Europe. The northern countries are rich and wealthy, whereas southern parts of Europe are relatively poor and to a large extent dependent on the support from the wealthier and richer northern community members. Such a division resembles a division of countries on the basis of differences in value orientations. People in the northern countries appear to be more 'modern' in their value orientations than people in countries as Italy and Spain where traditional values are still dominant (Dorenbos, Halman & Heunks 1987). It seems as if modernization, one of the main topics of sociology, has proceeded more rapidly in the northern countries than in the southern parts of Europe. Because of the differences in values and the often used division of Europe in North and South it will be better to use such a division of Europe in analyzing differences between Scandinavian and other European countries. Such a division is of course very rough and not at all reflecting the very complex situation. Figures from 1981 surveys yielded that both Irish countries are similar to southern parts of Europe. They are not at all modern in their values (Halman *et al.* 1987; Ester & Halman 1990; Halman 1991). Furthermore, although France is seen as part of Southern Europe, this will not be the case with respect to all kinds of values. In many respects, for instance with respect to religious orientations and behaviours, as well as orientations regarding family life and family structure, French people resemble Northern Europeans (Halman 1991). The same is true for Italy where a division in three parts is frequently used: Northern Italy is wealthy, rich and modern whereas the southern parts of Italy are poor and its population traditional. The area in between north and south is less modern and less rich than the north, and less traditional and less poor than the south (Gubert 1992). In other countries similar distinctions will be required, because very often it is found that "the differences *within* nations appear greater than the differences *among* nations" (Dogan 1988, 2f).

Our analyses will be based on the distinction of Europe in three parts:

1. Scandinavia or Nordic: Norway, Sweden, Denmark, Iceland;[3]
2. Northern Europe: Netherlands, Belgium, Germany, Great Britain;
3. Southern and Western Europe: France, Italy, Spain, Portugal, Ireland, Northern Ireland.

As stated above, in case the Scandinavian countries share value orientations in common, not shared by other European countries, these countries will be mutually coherent, which in analytical terms implies that the within group variation is small. Extreme scores within this cluster of countries have to be limited. In case this is not found the differences appear to be too large to consider the Scandinavian countries as mutually homogeneous.

Comparisons

The results of our comparative analyses will be presented and discussed for each domain separately. For more information on the measures and the way we have distinguished values we have to refer to Halman & Vloet (1992). In this article we first pay attention to the peculiarity of Scandinavia regarding religion. Next, political issues are the subject of our analyses, followed by the family and marriage. The presentation is closed by work related values.[4]

[3] Finland is not included in the analyses. Not only because Finland is officially not part of Scandinavia, but because data gathering in this country was not comparable with the way data were gathered in other countries.

[4] For information about the values we discuss here we refer to Halman (1991), Halman & de Moor (1992) and Halman & Vloet (1992).

Religion

The Scandinavian countries resemble each other in their Lutheran history and Lutheran church domination. "The Nordic countries still invest the Lutheran church with a special status. This is based on historical traditions and on the fact, that the majority belongs to the Lutheran churches" (Riis 1992, 2). This is reflected in church membership rates in the Scandinavian countries (Table 1).

A large majority in these countries belong to the national, Lutheran church. In this respect the Scandinavian countries are not at all fragmented (Lane & Ersson 1987, 57). However, this low degree of fragmentation disguises heterogeneous reality. There exist a large variety of Protestant churches and in fact the Nordic countries are fragmented. "Revival movements during the nineteenth century resulted in regional variety in the religious structure. In Norway the revival movements were particularly strong in Vestlandet around Bergen, in Denmark in West Jutland around Limfjorden and in Sweden on the west coast and in the province of Småland" (Lane & Ersson 1987, 58). Southern European countries as well as Ireland are also not fragmented. This part of Europe is more or less homogeneously Roman Catholic, whereas the countries in middle Europe (the Netherlands, Germany and Great Britain) are more or less religiously divided. However, in these parts of Europe church membership is not as widespread as in the Scandinavian countries (Halman 1992, 28). Particularly in the Netherlands a fragmented pattern exists with half of the population being unchurched, one third being Catholic, and the rest being members of one of the many Protestant churches. In Great Britain and Germany the number of unchurched people is far less extensive compared to the Netherlands. In other countries of Europe the number of unchurched people is also rather limited (Halman 1991; 1992).

Another important feature of Lutheran Scandinavia is the low church attendance, despite the fact that membership is extensive in these countries. Scandinavian people do not feel strongly attached to the church (Hamberg 1990). 45 % of the Scandinavians never attend a religious service, and regular church attendance (at least once a month) is limited to about 10 % of the population. In Southern European countries and in Ireland half of the population attends religious services rather frequently. The churchly committed form a minority in Scandinavian society as well as among church members (Riis 1992, 1). This appears very obvious in the typology based on active membership and church attendance.[5] Scandinavian people are not committed to the church, but nevertheless they consider themselves

[5] Five types of churched and unchurched people have been distinguished. Those who say they belong to a particular church and attend religious services regularly (at least once a month) and are otherwise actively involved in church activities are called *core members*. They have to be distinguished from those who say they belong to a church as well as attend religious services regularly (at least once a month), but who are otherwise not actively involved in church activities. They are called *modal*

Table 1. Church membership and frequent church attendance in Scandinavia and the rest of Europe (in %).

	Europe		
	South and West	North	Scandinavia
Church membership	85	69	87
Frequent participation (at least once a month)	50	26	11

Source: European Values Study 1990

members of the Lutheran church. In all four Scandinavian countries this pattern is dominant which seems to be typical for Scandinavia (Halman 1992, 29; Halman & Vloet 1992, 11). This distinctive pattern may be a consequence of the strong association of the Lutheran church with the state in these countries (Wilson 1982). Being a church member is almost a citizen's duty in the Scandinavian countries. When Scandinavians "move to a neighbour country, they generally adhere themselves to the national church of the host country" (Riis 1992, 2). The high level of affiliation in Sweden may "be seen as a way of expressing solidarity with Swedish society and its basic values" (Hamberg 1990, 39). However, being a member in the Scandinavian countries will be less religiously meaningful than in other countries.

The low degree of commitment to the church emerges also in the judgement of the importance of religious services for events like birth, marriage, death. The necessity for such religious services at these important events in life is lowest in these Scandinavian countries compared to other countries. However, about half of the population, ranging from 45 % in Denmark to 58 % in Norway, consider such events sufficiently worthwhile to merit a religious ceremony.

Although these figures apparently contradict the low levels of church attendance, participation in such ceremonies is not necessarily an expression of church involvement. It may be explained by the fact that in general the number of alternatives to mark such important transitions in human life is rather limited (Dobbe-

members. A third type of churched people say they belong to a church, but they do not frequently attend religious services. They are called *marginal members.*

The unchurched people, those who are not a member of a church, can be divided into unchurched of the first and unchurched of the second generation. The first generation unchurched people are no longer church members, but they once were, whereas the unchurched of the second generation have never been church members (see also Halman & Ester 1991).

Table 2. Churches have to speak out on sexual issues and social issues (mean standardized LISREL scores) according to Scandinavians and other Europeans.

	Europe						
	South and West		North		Scandinavia		
	mean	std	mean	std	mean	std	eta
Church and sex issues	.13	1.02	–.07	.98	–.01	1.02	.09
Church and social issues	.18	.97	–.09	.99	–.12	1.05	.13

Source: European Values Study 1990

laere & Voyé 1992, 128). Furthermore, it is more or less a habit or national custom to have such ceremonies without any further motivation or reflection.

Institutional religiosity has diminished and the role of church in society is no longer dominant. People in modern society are not attracted to the doctrine of the church, particularly not in private affairs. This is most obviously the case in the Nordic countries. Scandinavians reject the idea that the churches should speak out on personal issues like homosexuality, abortion, extramarital affairs, and euthanasia. However, Scandinavians are also less in favour of churches speaking out on various social issues, like unemployment, disarmament, third world problems, racial discrimination, ecology and so on (Table 2).

This may be explained by the fact that more than in other countries the Lutheran church in Scandinavia is an institution merely limited to providing religious services. The church is one among many other specialized institutions with a very limited role in society. As a consequence it is very difficult for the church in Scandinavia to get involved in issues which are ascribed to other institutions. "It is not legitimate to enter political discussions, about the policy of the government or about vital social problems such as unemployment" (Riis 1992, 3). It is therefore not unexpected that Scandinavians are least of all of the opinion that churches provide adequate answers to moral questions, problems of family life, spiritual needs and social problems (Halman 1992, 30; Halman & Vloet 1992, 9). So, they do not only favour less the idea that churches should speak out on private and social issues, they are also least of all convinced that churches react adequately to all kind of problems. And in this respect Scandinavian countries resemble each other to a large extent.

These figures may be interpreted in terms of individualization and institutional differentiation. Individualization implies that traditional collective shared meaning systems have disappeared and that religious feelings are increasingly based on

Table 3. Religiosity, religious orthodoxy, Christian world view and world-oriented world view in Scandinavia and the rest of Europe (mean standardized LISREL and Latent Trait scores).

	Europe						
	South and West		North		Scandinavia		
	mean	std	mean	std	mean	std	eta
Religiosity	.49	.85	–.24	.97	–.64	.89	.37
Orthodoxy	.26	1.06	–.11	.94	–.41	.85	.20
Christian world view	.37	1.03	–.18	.93	–.55	.76	.29
World-oriented view	.15	.84	–.15	.93	.65	1.82	.21

Source: European Values Study 1990

individual choices and preferences. The role of the church as representative and keeper of traditional, institutional religion has diminished. Increasingly, traditional institutional religion has become an option, not a necessity (Luckmann 1967).

This decline in this institutional religiosity is just one aspect of a broader development in society which is called secularization (Dobbelaere 1981; 1985). This process also refers to changes in religious content. Traditional church oriented religiosity has diminished, and this seems to be the case particularly in the northern part of Europe. A majority of the people in the Nordic countries belong to the Lutheran church but this affiliation is not accompanied by strong religious beliefs. People in these countries are not only less attached to the church, they are also less orthodox in their beliefs and less religious (Table 3) measured in a more neutral, not necessarily traditional way.[6]

Therefore, Riis seems to be right in stating that most people in Scandinavia "are belonging without believing" (Riis 1992, 2). 77 % of Southern Europeans declare themselves as religious, whereas this proportion in the Scandinavian countries is limited to almost half of the population. Almost as many people say they are not religious, which however, does not mean that they are atheists. Convinced atheism is even in these less religious countries a minority phenomenon, applicable to about 5 % of the Scandinavians. And in this respect Scandinavians are not

[6] This kind of general religiosity has been measured by items like belief in a personal God, being a religious person, the importance of God, taking moments for prayer, getting comfort from religion. It does not necessarily refer to traditional institutional religiosity. This religious orientation may also apply to people who do not belong to, or do not feel attracted to a church (De Moor 1987, 22; Ester & Halman 1990, 7).

different from Southern and Northern Europe. The decrease in religiosity seems to imply a change in the content or kind of religiosity. Instead of belief in a personal God, many people believe in some kind of spirit or life force, or people say they are uncertain and do not know what to believe. However, such a belief is not typical for the Scandinavian countries. The same is true for the Northern European countries. Scandinavia and Northern Europe resemble each other in their beliefs. About 20 % do not know what to believe, whereas 40 % believe in some kind of spirit or life force, and 21 % in Scandinavia, resp. 27 % of Northern European people believe in a personal God. Both geographical areas can be distinguished from Southern Europe, where 61 % believe in a personal God, 24 % in a spirit, and 9 % do not to know what to believe in.

People in the northern part of Europe are less traditional in their beliefs. This non-traditional way of believing is also expressed in the evaluation of the items referring to a traditional Christian meaning system. In the Scandinavian countries the meaning of life, death and suffering are found less in traditional Christian beliefs, but instead more in daily life itself. Christian doctrine seems to be less important in these countries, whereas a world-oriented view seems to prevail (see Table 3). In Southern European countries a reversed situation is found. Christian doctrine dominates here, whereas a world-oriented view seems to be less important.

To a certain extent it is possible to speak of a typical Nordic or Scandinavian religious pattern, particularly in the case of religious behaviour (membership as well as church participation) and the role of the church in society. Compared to other countries marginal membership is extensive in these countries. A large majority of the Scandinavians is not actively involved in church activities, but nevertheless retains membership of the Lutheran church.

The role of the church is limited to providing religious services which one is not attending, but churches should not speak out on private, political or social issues (Riis 1992).

However, such overall images masks the whimsicality of reality. The Scandinavian countries appear to be far from homogeneous. Compared to other European countries religiousness is low in the Scandinavian countries, but the differences within Scandinavian countries are sometimes not to be neglected. Norway and Iceland are often less extreme compared to Denmark and Sweden. Iceland is as religious as Northern Ireland, Ireland and Portugal, whereas religiousness is low in Denmark and Sweden (Halman 1992). We mentioned that about half of the Scandinavians consider themselves to be religious, but within the Scandinavian countries proportions range from 75 % of the Icelandic people to 31 % of the Swedes. Although belief in a personal God is limited in Scandinavia as such, there exist large differences between the continental Scandinavian countries and Iceland. 16 % of the Swedes, 20 % of the Danes, and 30 % of the Norwegians believe in a personal God. But on Iceland this proportion is no less than 51 %. So, on Iceland people are as traditional in their beliefs as for instance in Spain.

Scandinavians share a common Lutheran history which has led to similar behaviour, but which has not made the inhabitants of the various countries share similar religious orientations.

Politics

Modern society is an individualized society. Increasingly, the individual has become the yardstick of decisions, and point of reference. In traditional society issues of order, authority, discipline and obedience were emphasized strongly, whereas in modern society values emphasize autonomy, creativity, and emancipation. "Pflicht-" und "Akzeptanzwerte" have decreased whereas "Selbstentfaltungswerte" have become increasingly important (Klages 1985; see also Meulemann 1983; 1985; 1987). Self-development and personal happiness have become leading principles for individual actions. The ethic of modern society is described as one of "fulfilment" (Wood & Zurcher 1988).

According to Inglehart the fundamental shift that has taken place and still takes place in values is a shift from a materialist value orientation which is directed predominantly to order and prosperity, to a post-materialist value orientation stressing personal freedom, individual participation in politics and freedom of speech (Inglehart 1977; 1990). This shift has been facilitated by the high degree of security that was characteristic for most of the countries in Europe (Inglehart 1977, 3; 1990, 68). Inglehart's theory is based on two hypotheses: the scarcity and socialization hypothesis. The first hypothesis refers to the idea that individuals' priorities reflect the socio-economic situation during their socialization period, giving highest priority to those goods that are scarce in society. The second hypothesis states that the basic values one acquires during one's formative years remain stable during the rest of one's life. Being raised in rather wealthy periods in which the basic (material) needs are met implies that one will have a post-materialist value orientation. The emergence of the modern welfare state has undoubtedly contributed significantly to this shift from a largely materialist value orientation towards a dominant post-materialist value orientation. However, despite the fact that the Nordic countries are all advanced and very well developed welfare states, relatively wealthy, and that in these countries the basic needs of people are met, there is no empirical evidence for such a shift from materialism to post-materialism. In fact, the Scandinavian countries are not at all post-materialist, compared to other European countries (Halman & Ester 1991, 27). In Denmark and Iceland the support for post-materialist values has even decreased during the last decade whereas in Norway and Sweden no changes can be reported in this respect (Halman & Ester 1991, 13). Compared to other European countries the Nordic countries belong to the most materialistically-oriented countries. Least materialist are the Netherlands and West Germany.

Table 4. More emphasis on individual development is good and freedom above equality in Scandinavia and the rest of Europe (in %).

	Europe		
	South and West	North	Scandinavia
Individual development	89	83	90
Freedom above equality	46	61	65

Source: European Values Study 1990

The trend towards individualization in European countries appears in the widespread agreement with greater emphasis on personal development (Table 4). However, this trend is not limited to the Scandinavian countries, but appears in all countries in a more or less similar way.

In all European countries, the Scandinavian as well as the southern parts of Europe, such a future development in which personal development is emphasized is judged as good. A more significant difference can be found in the tendency to give priority to freedom above equality. A majority (65 %) of the people in the Scandinavian countries shares the opinion that individual freedom is more important than equality in society. In the northern countries of Western Europe approval with this statement is as high as in the Scandinavian countries (61 %), whereas in the Southern European countries agreement with this statement is limited to 46 %.

In advanced, individualized society the relevance of ideology has disappeared. People are no longer tied for their lifetime to one political party, but instead they increasingly switch from party to party as they like. Political orientations are increasingly becoming personal choices. People select and adopt ideas and concepts from the political menu à la carte (van Deth 1991), not hindered by a coherent political pattern. Political orientations have become fragmented and largely dependent upon the issue at stake. Modern politics is no longer ideological, but instead issue politics. All kinds of interest groups and movements "have come to play an increasingly active role in both local and national politics" (Ashford & Timms 1992, 87). Confidence in existing democratic institutions, especially in authoritative institutions, has decreased. This loss of confidence is really a problem to modern democratic government, for "the basis of a democratic system of government resides in the support of its electorate; a democracy which is unable to convince a substantial proportion of voters that it is functioning in a reasonably satisfactory way has lost its principle power base and has ceased to operate effectively" (Ashford & Timms 1992, 91).

Table 5. Confidence in government in Scandinavia and the rest of Europe (in %).

	Europe		
	South and West	North	Scandinavia
A lot of confidence	6	7	7
Quite a lot	31	42	41
Not very much	45	40	42
None at all	18	11	9

Source: European Values Study 1990

Confidence in government is not overwhelming in the European countries, although in the northern countries and in Scandinavia about half of the populations say they have confidence in their governments.

In Southern Europe the level of trust in the government is considerably lower. Particularly in Italy and Portugal people do not trust their governments. More than 20 % of these populations declare they have no confidence at all in their governments. In the Scandinavian countries this proportion is limited to about 10 % or less. The low governmental trust in Italy is nothing new and confirms the results of previous studies (Almond & Verba 1965; Sani 1980; Barnes, Kaase *et al.* 1979). The Italian lack of confidence is not limited to the government but concerns all kinds of institutions. However, in general it may be concluded that Scandinavians as well as people in Northern Europe have less confidence in authoritative institutions, which are trusted more in Southern European countries, whereas democratic institutions are trusted more in Northern European countries and Scandinavia than in Southern European countries.

It has been argued that as a consequence of modernization traditional cleavages such as ethnicity and religion have been replaced by functional cleavages such as class and economic structure (Lane & Ersson 1987, 65). Sustained individualization implies a more tolerant climate in contemporary society. As a consequence of emphasizing personal choices the individual is increasingly confronted with people who behave in a different or deviant way. These behaviours will be tolerated by large majorities in society which are more modernized and individualized. However, in contrast to these general expectations, tolerance towards ethnic groups as well as tolerance towards people with deviant behaviour declined during the eighties in most countries. But whereas tolerance towards ethnic groups decreased in Southern European countries in particular, in the Northern European countries and Scandinavia a decrease is found in tolerance towards people with

Table 6. Degree of intolerance against ethnic groups and deviant behaviours in Scandinavia and the rest of Europe (mean standardized Latent Trait scores).

	Europe						
	South and West		North		Scandinavia		
	mean	std	mean	std	mean	std	eta
Ethnic groups	.01	1.06	.00	.97	–.08	.92	.02
Deviant behaviours	.19	1.08	–.08	.94	–.23	.90	.14

Source: European Values Study 1990

deviant behaviour. Despite this decrease in tolerance, people in the Scandinavian countries tend to be more tolerant towards people of different ethnic and religious groups as well as people who behave in a deviant way (Table 6).

This decline in tolerance is rather unexpected and may be an indication of "a development toward hyper-individualism instead of a development toward open minded individualism. The reduced influence of traditional institutions may have brought along an increase in deviant behaviour [...], while simultaneously ethnic groups and refugees grew in number and became more visible, e.g. in the competition for jobs and houses. Perhaps these phenomena were perceived as a threat and thus led to a decrease in tolerance" (van den Broek & Heunks 1992).

Modernization of society and the process of individualization in particular involve the emancipation of the individual citizen. The individual has become self-reliant which has resulted in a rise in interest in politics as well as in political participation and especially unconventional political behaviour (Barnes, Kaase *et al.* 1979). According to Huntington participation is a key element of modernization. "Participation distinguishes modern politics from traditional politics" (Huntington 1974, 110). And following Inglehart it is to be expected that in modern society people will be more participatory than people in less advanced societies. Increasingly, people "are likely to demand participation in *making* decisions, not just a voice in selecting the decision makers" (Inglehart 1977, 367).

Political participation is stronger and more widespread in Scandinavian countries than in other European countries, no matter whether this participation has to do with political interest, or actual involvement and willingness to get involved in protest activities.[7] Interest is highest in Norway, whereas the other Scandinavian countries are less extreme (Table 7).

[7] Political interest is indicated by three items: self-judgement about political interest, membership of political party, and discussing political matters.

Table 7. Interest in politics, tendency to protest and protest behaviour in Scandinavia and the rest of Europe (means standardized count scores).

	Europe						
	South and West		North		Scandinavia		
	mean	std	mean	std	mean	std	eta
Political interest	–.30	.95	.14	.99	.32	.98	.22
Political participation*	–.13	1.01	.06	.99	.12	.93	.09
Tendency to protest*	–.04	1.03	–.00	.98	.29	.94	.06

* The score for Scandinavia is calculated only for Denmark, Sweden and Iceland. Due to a translation error in the Norwegian questionnaire one of the items (joining unofficial strikes) was not comparable.

Source: European Values Study 1990

The degree of political interest in these countries resembles the degree of interest in the northern parts of Europe. Southern Europe seems to be far less interested in politics. Actual participation in all kinds of protest activities such as signing petitions, boycotts, demonstrations, unofficial strikes and occupations, appears more frequently in the Scandinavian[8] and Northern European countries than in Southern Europe. However, as far as the willingness to get involved in these kind of actions is concerned the Scandinavian countries are more willing to be engaged than both Northern and Southern Europe.

These general patterns for the Scandinavian countries masks the (often large) differences among the Nordic countries. Of course there are similarities, e.g., all Scandinavian countries are tolerant towards various kinds of persons, but there also exist differences in the degree of tolerating other people. Danish people are more tolerant than Icelanders, but Danish as well as Icelanders tolerate ethnic and religious groups more than Norwegians do. Norwegians, and particularly Swedes and Icelanders, have confidence in democratic institutions, whereas Danish people have far less confidence in such institutions. Swedes are more post-materialist than the Danes, Norwegians and Icelanders, who in their turn are more materialisti-

[8] Norway has to be excluded in these comparisons, because in this country one of the items was mistakenly wrongly translated. Instead of joining unofficial strikes, one on joining official strikes was asked.

cally-oriented. In the socio-political area the Scandinavian countries appear to be far from homogeneous.

Family

Particularly in the domain of primary relations large differences between the Scandinavian countries and the rest of Europe are to be expected. The Scandinavian countries are the forerunners as far as demographic changes are concerned (van de Kaa 1987; Lesthaeghe 1983; 1987). These demographic changes may be interpreted in terms of modernization. It seems as if individualization, the main process of modernization, has proceeded in a quicker tempo in these countries than in other countries. From the Scandinavian countries the changes in behaviours spread with a certain time lag over the rest of Europe. Marriage rates decreased first in the Scandinavian countries, then in the other European countries. The increase in divorces occurred first in Scandinavia, followed by the rest of Europe.

The leading position of the Scandinavian countries in this process of modernization appears in attitudes towards abortion, homosexuality and divorce.[9] Compared to other parts of Europe Scandinavia is much more permissive towards these kinds of behaviour (Table 8).

Particularly regarding the acceptance of homosexuality and abortion relatively large differences exist between the Scandinavians and the other Europeans. However, this rather permissive attitude towards these behaviours does not imply that anything goes. The tolerance is limited to these kind of behaviours. In case of other behaviours like adultery and sex under 18 people in the Scandinavian countries are most severe. These behaviours are not at all tolerated in the Scandinavian countries. Particularly sex under the legal age of consent is not allowed by the Scandinavians.[10]

When asked whether individuals should have the chance to enjoy complete sexual freedom without being restricted 74 % of the Scandinavians disagree with this statement, and only 16 % agree with it. Despite the apparent permissive climate in these countries there is a strong need for rules (Halman 1991). In this respect the Scandinavians are very distinctive from the rest of Europe, particularly compared to the southern countries where a less strict climate prevails. In the Southern European countries only 40 % disagree with the idea that each individual

[9] Abortion was not measured in Denmark in 1990 due to a mistake in translating the questionnaire. However, the 1981 survey yielded that the Danes are the most permissive population regarding abortion. 41 % of the Danes share the opinion that abortion can always be justified (Halman 1991, 340).

[10] In 1982 almost all people in Norway (99 %) were convinced that this behaviour could not be accepted (Halman 1991, 219).

Table 8. Justification of homosexuality, abortion, divorce, adultery and sex under the legal age of consent in Scandinavia and the rest of Europe (mean scores on 10-point scale: 1 = never justified, 10 = always justified).

	Europe						
	South and West		North		Scandinavia		
	mean	std	mean	std	mean	std	eta
Homosexuality	3.40	2.92	4.22	3.15	4.40	3.47	.12
Abortion*	4.15	2.78	4.64	2.59	5.24	2.79	.10
Divorce	5.20	2.99	5.56	2.62	5.97	2.79	.07
Adultery	2.66	2.37	2.97	2.29	2.10	1.87	.10
Sex under 18	2.83	2.63	3.04	2.64	1.09	.64	.17

* By mistake the item about abortion was not in the Danish questionnaire. The calculated mean score refers to Norway, Sweden and Iceland.

Source: European Values Study 1990

should have the chance to enjoy complete sexual freedom, and in the northern countries the proportion is 47 %.

As a consequence of individualization marriage has lost its monopoly position and has become an option. All kinds of alternative living arrangements are considered to be equal to traditional marriage. Besides, marriage is no longer perceived as an everlasting obligation and hence divorce is acceptable. The widespread acceptance of divorce and of increase in alternative living arrangements in the Scandinavian countries, should not be interpreted as a rejection of marriage. A large majority, even in the Scandinavian countries is of the opinion that marriage is not an outdated institution (Halman & Ester 1991, 29). Highest rates of people who share this opinion can be found in France (29 %), The Netherlands (21 %) and Belgium (23 %). In the Scandinavian countries the proportions are lower, and in case of Iceland much lower. The Scandinavians resemble in this respect the populations in Southern Europe.

The increase in acceptance of divorce is a sign of increased individualism and above all a sign of the higher demands on modern relationships. The decision to have a divorce or not has become a personal matter and it is no longer self-evident that such behaviour is rejected in case a couple has decided to get a divorce. In advanced, modern, individualized society it is a question of people's own decision. Furthermore, the higher demands in a relationship and marriage imply that if these demands are not met people will separate and end the relationship.

Table 9. Adherence to traditional family pattern in Scandinavia and the rest of Europe (mean standardized count scores).

	Europe						
	South and West		North		Scandinavia		
	mean	std	mean	std	mean	std	eta
Traditional family	.01	.92	.01	1.03	–.14	1.15	.03

Source: European Values Study 1990

The increased divorce rates do not therefore indicate a rejection of marriage. This appears also in the proportion of divorced people who are of the opinion that marriage is outdated. The same is true for those who live separately from their partners (see also Halman 1987; 1991).

The conclusion is that marriage is still rather popular in modern society, even in those societies (the Scandinavian countries) where alternative forms of marriage are widespread. Most people want to get married and many of the alternative ways of cohabitation end up in a marriage. In fact, these alternative ways of living together may be seen as stages before a marriage rather than real alternatives (van de Kaa 1987, 17).

Not only marriage is still highly valued in modern society, the same is true for family life. Large majorities of the populations in Europe as well as in Scandinavia consider the family very important in their life. In all countries the family is considered to be more important than friends and acquaintances, leisure time, work, religion or politics. The value of family life appears also in the large proportions of people saying that more emphasis on family life in the near future would be a good development.

Of course people can think of a wide variety of "family types" nowadays, ranging from "single individual households, couples living together not married, single parents, gay couples, 'reconstructed' families containing children of earlier unions of one or more of the adult members, and so on" (Rapoport 1989, 56). But in general the ideas of a family do not alter very much. Despite the increase in different family types a traditional view on the family still seems to prevail. This is reflected in the large majorities saying that a child needs both parents in order to grow up happily. A traditional family model is thus still highly valued in modern society, even in the Scandinavian countries. In this respect Scandinavia resembles the rest of Europe (Table 9).

Table 10. Democratic parenthood in Scandinavia and the rest of Europe (means standardized count score).

	Europe						
	South and West		North		Scandinavia		
	mean	std	mean	std	mean	std	eta
Democratic parenthood	–.26	.87	.12	1.04	.40	.99	.20

Source: European Values Study 1990

In modern society children are no longer an economic necessity (Saporiti 1989). Parenthood is no longer an obligation, but has become an option, and the decision to have children is determined by personal choices and considerations. A decrease in fertility levels (even below replacement level) appeared first in the Scandinavian countries, followed by the other European countries.

Furthermore, there has been a change in the relationship between parent(s) and child(ren). Parental roles have changed. A significant part of education has been left to specialized institutions like schools. "The child's susceptibility to the immediate social environment is increased, while his susceptibility to tradition is decreased" (Slater 1969, 24). The status of a child has increased, whereas parents are no longer as a matter of course dominating in an authoritarian way their children's lives. The distance between a child and its parents has been reduced significantly. The family has become a democratic institution.

However, empirically there is not much evidence that democracy has penetrated in the parent–child relationship. In most countries there is widespread agreement on the statement regarding the duties of the child towards its parents. Exceptions to this rule are the Scandinavian countries and the Netherlands. In these countries a (small) majority favours the idea that a child does not have the duty to respect and love parents who have not earned it by their behaviour and attitudes. However, even in the Scandinavian countries and the Netherlands a majority is of the opinion that parents have to do their utmost best for their child(ren) even at the cost of their own well-being.

Hence, modern views concerning parent-child relationships can be found particularly in the Scandinavian countries, whereas the opposite opinion is dominant in Southern Europe, and in Ireland (Table 10).

In almost all countries there is an increase in the support of the traditional views on parental roles. Contrary to the ideas about individualization and the

Table 11. Acceptability of abortion (mean standardized count score) in Scandinavia and the rest of Europe.

	Europe						
	South and West		North		Scandinavia		
	mean	std	mean	std	mean	std	eta
Abortion	–.18	1.05	.08	.95	.41	.99	.15

Source: European Values Study 1990

expected decrease in authoritarian parental roles, the empirical data show increasing support of traditional views in this respect. Modern liberal, democratic views are not widespread, but instead only minority phenomena. And the situation in Scandinavia is not very different from the rest of Europe.

Abortion is tolerated more in Scandinavian countries than in other countries, but this tolerance should not be exaggerated. In no country a mean score higher than 5.36 on a ten point scale (1 = never justified, 10 = always justified), which was found in Sweden, can be found. So, people are not tending to accept abortion in any case and in all circumstances. The acceptance or rejection of abortion is dependent upon the situation and the circumstances under which an abortion is considered. Even in Ireland where abortion is judged as hardly ever justifiable behaviour, a majority of the population is willing to accept an abortion if the mother's health is put at risk by the pregnancy. In Denmark and Sweden a small majority (of resp. 63 % and 52 %) is of the opinion that abortion can be approved if children are not wanted by the partners. Abortion is approved least of all when a couple is not married. An exception to this rule is Denmark where a (again small) majority says abortion is approved under these circumstances, too.

In most countries the approval of abortion has increased during the last decade. However, Sweden and Denmark are striking exceptions to this general rule. In both countries the various reasons for abortion are less approved of in 1990 than in 1981. However, despite this decrease in approval, these countries remain very tolerant towards abortion (Table 11).

In the domain of primary relations, thus, the Scandinavian countries resemble to a large extent the values and attitudes in the other countries. In fact the Scandinavian countries appear to be less modern, less individualized than could be expected on the basis of demographic trends. Marriage is not outdated in these countries, nor is the traditional family pattern rejected there. It is true that in Scandinavia a more tolerant climate prevails, whereas Southern European countries remain more strict. But this permissive climate does not imply that anything goes. Some behaviours are indeed permitted, others are not. Sex under the legal age of consent and adultery are condemned by Scandinavians, and Norwegians in particular. There is a clear need for strict rules regarding this kind of sexual behaviour.

However, although the Scandinavian countries resemble each other to a large extent, there are also marked differences which are hard to explain for a non-inhabitant of one of the Scandinavian countries. For instance, why are there so many Danes of the opinion that a woman needs a child to be fulfilled? No less then 82 % of the Danes share this opinion, whereas the other Scandinavians appear to be less convinced of this necessity (Sweden 21 %, Norway 23 %, Iceland 42 %). It is not clear to a foreigner why 67 % of the Danes and 84 % of the people in Iceland approve if a woman wants to have a child without a stable relationship, whereas in Norway and Sweden the proportion of people sharing this opinion is limited to resp. 25 % and 27 %. These figures illustrate the heterogeneity which appears sometimes in the Scandinavian countries with regard to value orientations in the domain of primary relations.

Work

The number of items in the European Values questionnaire indicative of the values in the domain of work is rather limited. They are mainly personal evaluations about the quality of work which may be judged by all people whether they have a job or not. The issues mentioned in the questionnaire referred to three basic orientations (Zanders 1987; Ester & Halman 1990; Halman & Vloet 1992). One of these basic orientations is personal development and consists of items like using initiative, responsibility, achieving something, using one's abilities, interesting job. Another orientation is comfort, indicated by such preferences as not too much pressure, generous holidays, and good hours. The third dimension contains only two items, good pay and job security, and is called material conditions.

The Scandinavian countries do not differ much from the other European countries in the judgement of these items (Table 12).

The Scandinavians are a little bit more in favour of personal development qualities than other Europeans are. On both other orientations the differences between Scandinavia and Europe are even less significant. This may be due to the fact that Scandinavia is not at all homogeneous in this respect. Swedes and Icelandic people are strongest in favouring personal development characteristics in jobs, just as they are also more in favour of comfort aspects, whereas Danes and Norwegians are not so convinced about the importance of such job qualities. Material conditions seem to be not at all important for the Danes, whereas the negotiation of the importance of these material qualities is not that strong in the

Table 12. Personal development, comfort and material conditions are important characteristics of a job (mean standardized LISREL and Latent Trait scores) according to Scandinavians and other Europeans.

	Europe						
	South and West		North		Scandinavia		
	mean	std	mean	std	mean	std	eta
Personal development	–.19	1.01	.08	.98	.31	.96	.15
Comfort	.12	1.04	–.07	.96	.08	1.04	.09
Material conditions	.14	.96	–.08	1.02	.04	.97	.11

Source: European Values Study 1990

other Scandinavian countries. Regarding work orientations there seems to exist no specific Scandinavian pattern which distinguishes people in these countries as a group from the rest of Europe. However, Scandinavia is not as homogeneous in this respect as might be assumed.

Conclusion

The comparisons of some basic social value orientations in the Scandinavian and other European countries yielded similarities as well as some undeniable differences. However, it seems impossible to distinguish a typical Scandinavian value pattern, although in some respects similar orientations appear in the Nordic countries only.

The Scandinavian countries resemble each other to a large extent, particularly regarding a comparison of church attendance and church membership. Membership of the Lutheran church is widespread and is part of Scandinavian identity, but this membership is not accompanied by strong commitment to the church. Membership is therefore only marginal membership. The influence of the churches is rather limited to providing for religious services. In this respect the Scandinavian countries are internally homogeneous, and compared to other European countries more or less unique. Institutional religion is low in Scandinavia; lower than in the rest of Europe.

In belief content the Scandinavian countries are far less homogeneous. A general picture is that traditional beliefs are not widespread in these countries. More people believe in some kind of spirit or life force rather than in a personal

God. However, Scandinavia and the Northern European countries resemble each other in this respect, and such general pictures do no justice to the large differences which exists within Scandinavia. Particularly in Denmark and Sweden people are less religious, whereas Norway and Iceland are far less extreme in this respect (Halman 1992).

A similar conclusion can be drawn regarding the political orientations. In general, Scandinavians appear to be preponderantly materialist in their orientation, despite the fact that all Nordic countries are well developed welfare states. Materialism is even more widespread in these Nordic countries than in the Southern European countries, which are less advanced. Inglehart's theory on value changes is not confirmed by these results (Pettersson 1992). In Denmark and Iceland post-materialism diminished in the eighties and in Norway and Sweden hardly any changes appeared in this respect.

In political orientations the Scandinavian countries resemble the Northern European countries, and together these countries have to be distinguished from Southern European countries. Confidence in authoritative institutions is low in both Scandinavian and Northern European countries. Democratic institutions are trusted more in the northern and Nordic countries and less in Southern Europe. Scandinavians appear to be more tolerant against all kinds of persons, and political participation is stronger and more widespread in Scandinavian countries than in other European countries.

However, there seems to be no typical Nordic pattern. Although Scandinavians tolerate others more than other populations in Europe do, they differ in the degree of tolerance. Danes are more tolerant than Icelanders and Norwegians. Compared to the other Scandinavian countries the Danes show low levels of confidence in institutions and Swedes are more post-materialist than the other Scandinavians.

Regarding primary relations the Scandinavian countries resemble the values and attitudes in the other European countries. In no country investigated is marriage seen as an outdated institution, nor is the traditional family pattern condemned. Typical for the Scandinavian countries seems to be the relatively tolerant climate concerning various alternative (particular sexual) behaviours. This permissiveness should not be confused with unlimited liberty. Permissiveness is accompanied by strict rules, particularly regarding adultery and sex under 18.

Despite this congruence there remain marked differences. For instance, a large majority of the Danes is of the opinion that a woman needs a child to be fulfilled whereas in other Scandinavian countries a rather limited number of people shares this opinion. Approval of women wanting to have a child without a stable relationship is relatively strong in Denmark and Iceland, whereas people in Sweden and Norway are more reluctant to accept this behaviour.

The value orientations we have distinguished in the domain of work appear to be atypical for the Scandinavian countries. Scandinavia is in fact not at all homogeneous in this respect.

The Scandinavian countries have a common ethnic and cultural background. These countries are very well developed democratic welfare states sharing a common Lutheran history. These common histories at least suggest that these countries will resemble each other to a large extent as far as value orientations are concerned. Our analyses yielded no confirmation for such ideas. In some values there seems indeed to be a typical Scandinavian pattern, but regarding other values the Scandinavian countries resemble other European countries; the Northern European countries (Netherlands, Belgium, Germany and Great Britain) in particular. Besides, concerning many value orientations Scandinavia is not at all homogeneous. The mutual variation in value orientations is often too large to get at such a conclusion. There is no uniform pattern of values in the Scandinavian countries. As far as values are concerned Scandinavia is heterogeneous.

References

Almond, G. A. & S. Verba, 1965
The Civic Culture. Boston: Little Brown and Company.

Ashford, S. & N. Timms, 1992
What Europe Thinks. Dartmouth: Aldershot.

Barnes, S., M. Kaase *et al.*, 1979
Political Action: Mass Participation in Five Western Democracies. Beverly Hills: Sage.

Broek, A. van den & F. Heunks, 1992
"Political Culture. Patterns of Political Orientations and Behaviour". Manuscript for Dutch publication on the EVG study to appear in 1993.

Deth, J. W. van, 1991
"New Values and Old Cleavages". Paper presented at the XVth World Congress of the International Political Association, Buenos Aires, Argentina, July 21–25, 1991.

Dobbelaere, K., 1981
"Secularization: A Multi-Dimensional Concept". *Current Sociology* 29:1–213.

Dobbelaere, K., 1985
"Convergenties en divergenties in sociologische theorieën naargelang van de gebruikte paradigma's". *Sociale Wetenschappen* 28:237–259.

Dobbelaere, K. & L. Voyé, 1992
"Godsdienst en kerkelijkheid". Pp. 115–162 in: J. Kerkhofs, K. Dobbelaere, L. Voyé & B. Bawin-Legros (eds.), *De versnelde ommekeer*. Tielt: Lannoo.

Dogan, M., 1988
"Introduction: Strains on Legitimacy". Pp. 1–18 in M. Dogan (ed.), *Comparing Pluralist Democracies*. Boulder and London: Westview Press.

Dorenbos, J., L. Halman & F. Heunks, 1987
"Modernisering in West Europa: een tweedeling?". Pp. 234–254 in: L. Halman, F.

Heunks, R. de Moor & H. Zanders, *Traditie, secularisatie en individualisering*. Tilburg: Tilburg University Press.

Ester, P. & L. Halman, 1990
"Basic Values in Western Europe: An Empirical Exploration". Paper presented at the XIIth World Congress of Sociology, Madrid, July 9–13, 1990.

Gubert, R. (ed.), 1992
Persistenze e Mutamenti Dei Valori Degli Italiani Nel Contesto Europeo. Trento: Reverdito Edizioni.

Halman, L., 1987
"Waarden rond gezin, huwelijk, seksualiteit en opvoeding". Pp. 123–167 in: L. Halman, F. Heunks, R. de Moor & H. Zanders, *Traditie, secularisatie en individualisering*. Tilburg: Tilburg University Press.

Halman, L., 1991
Waarden in de Westerse Wereld. Tilburg: Tilburg University Press.

Halman, L., 1992
"Value Shift and Generations in Western Europe, Scandinavia and Northern America". Paper presented at the XIth Nordic Conference for the Sociology of Religion, Skálholt, Iceland, August 17–20, 1992.

Halman, L. & P. Ester, 1991
"Trends in Individualization in Western Europe, North America, and Scandinavia: Divergence or Convergence of Underlying Values". Paper presented at the symposium "Growing into the Future", Stockholm, October 22–23, 1991.

Halman, L., F. Heunks, R. de Moor & H. Zanders, 1987
Traditie, secularisatie en individualisering. Tilburg: Tilburg University Press.

Halman, L. & R. de Moor, 1991
Information Bulletin EVSSG 1991. Tilburg: IVA and Tilburg University.

Halman, L. & A. Vloet, 1992
Measuring and Comparing Values in 16 Countries of the Western World in 1990 and 1981. Tilburg: IVA and Tilburg University.

Hamberg, E., 1990
Studies in the Prevalence of Religious Beliefs and Religious Practices in Contemporary Sweden. Uppsala: Uppsala University.

Huntington, S. P., 1974
"Political Development and Political Decay". Pp. 108–130 in: N. J. Vig & R. P. Stiefbold (eds), *Politics in Advanced Nations: Modernization, Development, and Contemporary Change*. Englewood Cliffs: Prentice Hall.

Inglehart, R., 1977
The Silent Revolution. Princeton: Princeton University Press.

Inglehart, R., 1990
Culture Shift in Advanced Industrial Society. Princeton: Princeton University Press.
Kaa, D. J. van de, 1987
"Europe's Second Demographic Transition". *Population Bulletin* 42:1–57.
Kerkhofs, J., 1992
"The Meaning of Value Studies for the Future of Europe". Paper presented at the International Conference European Values, Trento, 1 and 2 October, 1992.
Klages, H., 1985
Wertorientierungen im Wandel: Rückblick, Gegenwartsanalyse, Prognosen. Frankfurt/ New York: Campus Verlag.
Lane, J. E. & S. O. Ersson, 1987
Politics and Society in Western Europe. Beverly Hills: Sage Publications.
Lesthaeghe, R., 1983
"A Century of Demographic and Cultural Change in Western Europe: An Exploration of Underlying Dimensions". *Population and Development Review* 9:411–435.
Lesthaeghe, R., 1987
"Gezinsvorming en -ontbinding: de twee transities". *Tijdschrift voor Sociologie* 8:9–33.
Luckmann, T., 1967
The Invisible Religion. New York: MacMillan.
Meulemann, H., 1983
"Value Change in West Germany 1950–1980: Integrating the Empirical Evidence". *Social Science Information* 22:777–800.
Meulemann, H., 1985
"Säkularisierung und Politik". *Politische Vierteljahresschrift* 26:29–51.
Meulemann, H., 1987
"Religiöse und Politische Werte in Alters- und Bildungsgruppen". *Politische Viertel-jahresschrift* 28:220–241.
Moor, R. de, 1987
"Religieuze en morele waarden". Pp. 15–49 in: L. Halman, F. Heunks, R. de Moor & H. Zanders, *Traditie, secularisatie en individualisering*. Tilburg: Tilburg University Press.
Peabody, D., 1985
National Characters. New York: Cambridge University Press.
Pettersson, T., 1992
"Culture Shift and Generational Population Replacement. Individualization, Secularization, and Moral Value Change in Contemporary Scandinavia". Paper presented at the XIth Nordic Conference for the Sociology of Religion, Skálholt, Iceland, August 17–20, 1992.
Rapoport, R., 1989
"Ideologies about Family Forms". Pp. 53–69 in: K. Boh (*et al.*) (eds.), *Changing Patterns in European Family Life: A Comparative Analysis of 14 Countries*. London: Routledge.
Riis, O., 1992
"Secularization in Scandinavia". Paper presented at the International Conference European Values, Trento, 1 and 2 October, 1992.

Sani, G., 1980

"The Political Culture of Italy: Continuity and Change". Pp. 273–324 in: G. A. Almond and S. Verba (eds.), *The Civic Culture Revisited*. Boston: Little Brown and Company.

Saporiti, A., 1989

"Historical Changes in the Family's Reproductive Patterns". Pp. 191–216 in: K. Boh (*et al.*) (eds.), *Changing Patterns in European Family Life: A Comparative Analysis of 14 Countries*. London: Routledge.

Slater, P. E., 1969

"Social Change and the Democratic Family". Pp. 20–52 in: W. G. Bennis & P. E. Slater, *The Temporary Society*. New York: Harper and Row.

Wilson, B., 1982

Religion in Sociological Perspective. Oxford: Oxford University Press.

Wood, M. R. & L. A. Zurcher Jr., 1988

The Development of a Postmodern Self. New York: Greenwood Press.

Zanders, H., 1987

"Opvattingen over arbeid in Nederland en Europa". Pp. 168–186 in: L. Halman, F. Heunks, R. de Moor & H. Zanders, *Traditie, secularisatie en individualisering*. Tilburg: Tilburg University Press.

ODD HELGE LINDSETH and OLA LISTHAUG

Religion and Work Values in the 1990s: A Comparative Study of Western Europe and North America

Max Weber's thesis on the relationship between religion and economy, most notably his work on "The Protestant Ethic and the Spirit of Capitalism", has had tremendous influence on theoretical and empirical sociology. While it certainly is of interest to discuss Weber's studies in a theoretical context, our study is limited to an empirical investigation of Weberian hypotheses linked to the relationship between religion and work values. This is a field of modern sociology where empirical research inspired by Weber has been considerable, and it is to this line of research that we hope this paper will contribute. In the next section we will present a brief review of earlier research. We then discuss data sources and the empirical operationalizations of key variables. In the third section we survey the main empirical findings. Finally, in part four we conclude and discuss if further studies along the same lines as ours would be worthwhile to pursue.

1. Introduction

It is beyond the scope of this article to attempt any degree of summarizing of Weber's thesis concerning the link between Protestantism and capitalism, not to speak of his general sociology of religion. Suffice to say here that Weber's argument that religion is linked to economic factors has inspired scholars to develop testable hypotheses covering quite a wide range of phenomena. Weber presented a careful analysis of specific aspects of the content of meaning of certain religious dogmas (i.e. the concept of "calling") in particular Protestant sects (i.e. Calvinists), and suggested that certain forms of Protestantism could have an elective affinity to the ethos of modern capitalism (i.e. the systematic effort to achieve wealth and profit). Later research has developed the general idea that religion in the form of Protestantism would constitute a more dynamic factor in social and economic life than Catholicism – the other major version of Christianity. In his classic, *The Religious Factor*, Gerhard Lenski (1963) introduced Weber's thesis to the methods of modern social science research. Based on data collected by the Detroit Area Study of the University of Michigan he concluded:

On the great majority of variables either the Jews or the white Protestants have ranked first with the other ranking second, the Catholics have usually ranked third, and the Negro Protestants fourth. With considerable regularity the Jews and the white Protestants have identified themselves with the individualistic, competitive patterns of thought and action linked with the middle class, and historically associated with the Protestant ethic or its secular counterpart, the spirit of capitalism. By contrast Catholics and Negro Protestants have more often been associated with collectivist, security oriented, working-class patterns of thought and action historically opposed to the Protestant Ethic and the Spirit of Capitalism (Lenski 1963, 113).

The conclusions of Lenski were radical in the sense that they both went against the conventional wisdom stated in the influential volume by Lipset and Bendix (1959) that the Weber thesis did not apply to modern society (Bouma 1973), and because Lenski demonstrated that the secularization process of modern society had not eliminated religion as a social force. Following Lenski's book there soon emerged a series of studies that partly sought to replicate his findings as well as extending the research to associated questions. This research, covering themes like social mobility, the social and religious bases for achievement motivation, and the use of education to get ahead, produced mostly negative findings (Bouma 1973). Moreover, a number of these studies pointed to a series of shortcomings in the modern empirical investigation of Weber's thesis – most of which were also seen as deficiencies of Lenski's book. First, the current research did not include measures of religious involvement, which along the lines of Weber's theory should be as significant as denomination (Schuman 1971; Bouma 1973). Second, the potential confounding impact of variables like class or ethnicity was not accounted for (Greeley 1964; Schuman 1971). Third, the hypotheses of the modern research were simplistic when compared to the analytically rich work of Weber (Greeley 1964; Lenski 1971; Bouma 1973; McAllister 1983). Fourth, most of the data were collected in the United States, and in some cases even from local or regional samples, which certainly was the case for the most important of them all – the Detroit Area Study data used by Lenski (McAllister 1983).

The mostly negative findings that accrued in the post-Lenski flow of empirical research on the Weber thesis hold even for work values; Protestants have not been demonstrated to be more driven in their work achievement motivation than have Catholics (Bouma 1973). The accumulation of negative evidence could lead us to close the case, and conclude that Weber formulated some interesting speculations on the relationship between religion and economy, but that these speculations are not corroborated by scientific evidence. His thesis could well be true for the period of nascent capitalism – although this is difficult to know since modern social science did not exist at the time. The validity for contemporary Western society, on the other hand, could be marginal – as the overall empirical findings would suggest. The negative findings could be attributed to the effects of secularization and to the general processes of convergence between Protestantism and Catholicism (Alwin 1986). However, there may still be research strategies that could improve on the production of evidence for or against the Weber thesis. Three such directions can be outlined. First, new research might attempt to define and measure more closely the impact of specific religious beliefs (i.e. the belief in predestination) on work values (Bouma 1973, 152). Second, new research could focus on the problem of establishing proper operationalization of work values as it is not always clear how these should be measured. Third, cross-national data that allow for comparisons between nations would be particularly useful as this would eliminate influences of national cultures that could mask the differential impact of religious denomination on work values. For example, the negative findings in the United States could be attributed to a strong cultural belief in the values of individual achievement that is adopted by Catholics and Protestants alike – thus masking the impact of variations in religious belief systems. The omnipresence of an American ethos (McClosky & Zaller 1984) could thus make the United States a deviating case. The research for this paper follows research strategies two and three; we use multiple measurements of work values and expand the data analysis to include 16 countries.

2. Data and Measurement

Data are from the 1990 EVSSG Study (Listhaug & Huseby 1990).[1] We analyse data from the following countries: Iceland, Norway, Sweden, Denmark, Great Britain, Northern Ireland, Ireland, West Germany, Netherlands, Belgium, France, Italy, Spain, Portugal, the United States, Canada. For six of the countries, Great Britain, Northern Ireland, West Germany, The Netherlands, the United States, and Canada, the populations can be split by Catholic and Protestant denominations. For these countries we can perform an elaborate analysis of the impact of denomination on work values. To simplify the analysis we have excluded members of religious denominations other than Protestants or Catholics from the data sets.

The concept of the Protestant work ethic includes a notion of a positive attitude toward work, that work is a dynamic activity, and that work in itself is good. We can also call such values work-directed. The questionnaire contains three sets of items that can be used to construct composite measures for work values. The first set presents a card with 15 aspects of a job that the respondent is asked to evaluate: "Here are some aspects of a job that people say are important. Please look at them and tell me which ones you personally think are important in a job?" Similar lists have been used in earlier research (Lenski 1963; Elizur 1984; Fogarty 1985; Harding *et al.* 1986; Borg 1986; Elizur *et al.* 1991; Ashford & Timms 1992). It

[1] Data were made available by the Norwegian Social Science Data Services.

seems fair to say that the resulting indices have been inconsistent and often lacking in conceptual and theoretical meaning (Timms 1992). The goal here is to construct a measure of work values that tap the concept of the Protestant work ethic. The first index, that we label LENSKI1, is constructed to be close to the operationalizations of Lenski in his original work (Lenski 1963). We have based this index on 6 of the 15 items in the list. The index is built by adding up the number of items that are mentioned by the respondent if these items are positive indicators of the Protestant work ethic or not preferred (not marked) by the respondent if the items are negative indicators of the Protestant work ethic. The positive indicators were the following: "Good chances for promotion"; "a job in which you feel you can achieve something". The negative indicators were: "Good pay", "Good hours"; "Generous holidays"; "Good job security". This index goes from 0 to 6 with a high value indicating preference for the Protestant work ethic. The second index uses information from all 15 items employing identical principles for its construction. Four more positive items were added from the list: "A job that is interesting"; "An opportunity to use initiative"; "A responsible job"; "A job that meets one's abilities". The five additional negative indicators were: "Pleasant people to work with"; "Not too much pressure"; "A job respected by people in general"; "A useful job for society"; "Meeting people". The resulting index, labeled LENSKI2, runs from 0 to 15 with high values marking a support for a Protestant work ethic.

The second set of items consisted of a description of motivations for work: "Here are some statements about why people work. Irrespective of whether you work or not, which of them comes closest to what you think?" Among the five alternatives listed, two were positive indicators of the Protestant work ethic: "I will always do the best I can, regardless of pay"; "I enjoy my work; it's the most important thing in my life". The three negative indicators were: "Work is like a business transaction. The more I get paid, the more I do; the less I get paid, the less I do"; "Working for a living is a necessity; I wouldn't work if I didn't have to"; "I enjoy working, but I don't let it interfere with the rest of my life". The resulting index, LENSKI3, goes from 0 to 5, with a high value signifying the acceptance of a Protestant work ethic. We note that all or parts of the relevant questions was not asked in Canada, the United States, and Sweden. These countries are then excluded from the analysis of this index.

The third set consists of two items, taken from a longer list of statements, measured on a 10-point scale. The first tapped preference for competition and the second preference for hard work. The scales for both questions were reversed such that the low value (1) on the scales were linked to the following statements for the respective item: "Competition is harmful. It brings out the worst in people", and, "Hard work doesn't generally bring success – it's more a matter of luck and connections". The high value on the scales (10) was associated with support for the following positions on the items: "Competition is good. It stimulates people to work hard and develop new ideas"; "In the long run, hard work usually brings a better life". The resulting index, COMPWORK (this index might be sufficiently divergent from the empirical work of Lenski to avoid a label that calls on his name), runs from 2 to 20, even this measure with the positive end tapping support for the Protestant work ethic. Further details on index constructions are available from the authors. An examination of the correlations between indices shows that it is only LENSKI1 and LENSKI2 that are significantly correlated – which of course is an effect of the way these measures are constructed. The correlations between indices across the three sets of items are virtually zero. This is an indication that our operationalizations do not measure the same underlying concept. Elusive as this concept might be, an approach that uses variegating operationalizations could possibly produce empirical findings of some inconsistency, but at the same holding the potential to uncover ways of measuring the concept of the Protestant work ethic that could show more promise than others.

3. Empirical Results

The first step in the analysis is simply to inspect the means on the indices for the countries in the study. We have to remember that we have excluded members in religious denominations other than Catholics and Protestants, including those without a religious affiliation. The results (in Figures 1–4) are presented for Protestant and Catholic countries, and for Catholics and Protestants within split countries. The results for LENSKI1 (Figure 1) show Catholics in France to have the strongest Protestant work ethic with an average of 3.4 on the scale, slightly ahead of Protestants in Britain (3.3) and the Protestants of Denmark (3.1) and Norway (3.0). The spread among Catholics is somewhat larger, ranging from 3.4 in France to 2.6 in Spain and Portugal. The comparable spread on the Protestant side of the divide goes from 3.3 in Britain to 2.8 in West Germany and the United States. Checking an unspecified number of items from a list is a form of survey measurement that might be susceptible to be influenced by the procedures of the companies that do the interviewing, for example in how much time that respondents are given to check items on the lists. Diverging survey procedures, and other country-specific factors, make comparisons within religiously divided countries especially intriguing. The means for Protestants and Catholics in divided countries are almost identical. It is only Britain that records a difference of .2 on the scale, with Protestants scoring higher than Catholics. The gross similarity between the two denominations in the six religiously split countries together with the mixed rank order of homogeneous countries of either faith, suggests a first conclusion that work ethic is not convincingly related to religious denomination.

The empirical pattern for LENSKI2 (Figure 2) is not remarkably different from what we found for the less encompassing measure. France is again on top and the pattern by Catholic and Protestant countries is utterly inconsistent. Again, among

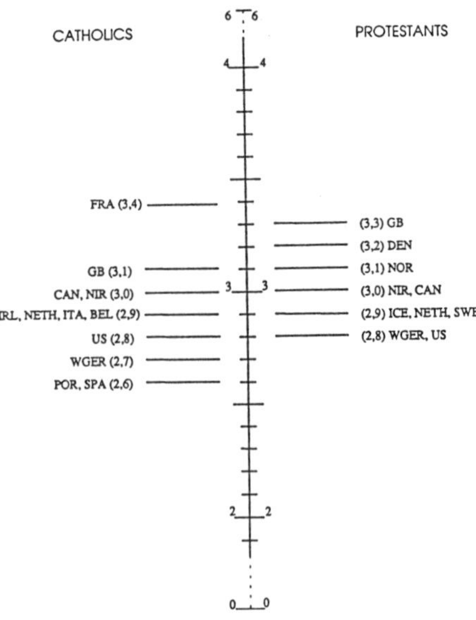

Figure 1. Work values and Religious Denomination. Average values on LENSKI1.

divided countries it is only Britain that shows some difference in the expected direction.

The index LENSKI3 accounted for above probes into motivations for work. The ranking of countries is somewhat different from what we observed for LENSKI1 and LENSKI2, but there is no clear order by religious denomination. We note that Catholics countries that tended to have low scores on LENSKI1 and LENSKI2, notably Portugal and Spain, record relatively higher scores here. The analysis for split countries is less complete as we lack data for Canada and the United States. The results for the remaining countries in this group, the Netherlands, West Germany, Britain, and Northern Ireland, show small differences, although Protestants in these countries seem to be a trifle stronger in their work ethic than their Catholic brethren.

COMPWORK is constructed from two items tapping support for competition and hard work. The ordering by nation and denomination is again fuzzy. The United States, Canada, and Iceland score highest, and Portugal and Denmark lowest. The differences between Catholics and Protestants in divided nations are small, with a partial exception for Northern Ireland and Britain, where Protestants are slightly more inclined to have high scores than are Catholics.

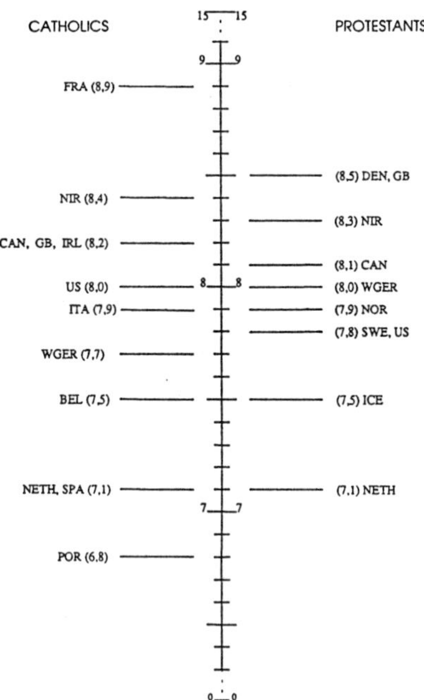

Figure 2. **Work values and Religious Denomination. Average values on LENSKI2.**

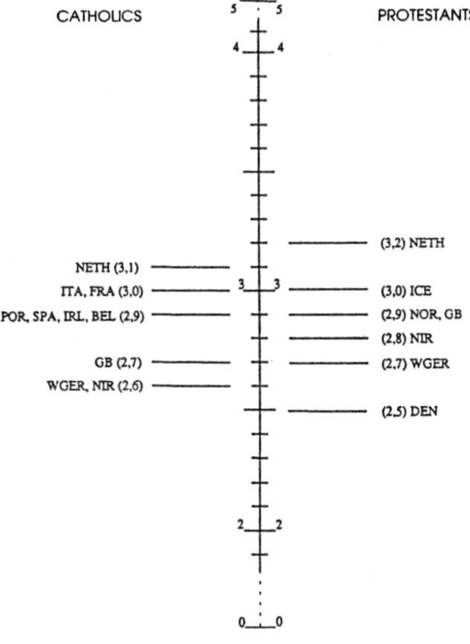

Figure 3. **Work values and Religious Denomination. Average values on LENSKI3.**

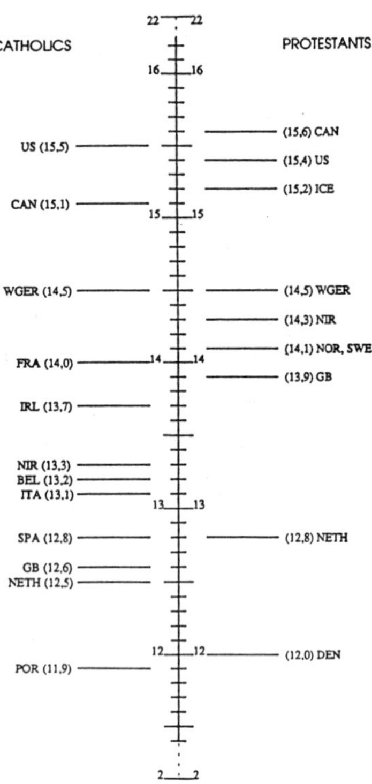

Figure 4. Work values and Religious Denomination. Average values on COMP-WORK.

In sum, the analysis by country has not given strong evidence for the proposition that the work ethic of Protestants and Catholics differs in kind. This holds true across the three sets of measures that we use as operationalizations. The only exception to the negative evidence is some support for the Weberian hypothesis in Britain. A crude analysis of the kind that we have performed above raises many questions – of methodological and substantive kind. To somewhat reduce the complexity of the analytical task we will restrict the empirical analysis to the cases where we can compare Catholics and Protestants within the same country context. This would eliminate the potential confounding impact of variations in survey procedures on the measurement of the listed items used for the LENSKI indices – although it is difficult to see that these variations could introduce a bias correlated with religion.

A within-country analysis also makes it possible to control for other relevant factors that might have an impact on work values. First of all it is important to introduce a control for religious involvement as we expect that the religiosity among Catholics is somewhat stronger than among Protestants. By controlling for the strength of religiosity we can sort out more clearly the impact of religious denomination – which is the main concern in this article. We have constructed a

Table 1. Multiple regression with LENSKI1 as dependent variable.

Regression coefficients	GB		NIR		WGER		NETH		USA		CAN	
	B	Beta	B	Beta	B	Beta	B	Beta	B	Beta	B	Beta
Sex	.29	.11*	.51	.19*	–.06	–.02	.18	.07	–.03	–.01	.10	.04
Age	.00	.03	–.00	–.04	.00	.03	.01	.11	.00	.03	.00	.01
Religious denomination	.12	.01	–.08	–.03	.11	.04	–.10	–.04	–.05	–.02	–.05	–.02
Religiosity	.01	.05	.01	.03	.02	.12**	.02	.09	–.00	–.01	–.01	–.05
Social class	.09	.23**	.08	.17	.11	.18**	.09	.19**	.05	.15**	.05	.14**
Adjusted R^2	.06		.04		.05		.04		.02		.02	
N	771		256		1 789		424		1 124		1 125	

Table 2. Multiple regression with LENSKI2 as dependent variable.

Regression coefficients	GB		NIR		WGER		NETH		USA		CAN	
	B	Beta	B	Beta	B	Beta	B	Beta	B	Beta	B	Beta
Sex	–.09	–.02	.40	.09	–.46	–.10**	–.35	–.08	–.15	–.04	.06	.01
Age	–.00	–.01	–.01	–.07	–.01	–.05	.00	.02	–.00	–.02	–.00	–.00
Religious denomination	.23	.04	–.19	–.04	.13	.03	–.01	–.00	–.17	–.04	–.10	–.03
Religiosity	–.00	–.01	.01	.04	.01	.02	.00	.01	–.02	–.04	–.03	–.09*
Social class	.18	.29**	.17	.25**	.23	.24**	.20	.26**	.10	.16**	.10	.16**
Adjusted R^2												
N												

Note:
Sex is coded 1 male, 2 female.
Age is coded in years.
Religious denomination is coded 1 Catholics, 2 Protestants.
Religiosity is a composite measure of beliefs in dogmas and religious involvement. The scale goes from 0 (weak religiosity) to 22 (high religiosity). Details on index construction are available from the authors.
Social class is coded from 1 (low) to 12 (high). The measure is based on the occupation code of the respondents or, if these data are missing, on the occupation code of the chief wage earner of the household.

* Significant at the 0.01 level. ** Significant at the 0.001 level.

Table 3. Multiple regression with LENSKI3 as dependent variable.

Regression coefficients	GB		NIR		WGER		NETH	
	B	Beta	B	Beta	B	Beta	B	Beta
Sex	–.04	–.02	–.18	–.09	.04	.02	–.02	–.01
Age	.01	.09	.01	.15	.01	.14**	.00	.07
Religious denomination	.22	.08	.13	.06	.08	.05	.13	.07
Religiosity	.02	.11*	.03	.15	.02	.14**	.00	.02
Social class	.01	.04	.05	.15	.04	.09**	.00	.00
Adjusted R^2	.03		.08		.06		.00	
N	771		256		1 789		424	

Table 4. Multiple regression with COMPWORK as dependent variable.

Regression coefficients	GB		NIR		WGER		NETH		USA		CAN	
	B	Beta	B	Beta	B	Beta	B	Beta	B	Beta	B	Beta
Sex	–.54	–.06	–.36	–.05	–.71	–.09**	–.10	–.01	–.71	–.09**	–.51	–.06
Age	.01	.05	.05	.21	.03	.13**	–.00	–.00	.01	.03	.03	.11**
Religious denomination	.97	.09	.47	.06	.10	.01	.20	.03	–.12	–.01	.28	.03
Religiosity	.01	.01	.05	.06	.07	.12**	.03	.06	.07	.08*	.05	.07
Social class	.18	.13**	.29	.23**	.28	.17**	.18	.16*	.14	.10**	.10	.08*
Adjusted R^2	.03		.11		.08		.02		.02		.03	
N	754		251		1 641		400		1 091		1 110	

Note:

Sex is coded 1 male, 2 female.

Age is coded in years.

Religious denomination is coded 1 Catholics, 2 Protestants.

Religiosity is a composite measure of beliefs in dogmas and religious involvement. The scale goes from 0 (weak religiosity) to 22 (high religiosity). Details on index construction are available from the authors.

Social class is coded from 1 (low) to 12 (high). The measure is based on the occupation code of the respondents or, if these data are missing, on the occupation code of the chief wage earner of the household.

* Significant at the 0.01 level.　　** Significant at the 0.001 level.

composite measure for religiosity covering both religious activity and beliefs in dogmas. Work values is expected to reflect the occupational class of the person. We expect that middle class and upper class occupations will tend to develop value preferences that see work in itself as a good thing, while lower class positions will develop preferences for work values that see work as a means to other ends. Class differences in work values can be accounted for both by a socialization effect of the family whereby the preference for work values are transferred from parents to the children, or by a socialization effect of the workplace. In the latter case the generally more favourable working conditions of the middle classes will work to develop a stronger commitment to work-directed values. We hypothesize a positive relationship between social class and the various measures of work values that we have constructed. Moreover, the argument for including class is the fact that in a number of countries Catholics tend to have lower class positions than Protestants such that differences in work values between the two groups might be a reflection of class rather than religion. Finally, we include controls for sex and age. These variables have a strong impact on religiosity, and they are at the same time potentially relevant in explaining variations in work values.

We have run a series of regression models separately for the six countries. Catholics are coded 1 and Protestants 2 such that we expect a positive coefficient if the basic hypothesis is supported. The results are documented in Tables 1–4. Starting with LENSKI1 and LENSKI2, we find no impact of religious denomination on work values (Tables 1–2) as the regression coefficient hovers around zero. Social class is the only variable that records a consistent impact on work values. The relationship goes in the expected direction with the higher classes having stronger work-directed values. The results for LENSKI3 are also negative as for none of the four countries (we lack data for the United States and Canada) is a statistical impact of denomination observed. We note, nonetheless, that the coefficients of countries are all positive. Religiosity has a positive influence on work values in Great Britain and Western Germany. In contrast to what we found above the impact of class is almost non-existent, with the expected positive impact recorded only in Western Germany. Lastly, on COMPWORK no statistically significant differences between Catholics and Protestants are observed, although the signs here are positive except for the United States. Class is again the only factor to have a consistent impact on work values. This holds up in all six countries.

The models that we have presented in Tables 1–4 do not exhaust all relevant statistical models. One could argue that a line of modelling that is maybe closer to Weberian thought is to see the impact of religiosity – beliefs and activity – to be different among Protestants and Catholics. While a strong religiosity might lead to a strengthening of work-directed values among Protestants a comparable effect might be lacking among Catholics. The appropriate statistical specification of this class of models would be to estimate the models separately for Catholics and

Protestants. We have rerun the new model across the four dependent variables. The results fail to support the hypothesis. (Tables can be obtained from the authors).

The conclusions from the multivariate analysis of the six religiously divided countries are in line with what we found for the simpler analysis of the sixteen countries: Systematic differences in work values between Catholics and Protestants cannot be observed.

4. Conclusion

This paper has sought to elaborate on Weberian inspired hypotheses on the relationships between religion and work values. We have done this by expanding the research in two directions, one by employing a classification of work values that uses three distinct operationalizations, second by analyzing data from a large number of countries. The negative evidence that has turned up leads us to conclude that it is unlikely that we will find systematic differences between Catholics and Protestants in the realm of work values when we compare samples from general populations. Any merits that the theory still might hold will most likely be restricted to specific religious groups in particular historical settings. But this tempered version of the theory – which we have not investigated – might be closer to Weber's own ideas on the subject than the derivations that we have entertained here.

References

Alwin, Diane F., 1986

"Religion and Parental Child-Rearing Orientations: Evidence of a Catholic–Protestant Convergence". *American Journal of Sociology*, vol. 92, no. 2 (September).

Ashford, Sheena & Noel Timms, 1992

What Europe Thinks: A Study of Western European Values. Dartmouth: Aldershot.

Borg, Ingwer, 1986

"A Cross-Cultural Replication on Elizur's Facets of Work Values". *Multivariate Behavioral Research*, vol. 21 (October).

Bouma, Gary D., 1973

"Beyond Lenski: A Critical Review of Recent 'Protestant Ethic' Research". *Journal for the Scientific Study of Religion*, vol. 12.

Elizur, Dov, 1984

"Facets of Work Values: A Structural Analysis of Work Outcomes". *Journal of Applied Psychology*, vol. 69, No. 3.

Elizur, Dov, *et al.,* 1991

"The Structure of Work Values: A Cross-Cultural Comparison". *Journal of Organizational Behavior*, vol. 12.

Fogarty, Michael, 1985

"British Attitudes to Work", in: Abrahms, Mark, David Gerhard & Noel Timms (eds.), *Values and Social Change in Britain*. London: Macmillan.

Greeley, Andrew, 1964

"The Protestant Ethic: Time for a Moratorium". *Sociological Analysis*, vol. 25.

Harding, Stephen, David Phillips & Michael Fogarty, 1986

Contrasting Values in Western Europe: Unity, Diversity and Change. London: Macmillan.

Lenski, Gerhard, 1963

The Religious Factor: A Sociological Study of Religion's Impact on Politics, Economics, and Family Life. New York: Doubleday, Anchor Books.

Lenski, Gerhard, 1971

"The Religious Factor in Detroit: Revisited". *American Sociological Review*, vol. 36 (February).

Lipset, Seymour Martin & Reinhard Bendix, 1959

Social Mobility in Industrial Society. Berkeley: University of California Press.

Listhaug, Ola & Beate Huseby, 1990

Values in Norway: Study Description and Codebook. ISS-rapport no. 29. Trondheim: Department of Sociology, University of Trondheim.

McAllister, Ian, 1983

"Religious Commitment and Social Attitudes in Ireland". *Review of Religious Research*, vol. 25, no. 1 (September).

McClosky, Herbert & John Zaller, 1984

The American Ethos. Cambridge, Mass.: Harvard University Press.

Schuman, Howard, 1971

"The Religious Factor in Detroit: Review, Replication, and Reanalysis". *American Sociological Review*, vol. 36 (February).

Timms, Noel, 1992

Family and Citizenship: Values in Contemporary Britain. Dartmouth: Aldershot.

OLE RIIS

Patterns of Secularization in Scandinavia

The Problem

Scandinavia forms a paradoxical case of secularization. The influence of the religious institution is limited to a narrowly defined scope. The spokesmen of the churches have little influence in society. Few believe in the Christian dogma and few attend mass on ordinary Sundays. Scandinavian countries thereby seem singular examples of secularization. However, this does not form the whole picture. The majority of the people remain members of the Lutheran state churches, and faithfully pay church taxes. Scandinavian religion thus seems to be a case of "belonging without believing". Despite the impression that the churches are half-empty at mass, Scandinavian taxpayers have financed a wide-spread building of new churches during the last decades. Despite that churches may seem half-empty on normal Sundays, they are full on special occasions, such as on the 24th of December. Despite that religion does not seem to have much influence on the interpretation of life for most modern Scandinavians, they still use churches for the *rites-de-passage*. For sociologists, it is worth stressing that the churches are used for the solemn overtures to the festivities which reunite kin and friends. Despite that pastors have limited influence in public matters, they still retain the social prestige as high-ranking officials and are paid accordingly.

Martin regards the Scandinavian case of an example of the Protestant monopoly, where the close historical association of the Protestant church with the state forms the cultural basis for a wide-spread membership, though the protection of the church also prevents it from adopting to the modern conditions (Martin 1978). Martin's description closely follows the Scandinavian self-understanding. The Lutheran churches formed an ideological basis of the formation of the Scandinavian nations. The monarchies were legitimated by the churches, and the democratic emancipation found inspiration from the Protestant revivalist movement of the early 19th Century. The Haugean revival in Norway and the Grundtvigian revival in Denmark endowed the national churches with a sense of national heritage and contained – as phrased by Martin "a Protestant 'seed' of voluntary association" (Martin 1978, 34).

The position as a state church implies that the Lutheran churches are affiliated with the state apparatus, and receive benefits from it. The privileged status implies a subtle distinction between political and religious issues. The national church is not supposed to interfere in strictly political matters. On the other hand, the politicians are not supposed to interfere in the internal, theological debates of the church. This is therefore a case of institutional differentiation.

The emergence of the labour movement challenged the ideological status of the state churches. The tone of the Scandinavian labour movement was originally anti-clerical. However, as the Social Democratic parties came to power and influenced the formation of the welfare states, the churches became a part of the public service scheme. The secularist policy of the Social Democratic regimes led to an institutional differentiation, which limited the authority of the church, especially in relation to the educational system. However, the Protestant church is ascribed with an important role as a carrier of the national heritage. Martin is probably right in stressing the importance of the Social Democratic church policies behind the Scandinavian welfare state model in an international, comparative perspective. However, the support for such a church policy is not limited to the Social Democratic parties. There is a wide consensus about the general lines of the church policy. The Christian parties form the major exception. They are spokesmen for the view, that a renewed Christian morality should guide society. It is worth noticing that only few of the electorate support these parties. The majority adhere to the view that religious belief is fundamentally a private matter, and as such not a topic of public, political discourse. The main function of the state church is to deliver a common, ritual framework for the members. This policy may explain why the Lutheran churches can maintain a near-monopoly, combined with a high degree of toleration of other forms of religiosity. It may also explain why attendance a normal Sunday services is generally regarded as rather unimportant, whereas most ascribe the *rites-de-passage* as important events.

The following study tries to look into the Scandinavians' religious attitudes in order to illustrate this pattern of secularization. The empirical basis for the analysis is the EVS survey of 1990 with occasional glimpses back to the 1981 survey.

Secularization

Secularization is a concept with many meanings. Therefore, it has often been suggested to give it up. Nevertheless, even some of its critics have reverted to the term.[1] As a sociological concept, it covers the manifold processes of religious change affiliated with the European variety of the processes of modernization.[2]

[1] D. Martin (1969) criticizes the concept, but still uses it.

[2] It is quite problematic to use the concept outside the West-European context. The process in Eastern Europe is the result of a secularist policy, rather than a voluntary secularization. As for the U.S.A., secularization has implications which are very different from the West-European one. The institutional differentiation is expressed by the Constitution, and processes of rationalization can be found within the major religious organizations. However, the religious commitment of the people

The diffuse character of the term is thus derived from the multiple meanings of religion on the one hand and modernization on the other. Religion may be conceived of as an institutional concept. It may also be seen as an expression of individual attitudes, which imply beliefs in a cosmological and existential framework, inspired by a postulated supernatural authority and affective associations of these beliefs. The first approach focuses upon the reduced dominance of the church in the institutional setting of modern, European society. The main themes are institutional differentiation and power. The second approach focuses upon changes in religious attitudes: Whether people become more or less religious in the sense that supernatural authorities are ascribed with more or less plausibility for a meaningful interpretation of life. The changes in the authority of the religious institution and the changes in religious attitudes of people are not necessarily interlinked. A religious institution may have much societal influence, in a society where people are not very religious-minded, and *vice versa*.

Dobbelaere has clarified the multidimensional processes of secularization by a distinction between the processes at the societal, the organizational and the personal level (Dobbelaere 1981). The processes, which have been described above as institutional, are labelled "laicization", derived from the French term. Another complex of secularization may occur within the religious organizations, for instance bureaucratization and a de-mythologization of the beliefs. Dobbelaere labels these processes "religious changes". The processes at the personal level are called "changes in religious involvement". Doebbelaere stresses that the processes at these three levels are not necessarily linked together, and therefore may be regarded as three dimensions. The institutional approach focuses upon religious changes at a societal level, whereas the attitudinal approach points at religious changes at a personal level.

Martin's general theory of secularization relates mainly to the institutional level. The inherent logic of the institutional approach is that secularization is regarded as the vanishing of an institutional order. The institutional analysis focuses upon the limitation and relativization of the church as an ideological authority. This may be supplemented with studies of how much the personal beliefs deviate from the official mode. The limitation of such an approach has been pointed out by Luckmann. His well-known discussion tried to change the focus from the "visible", institutional forms of religion to the cultural and attitudinal forms. The main argument is that due to changes of the societal structure, individual orientations are not any longer based upon socially obligatory modes (Luckmann 1967; 1985).

remains much higher among Americans than among equally modernized West-Europeans. The concept becomes even more dubious when it is transferred to societies with non-Christian traditions. The *Journal of Oriental Studies* vol 26, 1, 1987, discusses the problems with the concept in a Japanese context. Other discussions of the problems with the concept in different contexts can be found in the Acts from 19th CISR conference, 1987. Voll discusses the concept in an Islamic context and Isar in a Hindu one.

Peter Berger's famous essay follows a parallel line. Berger's approach is also essentially cognitive, inspired by Alfred Schutz' seminal work. It regards religion as a process of constructing a meaningful world view. Berger regards secularization "the process by which sectors of society and culture are removed from the domination of religious institutions and symbols" (Berger 1967, 107). The main theme is the plausible scope of the world construction ascribed to the religious institutions. Berger makes a useful distinction between the secularization of society and culture on the one hand, and the secularization of consciousness on the other. There is, of course, a link between processes of institutional differentiation and the segregation of a sacred cosmos, though not a direct, causal relation. Furthermore, these changes of the social structure and cultural system are often reflected at the individual level in a specialization of roles and a compartmentalization of life-worlds. These themes point at secularization as a dwindling influence of religion upon society and everyday life of the individual, though not the dissolution of religion. The core of the argument can already be found in Durkheim: "Il y a donc dans le religion quelque chose d'éternel quit est destiné à survivre à tous les symboles particuliers dans lesquels la pensée religieuse s'est successivement enveloppée" (Durkheim 1985, 605).

Berger's and Luckmann's approaches are based upon the dialectical processes which link the individual with society. Therefore, they include individual reactions to the processes of secularization. However, they tend to focus upon the cognitive aspects. The main theme is how people re-construct a meaningful life-world despite the unavoidable experiences of crises.

As the material at hand stems from a survey of religious attitudes, the closest approach is an attitudinal one. The main reason for this is that the available data illustrate religious attitudes. Thurstone's brief definition will suffice here: an "attitude is the affect for or against a psychological object".[3] Some questions relate to religious behaviour or religious beliefs. However, many studies have demonstrated that the responses to these questions are coloured by affective significations. A consistent attitudinal approach to secularization raises the question about the saliency of religious symbols and the affective associations which they inspire. The focal theme is thus whether religious symbols may inspire "long-lasting moods and motivations": whether religious rituals are outlets of catharsis; whether religious authorities are ascribed with charisma, et cetera.[4] According to this approach, secularization of religious attitudes implies indifference to religious symbols.

A secularization of religious attitudes need not coincide with other types of secularization. A high rate of church-attendance may be based on conventions

[3] Quoted from "The measurement of social attitudes", *Journal of Abnormal and Social Psychology*, vol. 26, 1931, p. 249.

[4] The implicit use of C. Geertz's definition of religion is not accidental. The Scandinavian respondents have not been asked how they define "religion". However, the common impression is that many associate "religious" with an affective aspect, even a fanatical one.

rather than convictions. The sacred cosmos may be indisputable, but not awaken a sense of awe. The authority of religious spokesmen in society may be due to political power rather than spiritual influence.

Hypotheses

Secularization covers a complex of hypotheses concerning religious changes, which relate to both institutional religion and more diffuse forms. On the individual level, the hypotheses expect that a decreasing proportion of the population demonstrate a deep commitment to religious institutions. Several possible alternative points of reference evolve. Some turn from super-natural sources to scientific or political frames of reference. Others maintain a religious view, based on their personal opinions. On the organizational level, the hypotheses expect a change within the religious organization, where secular motives mix with religious aims. Secular activities may eventually dominate in the religious organizations. At the same time, new types of religious organizations evolve, which are adapted to the diffuse, personal type of religiosity, characteristic of modern society. On the societal level, institutional religion have less importance as a definer of societal values. As an institution, the church has very little influence on major societal decisions. However, the tradition deceived from the church may still be used as a rhetorical point of reference. References to the bases of the social integration point to a more diffuse civil religion, which hints at a common denominator behind the diffuse, personal types of religiosity. This common denominator may still be associated with the historical roots formed by the church.

Secularization processes at the institutional level can only indirectly be traced by interviews. For instance, the interviews cannot tell us about institutional differentiation or functional equivalents. They can, however, tell us whether people adhere to the institutions, whether they compartmentalize their life-world, and whether religious and political commitments alternate.

The interviews reflect individual responses to standardized questions about religion, and especially to the type of religiosity associated with the European Christian tradition. The general hypothesis therefore becomes that commitment to the church declines. This decline is most marked in the most modernized segments of society. A decline of the commitment to the church may be expressed in several ways: participation in ritual activities may decline; disbelief in the orthodox dogma may spread; reaction to symbols of the church may become indifferent; the authority of the church in social life may decline. There is not necessarily a close relation between the conative, cognitive, attitudinal and political dimensions.

This general hypothesis can be expanded by several supplementary hypotheses: One set of theories associates secularization with a process of rationalization. The derivation from this argument is that the decline of the commitment to the church is followed by atheist views and belief in scientific explanations and technical, bureaucratic or political solutions. Some expect that people will instead turn to a positive science, others that they become Marxists, and there are many varieties in between. The operationalization of the hypothesis about a rationalization process could be that atheistic tendencies can be found among either those who put their trust in science and technology or among the Socialist-oriented part of the population.

The Structural-Functionalist strand of sociologists represent another interpretation of the process. They concede that the authority of the church declines. However, the general decline of a central social institution, such as religion, would imply a profound crisis in the value consensus of society. Therefore, the decline of the churchly commitment is interpreted as a prelude to a change towards a different type of religiosity: It may be regarded as privatized, in the sense that it is founded upon individual beliefs rather than on an institutionalized religious authority. This change implies that religion becomes more diffuse. The sociological precondition for a milieu of privatized religious views is a state of religious pluralism and toleration. It is rather difficult to operationalize the hypothesis derived from this type of approach to secularization. The expected trend is that a specific type of religiosity, a church-oriented one, is followed by many non-specific kinds of vague religious views. The only common denominator is a belief that "there is more between heaven and earth...".

Operationalizations

The following analysis is based on data from a survey which was performed in 1990 in all the Scandinavian countries. Data are both analyzed on a national level and on an inter-Scandinavian one. In the latter-mentioned case, data are weighted according to the relative size of the populations.

The questionnaires contain regrettably few questions about religiosity in the non-official modes. The simple reason for this is that it is quite difficult to ask about such matters in a questionnaire. It is much easier to construct measures of religiosity based upon official and institutionalized modes of religiosity. The only directly relevant item asks about belief in re-incarnation. However, the Danish questionnaire includes a few relevant items, such as experience with yoga, meditation or healing.[5] The proportion of "don't know" answers vary between the Scandinavian countries. Therefore, these answers are left out in the following percentages.

[5] The narrow range of issues illustrated through the religious items may give some of the explanation to why the results seem to point at one single dimension of religious attitudes, e.g. one related to orthodox beliefs.

The hypotheses relate to long-term trends, whereas the material at hand only describes religious attitudes within a short interval, from 1981 to 1990. In order to illustrate these hypotheses, several attitude-scales have been constructed. Mokken's analysis has been utilized in order to test whether a set of items fit into a cumulative Guttman scale.

The attitudes of *orthodox beliefs*, i.e. belief in God, life after death, a soul, the devil, Hell, Paradise, sin and resurrection, fitted into a cumulative Guttman scale (Loevinger's H = 0.677).[6] This index correlated highly with a general index of *churchly* commitment, which includes the items, service attendance at least monthly, that one is a religious believer, that one believes in a personal God, and that one ascribes God with high importance (Loevinger's H = 0.68). The *atheistic* belief deny that life, death or sorrow is meaningful because God exists, deny belief in God, neither as a personal God nor a spirit force, express that God is not important at all, and, finally, affirm that one is a convinced atheist. These items also formed a neat, cumulative scale. Furthermore, the correlation between the scales of orthodoxy and atheism was highly negative (Pearson's r = –0.6357). A scale was formed relating to a more *diffuse religiosity*: It covers that religion is important in one's life, one is a religious believer, that one believes in either a personal God or a spirit force, that one finds comfort and strength in religion, and that one takes a moment of prayer or meditation. The items here also formed a Guttman scale (Loevinger's H = 0.57). Some of the items on the scale of diffuse religiosity are also included in other scales. This may partially explain high correlation between the scale of diffuse religiosity and the scale of orthodox belief (r = 0.64) and churchly commitment (r = 0.72). The high correlation also indicates that a high degree of religious commitment is often associated with the church. Items concerning the *authority of the church* were also scalable, i.e. trust in the church, and the credibility of the church on moral problems, family problems or spiritual questions (Loevinger's H = 0.63). However, the correlations between this and the other scales of orthodox belief and churchly commitment were somewhat lower. For instance, the correlation between orthodox belief and the authority of the church was only 0.438. This hints at a privatization of the religious views even among orthodox Scandinavians.

The items which may indicate a New Age-religiosity, i.e. belief in re-incarnation, a soul, a spirit force, and practising prayer or meditation, did not fit into a scale. The Danish items which relate to "new religions", i.e. belief in re-incarnation, and the practices of yoga, meditation or healing, fitted only weakly in a

[6] Mokken's analysis is preferred here because it is more in accordance with the actual measurements than the commonly used factor analysis. Furthermore the unidimensionality of a Guttman scale is easier to interpret sociologically than the results of a factor analysis. The items of the scales identified are not additive. The usage of an additive index based on an ordinal scale is questionable. However, this methodological simplification will probably not distort the conclusions.

Guttman scale. Therefore, it can not be confirmed that they belong to a single dimension.

It should be stressed that the data do not illustrate how people cope with the marginal life-situations, how they react in acute crises, who they talk with, and how they re-interpret their life-world, in a manner which may make sense to them. The reactions to such situations are probably more relevant to the basic themes of religion rather than the relaxed answers to standard questions about belief and commitment to the church. This general warning leads to a hermeneutical interpretation of the findings. Instead of regarding the correlations as behaviouristic patterns, they are regarded as hints of the plausibility structures, which people relate to as frames-of-reference in their re-interpretations of life-worlds.

The further discussion therefore focuses upon three major plausibility-structures among the Scandinavians: One, which is especially traceable among the older population of the country-side, and which focuses upon the church. Another, which is especially marked among the industrial workers, and which has an atheist focal point. The third one is diffusely religious, and is especially remarkable among women in the social, clerical and teaching professions.

The General Patterns

The data confirm that Scandinavians seldom attend church services. The average attendance rate per year is only 3.1. The variation between the Scandinavian countries is not very large. Danes attend 2.5 times on the average, and Swedes 3.2 times, whereas Norwegians attend 3.7 times a year.

With an attitudinal approach, the saliency of the religious issues are of vital interest. One of the questions, which may be regarded as a measurement of the saliency of the religious beliefs concerns the importance of God. Measured on a scale from 1 to 10, the mean value is 4.0. This demonstrates that it is only a minority of the Scandinavians who ascribe great importance to God in their lives. The typical attitude is lukewarm and a bit sceptical. This impression can be corroborated by the mean on index of atheism. It is 3.6, which is not very high, compared with the maximum of 8. Therefore, the typical Scandinavian is not an outright atheist. The index of the diffuse religiosity has a mean value of 2.7, with a maximum of 6. This indicates that some kind of religious interest is very common, though not a high degree of religious commitment. As the index of churchly commitment is only 0.9, with a maximum value of 4, only a minority among the Scandinavians show a deep commitment to the churches.

The mean value on the index of orthodox belief is low, 2.4, as the maximum is 8. A typical response accepts belief in God and a soul, but not much more. Most of the respondents reject the dark tenets about sin, the Devil or Hell. Many respondents avoid precise answers to the questions about religious beliefs. These are necessarily excluded from the calculus of the index of orthodox belief. The mean of this index did not change much during the decade. It is, however, worth noticing that fewer Swedes and Norwegians believe in God (Sweden 1981: 52 %; 1990: 38 %; Norway 1981: 68 %, 1990: 58 %). This does not mean that fewer believe in all the religious dogma. At a more specific question about the image of God, the rate which believe in a personal God declined in all Scandinavian countries, whereas somewhat more expressed a belief in a spirit force. Furthermore, one item of belief gets more support, namely belief in a soul (Denmark: 1981: 32 %; 1990: 41 %; Sweden: 1981: 40 %, 1990: 51 %). This pattern corresponds with the hypothesis that fewer believe in the traditional dogma of the churches, whereas more associated with a diffuse, spiritual world view. A swing towards belief in re-incarnation would give further support to this hypothesis. Regrettably, the question about re-incarnation could be misunderstood in the Norwegian questionnaire. The proportion of the Scandinavians who believe in re-incarnation is 17 %, whereas the proportion who believe in resurrection is 23 %.[7] There is some overlap between these beliefs, as a third of those who believe in resurrection also express belief in re-incarnation. Such a response pattern could be interpreted either as confused or as typical of a diffuse belief that the soul continues to exist somehow after physical death.

The Danish survey of 1990 used a few simple questions, which may be used as rough indicators of the support of the practices of these movements. According to the survey, 4 % of the Danes practice yoga, 4 % practice meditation and 5 % have some experience with healing. These experiences are most widespread in the sectors employed in social work, teaching or academic professions. They are less common in the industrial sector. The youngest generation is not specially involved in yoga (1 %) or meditation (3 %). It is rather their middle-aged aunts – in other words the generation, which was young in '68.

The service attendance rate correlates with the index of orthodox belief (r = 0.47), and negatively with the index of atheism (r = –0.34). Belief and behaviour are thus connected.[8] It is also related to the index of diffuse religious interest (r = 0.41). Therefore, service attendance may be used as a practical indicator of religious commitment.

The Majority and the Minorities

The Lutheran churches have retained their monopoly status, even after religious toleration was secured in the constitutions. The status as a state church for the whole population implies a latitudinarian profile. At the same time some part of

[7] Still excluding the "don't know" answers.

[8] A note of warning is needed: The answers about service rates express attitudes towards services as well as actual behaviour.

Table 1. Indicators of religious commitment among state church members, members of religious minority organizations and non-members.

	Members of the state churches	Members of the religious minority organizations	Non-members
Per cent of Scandinavian population	82	4	13
Attends religious services once a month or more often, pct.	10	64	2
Index of orthodox belief	2.2	5.7	1.6
Index of atheism	3.5	1.5	4.9
Index of importance of God	3.4	4.9	1.5
Religion very important	9	62	5
– not at all important	27	5	52
Religious person	50	92	22
Convinced atheist	3	0	21

the membership feel a special commitment to the specific Lutheran tradition of the state churches. Thereby the Lutheran churches come under a functional cross-pressure as they have on the one hand to maintain their specific theological profile, whereas they on the other hand have to perform religious services for the broad membership. The other religious organizations in Scandinavia – the "free churches" – may keep a sharper profile. Their very *raison d'être* is based on a distance from the broad and vaguely defined state churches. Some also have a traditional background in ethnic minorities, which by their church membership keep their common roots *vis-à-vis* the Scandinavian minorities. The minority churches can offer a better template of religious views, and a tighter community of members with similar interests. Therefore it is expected that the religious commitment is especially high among the members of the minority organizations.

The data demonstrate a close correspondence between formal membership and religious attitudes (see Table 1). The members of the religious minority organizations show a marked religious self-identification, whereas the non-members show an equally marked religious indifference. Most of the members of the religious minorities describe religion as "very important", and most of the non-members as "not at all important". The members of the state churches have more varied views, which tend to concentrate in the lukewarm category "not very important". It should be noted that some of the indicators point to orthodox Christian views, which some of the religious minorities expressly reject. Nevertheless, all the indicators of religious commitment are thus much higher among the religious minorities. Those who stand outside the religious organizations demonstrate very little religious interest. However, the high index value for atheism hints that many of the non-members have a clear view of life which excludes a supernatural power. The religious minority members tend to be female, young, live in the larger cities. The non-members tend to be male, live in the large cities, and be either skilled workers or larger employers or professionals.

The theories of secularization point at some hypotheses, which relate to the distribution of membership of religious organizations: According to the Marxist theories, the membership rates should decline among the workers. This hypothesis can only be confirmed as for the skilled workers. The membership rates remain high among the un- or semiskilled workers. Furthermore, the low membership rates among the professionals and larger employers can hardly be explained by the class-based theory. Another hypothesis may be derived from the classical theories of Troeltsch and Durkheim, namely that the religious orientation becomes more person-directed, and therefore changes from a church- or sect-basis to a more cultic one. The data at hand do not enable a distinction between members of various types of religious minority organizations. The data do not make it clear how many retain a formal membership of the state churches and at the same time are attached to some cultic group. However, it is clear that the proportion who leave the state churches is low in Scandinavia, and that the minority churches remain marginal. The discussion above hints at the possibility that the wide-spread membership of the state churches may be due to its civil religious status rather than to its theology. The Lutheran churches are neither independent of the state or the church, and thus exemplify the category missing in Hammond's well-known scheme (Bellah & Hammond 1980). The available data can not provide a direct estimate of the influence of the religious versus the civil religious motives behind the membership of the state churches. They can, however, give some simple hints. For instance, the proportion who state that they are very proud to be a Dane, Swede or Norwegian is somewhat higher among the members of the state churches: 44 % against 35 % among the minority religions and 33 % among the non-members. Similarly, a rather large proportion (38 %) of the religious minority groups are not willing to fight for their country, in comparison to the figure among the members of the state church (8 %). This is quite understandable, as some of the minorities have pacifist views. (The figures have been corrected for missing values, e.g. those who can not answer since they have a foreign nationality.) Nevertheless, these patterns affirm the association between membership of the state churches and Scandinavian nationalism. The most religiously committed members of the state churches also demonstrate more nationalistic opinions. The tendency is, however, weak, and can mainly be explained by a common background factor, namely age.

Religious behaviour has a public form by participation in church services, and a private form in prayer. It is worth noticing the degree of congruence between these forms. Both among members of the minority churches and among non-members, the degree of congruence is very high. The typical member of the minority churches both pray often and go often to services, whereas the typical non-member neither pray nor go to church. The discrepancies can be found mainly within the membership of the state churches. 11 % pray often, but only half of them attend services more than once a month. Further 15 % pray sometimes, but only half of these attend services more than once a year. This hints at a privatized religiosity among the membership of the state churches.

Religion and Individualization

One variety of the hypotheses of secularization points to the religious changes which follow from the increased individual autonomy in modern society. Religion becomes a private matter. The inherited world view is not accepted as a taken for granted truism. The world view becomes a matter of personal choice. Religion is transferred from the public domain to the "private sphere". Several theories have provided convincing arguments for a hypothesis about the affiliation between individualization and the de-institutionalization of religiousness, e.g. Berger (1967) and Luckmann (1967). What remains is to test the hypothesis empirically.

The hypothesis points to long-term trends. In a survey study such a hypothesis can only be tested by indirect indicators. As a corollary from this hypotheses, indicators of an individualistic orientation should be connected more with a diffuse type of religiosity than with a churchly commitment. The indicators of individualistic values do not seem to form a clear, single dimension. Items, which point to the theme of individualization correlate only weakly or not at all. Factor analysis indicate that several dimensions of individualism may be constructed, though these form rather weak scales. This indicates that isolated items should be selected in order to test the hypothesis. One indicator of individualism is when the respondents see it as good that there is greater emphasis on the development of the individual. Not any of the statistical tests of all the religious indexes presented here are significant. In other words, it is not possible to demonstrate an empirical relation between individualistic values and religious ones. Another indicator of individualism can be found in the values, which the respondents wish to encourage their children to develop. There is hardly any relation between mentioning "religion" and "independence" as important values for the children. Again, the general version of the hypothesis cannot be supported by the indicators available. Therefore, a further elaboration of the hypothesis seems to be needed.

Individualism may be interpreted in several ways. It is possible to regard "cultural individualism" as a pole opposite to authoritarianism. This dimension is underlying the measurement used by Ester *et al.* (1993). It consisted of only two items, namely respect for authority and willingness to follow instructions one does not fully agree with. Those who find greater respect for authorities good and at the same time are willing to follow order at work, despite that they do not agree with them, may be labelled as authoritarians. On all the indexes utilized, the authoritarian category is significantly more religious than other respondents. The authoritarians have a significantly higher mean on the indexes of orthodox belief, of commitment to the church, and acceptance of the authority of the church, whereas their mean on the index of atheism is significantly lower than that of the other respondents. The authoritarian group have a significantly higher number of service attendances per year. Also the index of general religiousness is significantly higher for the authoritarian category. On this background, it is noteworthy that the authoritarians do not differ from other respondents on one special indicator of religiousness, namely on the question about re-incarnation. Authoritarian views are somewhat more widespread among the older generations. Therefore, age could be hypothesized as a background factor, which contributed to explaining the above-mentioned relation. However, this relation does not disappear completely, when age is controlled for. The age category from 30 to 60 years still demonstrates a significant relation between authoritarianism and religious values. It disappears in the youngest category and is weakened in the oldest. These findings indicate that individualism is only related to secularization in one specific manner. People with authoritarian views also tend to adhere to religious values. People who are not prone to follow order unquestioningly, and who do not appreciate authorities, also tend to question religious authorities and to dissolve their affiliation with religious institutions.

Ideology Versus Religion

The Lutheran churches in Scandinavia have a historical affiliation with the ruling establishment. The state church was one of the pillars which supported the social order. A good, Conservative Scandinavian was therefore supposed to venerate God, the King and the Fatherland. The emerging labour movement combined a critique of the ruling class with anti-clerical attitudes. Eventually, the Social Democratic parties aligned themselves with the state churches during the thirties. The Marxists maintained a critique of religion up till this date. It has often be pointed out that the commitment to the Churches or to the Christian parties often occurs in peripheral communities where the labour movement and the left-wing-parties are rather weak. The labour movement tried to form a functional alternative to religion. For instance, the Scandinavian labour movement established a set of rituals, parallel to the Christian ones. The Danish labour movement thus installed a "civil confirmation" instead of the Lutheran Confirmation, and a "solstice feast" instead of Christmas. The success of these rituals was limited to the major cities during the middle of the 20th century.

Table 2. Correlation between left/right political attitude and the importance of God.

	Denmark	Norway	Sweden
1981	.27*	.16*	.15*
1990	.18*	.12*	-.01

* The coefficients differ significantly from 0, at a 1% level.

These arguments support the hypothesis that the more church-minded part of the Scandinavians still have Conservative leanings, whereas those with left-wing sympathies tend to have more atheistic views. An initial analysis of the Scandinavian 1990 data supports the hypothesis. The correlation between a self-placement on a left–right scale and the religious indicators are all significant. The index of atheism gives the highest coefficient (r = –0.13), followed by the importance of God (r = 0.12), and general commitment to the church (r = 0.12), with the index of orthodox belief at a barely significant level (r = 0.08).

Further analyses of the trends in the individual Scandinavian countries show that the correlation between political and religious views has declined during the 1980s (cf. Table 2). Religion and politics are regarded as arenas which become less interrelated. Values and attitudes expressed in the one arena are more seldom associated with those stated in the other. This trend corresponds with an increasing institutional differentiation. More surprising is the result that the relation between religion and politics is stronger in Denmark than in the other Nordic countries. This could be explained by the different profiles and strengths of the Christian parties in the Nordic countries. It is worth noticing that the adherents of the Christian parties tended to put themselves at the same point on the left–right-scale in all Scandinavian countries, namely a little bit right of the centre. The average was 6 on a 1 to 10 scale.

Both religiosity and the affiliation with the right side of the political spectrum are related to one common background variable, namely age. The older part of the population tend to be more religious, and it also tends to be more Conservative. By combining the data for Scandinavia, it is possible to look at the correlations within different age segments. The relationship between left–right-placement and indicators of religiosity disappears in the youngest category. However, the correlation remains significant, when the age categories from 30 to 59 years (r = 0.12), and above 60 years (r = 0.14) are considered. The correlation is somewhat higher with the index of atheism than with the index of orthodoxy.

Self-placement on a left–right scale is not the best way to measure Conservatism or Leftism. One may consider more direct indicators of political values. The 1990 survey included a series of items which related to the economic politics. These included views on private ownership versus government ownership of industry, individual or state responsibility, whether competition is good or harmful, whether hard work brings a better life, and whether the unemployed should take any job available. Factor analysis confirmed that most of these items formed a single factor. These items were, however, not correlated with the importance of God. Only the item on economic policy, which did not relate to the set, correlated with religiousness, namely whether people can only accumulate wealth at the expense of others. The correlation coefficient between this item and the importance of God is significant, though not high ($r = 0.10$). Low correlations between the importance of God and politically salient issues, such as the preference of private or public ownership, indicates that religion is not associated with Conservatism in a narrow, political sense. Neither is irreligiousness associated with left-wing views on the economic policy. For the majority of the Scandinavians, more concrete religious and political values form two separate patterns, which are not related to each other. This compartmentalization of the value system gives support to the secularization hypothesis about the differentiation between the religious and political spheres.

Conservatism is also an expression of the valuation of social stability. The 1990 survey included three items, which expressed traditionalist or innovative attitudes. A factor analysis indicated that these items could be considered as expressing the same factor. This combined indicator correlated significantly with the importance of God ($r = -0.15$). Traditionalism is also related to age. When age is controlled for, the correlation between the importance of God and traditionalism declines in the youngest and oldest categories, though remains significant in the age category between 30 and 60 years. This indicates that religiosity is moderately associated with Conservative values, in the basic sense of supporting the status quo.

According to the hypothesis of class consciousness, workers should tend be more atheistic whereas members of the bourgeoisie should be more church-minded.[9] The data at hand demonstrate only minor variations in religious views among the different employment groups. The same pattern emerges, whether the index of orthodoxy, atheism, churchly commitment or general religiosity is used (see Figure 1). Only skilled workers and farmers show marked divergences from the general pattern. The skilled workers have more pronounced atheistic leanings, whereas the farmers and farmhands are much more churchly committed and orthodox in their beliefs.

[9] The hypothesis is rendered here in the most simple form. More subtle variations of the hypothesis may be found, e.g. the Gramscian ones. However, for the present purpose of analyzing the available material, the simple version will suffice.

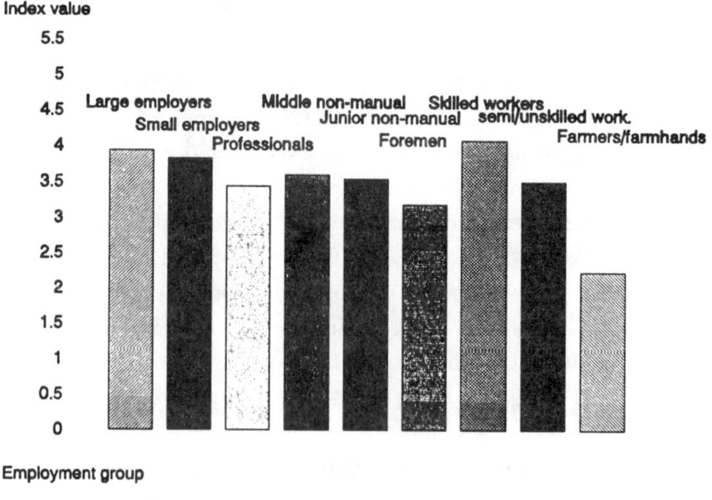

Figure 1. Index of atheist belief in different professional groups.

The differentiation between religious and political values can be demonstrated by other data. Few Scandinavians find it proper that churches speak out on government policy (27 %). Those issues, which are acceptable for a majority, relate to more distant or abstract ethical problems, such as Third World problems (74 %), racial discrimination (64 %) or euthanasia (61 %). Scandinavians perceive the church as a spiritual institution rather than as a moral guide. A majority (51 %) think that their church answers their spiritual needs, but only 24 % say that it answers moral problems and 17 % that it answers problems of family life. The members of the religious minorities are highly represented among all these three answers. In other words, a clear majority of the members of the state church regards it as a purely spiritual institution.

The differentiation between religious and other social values can be further illustrated by looking at the relation between religiosity and morality. Former studies have underlined that morality in Scandinavia must be split up in a public and a private sector (e.g. Harding *et al.* 1986). Whereas the Scandinavians tend to be quite strict in matters of public morality, they are more liberal in matters which take place within people's own homes, as long as they do not harm others. We may construct a scale of public morality, which includes the issues whether one accepts people who get public benefits without any right, accepts going with public transportation without a ticket, or accepts tax-fraud. Factor analysis indicates that these items express a single factor. The correlations between this index of public morality and religious indicators (like orthodoxy: r = –0.09, atheism: r = 0.15, or commitment to the church: r = –0.13) are low but still significant. An index of private morality may be constructed on basis of attitudes towards homosexuality, prostitution, divorce, suicide, euthanasia and killing in self-defense. A factor analysis indicates that these items express a common factor. The coefficients between this index and the religious indicators are much higher (orthodoxy: r = –0.23, atheism: r = 0.30, commitment to the church: r = 0.28). These coefficients are not reduced notably, when the factor of age is brought under control. This indicates that religious values are somewhat related to private morality and only weakly related to public morality. Religion does indeed seem to belong to a "private sphere". The fact that the church do not seem to answer family problems according to most Scandinavians does not nullify the above-mentioned statement. It rather demonstrates that interference of the church in family matters is not very welcome. This is underlined by the fact that less than half of the respondents accept that the church talks about extramarital affairs or abortion.

Science Versus Religion

One of the hypotheses of secularization argues that religious views are replaced by rationalistic or scientific views. The argument may find support in classical sociology, such as Max Weber's analysis of the process of *Entzauberung*.

These changes take place over a long span of time. The empirical corollary is that the religious-minded part of the population is more sceptical towards science and technology, whereas the more pro-scientific oriented part of the population tends to be have an atheistic world view.

Again, the EVS questionnaire provides rather crude indicators about the subject. Two relevant questions are included. The first asks whether scientific advances help or harm. The second asks whether it is good or bad that there is more emphasis on the development of technology. The theme of the questions is therefore the societal consequences of science and technology more than the credibility of a scientific foundation of a world view. The Scandinavian data at first glance confirm the expected pattern, albeit in a weak form. Among those who find that scientific advances will help mankind, the index of orthodoxy is 2.02, and the index of atheism is 3.91. The corresponding values among those who find scientific advances harmful are 2.72 and 3.33. These differences are significant at a 1 % level. The divergence is not quite as large between those who are pro-technology and those who are more sceptical. The indices of orthodox faith and atheism among those who find it good that there is more emphasis on technology are 2.15 and 3.70. The equivalent indices for those who regard such a development as bad are 2.56 and 3.32. These differences are still significant at a 1 % level.

Table 3. Index of ahteism according to age groups and attitude towards science and technology.

	Pro-scientific group	Anti-scientific group
19–29 years	4.31	4.18
30–59 years	3.96	3.27*
60 years and above	3.19	2.66*

* Marks a difference, which is significant at a 1% level.

The evaluation of science and technology is, however, related to age. The older are more sceptical and at the same time more religious. The views on science and religion may therefore be related because they occur simultaneously in the same generations. The material at hand is large enough to subdivide into meaningful age-groups. Table 3 shows that the difference in religious views is most pronounced in the older categories. The difference is insignificant in the youngest category. The same pattern emerges, when the index of orthodoxy is utilized instead of the index of atheism.

The difference in religious views among those for or against technology tend to disappear, when the factor of age is controlled. There is, however, still a significant difference in the age category from 30 to 60 years. In this category the pro-technological fraction has an index of atheism of 3.8 versus the value of 3.5 among those who are sceptical towards technology. Studies of the index of orthodox belief yield similar results. Among the age category from 30 to 60, the index of orthodoxy among the pro-technological group is 1.95, against 2.49 among the sceptical group. This difference is statistically significant, though not very large.

The conclusion seems to be that the youngest category is generally sceptical to religion. This attitude is not clearly related to scientific or technological leanings. Among the middle-aged category, religious scepticism tends to be related to a leaning towards a belief in science and technology.

It is possible that education is an important factor behind this relationship. The educational systems of the Scandinavian countries are so different that it is too difficult to construct a combined code. Therefore, the influence of the educational background must be tested within the single countries.

Education is the most important vehicle for socializing new generations into the scientific views. Therefore, one could expect that the level of education and the acceptance of a scientific world view were closely related. One major problem is that the educational systems diverge very much in Europe, and also between the Scandinavian countries. The universal measurement of the educational level in the

Table 4. Attitudes towards science and religion in the educational categories; Denmark 1990; pct.

	Low	Middle	High
Believes in both science and God	21	20	26
Believes in science but not in God	8	16	16
Believes in God but not in science	15	13	9
Believes in neither God nor science	6	7	4
Mixed group	50	44	45

EVS study is the age when education was finished. In countries, where education-for-life is instituted, such a measure is too crude. Further analysis of the relation between the educational level, and the belief in science and religion, is therefore limited to a single country. Denmark is chosen, because the information about the respondent's background is most detailed here. Initial analyses show that the attitude towards science is more positive among those with longer education (see Table 4). Among the third with the longest education, 47 % evaluate science as beneficent, and only 15 % as harmful. Among the third with the shortest education, 33 % find science good, whereas 26 % see it as harmful. As a crude measurement of the religious views, belief in God may be used. This will provide simple but meaningful categories. Among those with the shortest education 69 % believe in God, whereas the proportion in the middle category is 56 % and in the category with the longest education is about the same, 57 %. This seems to indicate that the relation between science and religion may both be influenced by education.

Four distinct patterns can be identified: The first pattern consist of persons who are both religious and pro-scientific. The second consists of persons who are pro-scientific but sceptical towards religion. The third is composed by persons who are religious and sceptical towards science. The fourth comprises persons who are sceptical towards both science and religion. In order to establish simple categories, only a crude measurement of religiosity is used here, namely belief in God.

The results show that relatively many among those with middle or high education believe in science but not in God. Furthermore, quite a few in the low and middle educational bracket believe in God but are sceptical towards science. So far the pattern follows the expectations. However, relatively many in the category with the highest education answer positively to both the question about science and God. This indicates a more complex relationship. It seems that a longer education may open for both religious scepticism and a world view, which mitigates between science and religion.

Table 5. Proportion who attend religious services at least once a month of persons thinking/not thinking often about death in different ages.

	59 years and below	60 years and above
Think often about death	21	34
Do not think often about death	7	17

Religion and Age

The attendance rate is related to age. From 19 to 54 years, the rates oscillate at very low levels, from 2.3 to 3.3. For the age group 55–59 years, the rate creeps up to 3.8, increasing further to 4.1 for the group aged 60–64 years; the peak occurs with 5.2 in the age group above 65 years of age.

This age pattern could be interpreted in several ways. Older people may have more leisure time for church activities. This hypothesis can be supported by the high service rates among those out of work. Another interpretation could be that the felt nearness of death leads to higher commitment to the church. As the questionnaire asks about whether one thinks about death, this hypothesis can be tested. The proportion of frequent church attendants is especially high among those who often think about death. This relation may, however, be linked through the factor of age.

As one may expect, older people think more often about death than young persons. About a fifth (18 %) of those above 60 years of age think often about death, whereas the proportion among the remaining age groups is 13 %. The proportion of frequent church attendants is higher among those who think often about death, among those above 60 years as well as below 60 years.

The data indicate that the age-variation in church attendance can only to a limited degree be explained by the actuality of the unavoidable question about the finality of the human life. Even among the younger respondents, a noteworthy proportion of those who often think about death go frequently to church services (see Table 5). Thinking about death may express many kinds of reaction. It may follow from a psychological disposition, a pattern of socialization, or some specific life experience. It may also follow from a frequent church attendance, which spotlights some issues, which are otherwise taboo in everyday discourse.[10] Most important is

[10] Whereas the procreation of life has become a public theme in Scandinavia during the last generation, the ending of life has become taboo. This can be seen directly in Danish death notices, which most often notify that the person has died and been buried "in silence", as well as in the now common anonymous graveyards.

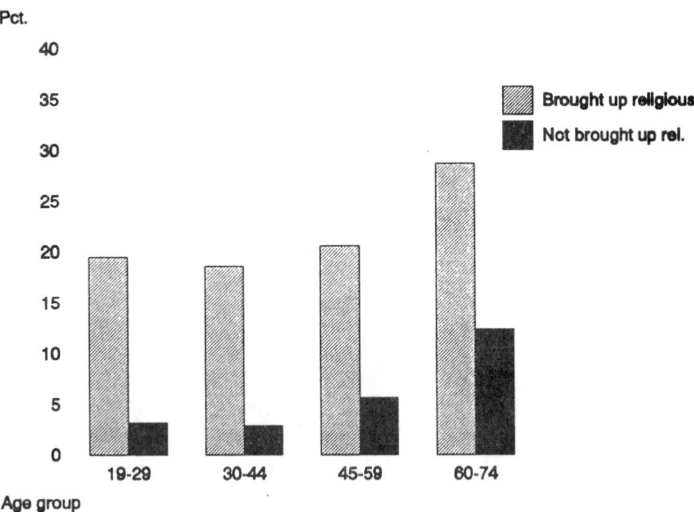

Figure 2. Frequent church attendance (at least once a month) among persons brought up/not brought up in a religious home.

the demonstration that other factors must be taken into consideration in order to clarify the special churchly commitment among the older Scandinavians.

Age indicates membership of a specific generation, with some common life experiences. According to their own evaluation, the older respondents have more often been subject to a religious socialization than the younger ones. Many of the youngest respondents find it difficult to grasp the meaning of a question about their religious upbringing in their childhood home, whereas few old respondents hesitated to answer. The proportion of frequent church attendants is much higher among those with a religious socialization than among those without it (see Figure 2). Therefore, some of the age variation may be explained by differences in the patterns of primary religious socialization. The variation in the church service rates is not very large among those who had a primary religious socialization. However, among those who did not have a religious upbringing, the church attendance rates increase clearly with age. This may be due to early religious influences from other sources than one's childhood home. One such source is the grandparents. It could also be due to indirect influences from the other members of the same generation, who had a religious upbringing. However, as underlined above, factors connected with age may inspire a reflection upon existential issues, and the answer may be sought in the church.

Church attendance may be a dubious indicator of religious commitment. However, other indicators of the religious involvement of the respondents confirm the importance of a primary religious socialization. The level of orthodox belief seems to decline generation for generation. This seems to be an effect of a decline in the

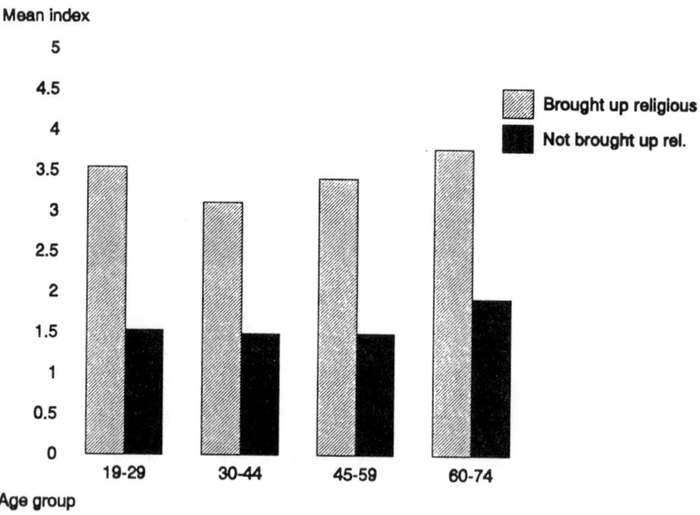

Figure 3. Index of orthodox belief among persons brought up/not brought up in a religious home.

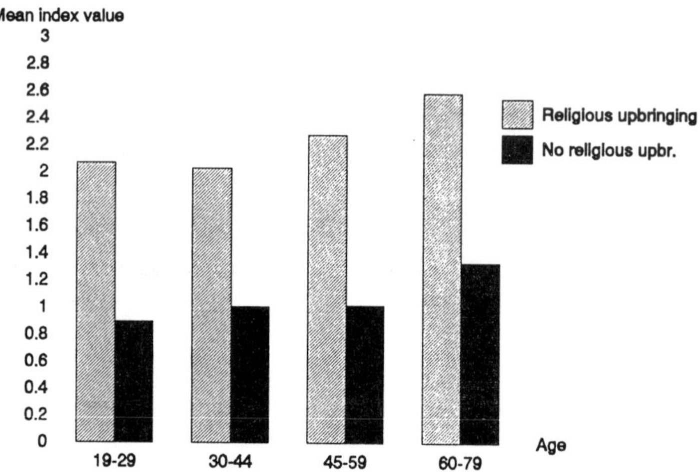

Figure 4. Index of general religiosity among persons brought up/not brought up in a religious home.

primary religious socialization. The age groups do not differ much in their levels of orthodox belief, when those who have a religious upbringing are considered (see Figure 3). It is noteworthy that the importance of the primary religious socialization is not only observable when indicators of church-oriented religiousness are considered, but even on the index of diffuse religiosity (see Figure 4).

The older generations had religious role models at home in their childhood. Their grandparents may have taken part in the great revivals of the 19th century, and conveyed their memories and enthusiasm to the grandchildren. Many in the oldest generations had been subject to a Christian indoctrination at home and in school. It was common to learn the Catechism and hymns by rote in the old school system. Today, the Danish and Swedish school systems are completely secularized and religious education is strictly a matter of information. Norway still retains a Christian orientation, as the Parliament as late as 1984 decreed that the school should be based on a "Christian-humanistic" foundation. The added word, humanistic, gives the important hint. The new school laws in all the Scandinavian countries stress a pluralistic and tolerant view. The former generations often attended voluntary Bible classes, so-called Sunday Schools. These still exist, albeit with much fewer children.

These results point at one important conclusion concerning the hypotheses of secularization. The decline in church-related religiousness seems, at least partially, to be affiliated with a decline in the early religious socialization. The primary religious socialization seems to form one important pre-condition for a later deepening of a religious identity and a closer association with a religious community.

Religion and Gender

One of the recurrent findings in empirical studies is that women score higher than men on many indicators of religiosity. T-tests on all the indexes of religious values show significant differences between men and women, except for the index concerning the authority of the church (see Table 6). The issue under discussion here concerns how to explain this difference.

Age and gender are both related to religious values. This is, for instance, observable in the proportion of regular churchgoers (see Figure 5). There is a difference, however, between the effect of these variables. A Multiple Classification Analysis reconfirms that gender does not contribute to explaining the authority of the church, whereas age does. The beta-weight for gender is 0.0, whereas the beta-weight for age is 0.20. Age also explains more concerning commitment to the church than gender. The respective beta-weights are 0.21 for age and 0.13 for gender. Also regarding atheism, age is more important than gender, though both factors contribute considerably to explaining the variation. The beta-weights are, respectively, 0.27 and 0.19. As for the index on general religiosity, gender and age

Table 6. Gender index values for indicators of religiosity (1990).

	Men	Women
Orthodox belief	1.94	2.62*
Commitment to the church	0.75	1.08*
Authority of the church	0.81	.83
Atheism	4.03	3.15*
General religiosity	1.69	2.39*

* Difference between the two genders significant at a 1% level.

have similar explanatory powers, with beta-weights of 0.19 and 0.21, respectively. Also concerning orthodox belief, age and gender contribute similarly. The beta-weights are in both cases 0.13. MCA-analysis is admissible here, since age and gender are not correlated. Whereas age is generally important for analyses of religiousness, gender is relevant for some types of religious attitudes. It seems especially important for analyses of personal, religious views, such as those expressed as general religiosity or the attitude to atheism. Gender is less important for analyzing institutionalized religiosity, such as the authority ascribed to the church.

It has often been observed that women in paid employments are less religious than women working at home (e.g. Lenski 1953; Luckmann 1967; de Vaus 1987; Ulbrich 1987; Hertel 1988). Therefore, employment differences between men and women must be taken into account. In Scandinavia, the employment rate for women is very high. There is only a small difference between the employment rate of women and men in the age groups of 20–50. The norm for Scandinavian women is to get a career. Status of a home-working woman often reflects a choice of values: reproduction, the family, and the local community are put in front of production, material standards, economic independence and the collective of workers. Career chances are not equal for the gender groups. Women are often given the most menial, and worst paid jobs. Nevertheless, Scandinavian women are more widely distributed on branches and statuses than in most other countries. In order to make a fair test of whether the religious views of women in employment converge with those of their male colleagues, comparable status groups must be utilized. This necessitates detailed employment categories.

The most basic comparison must distinguish between manual workers and those in white-collar jobs. It is a well-known fact that the religious criticism is more wide-spread among the workers, especially those with commitment to the political left-wing. The Scandinavian data indicate that female workers are less religiously

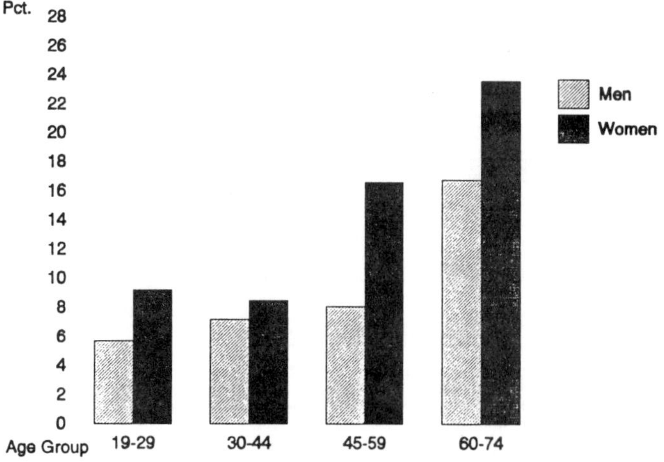

Figure 5. Frequent church attendance (at least once a month) among men and women.

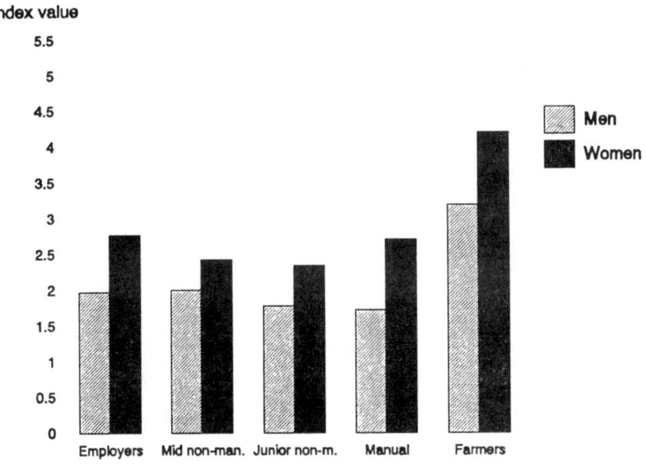

Figure 6. Index of orthodox belief in different professional groups.

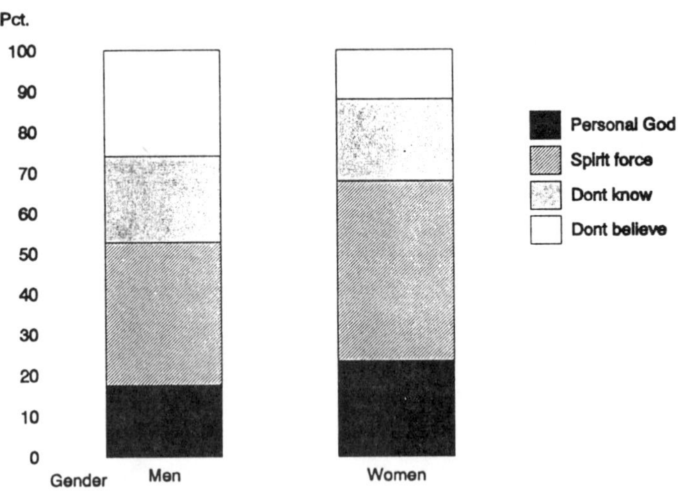

Figure 7. Forms of religious belief among men and women.

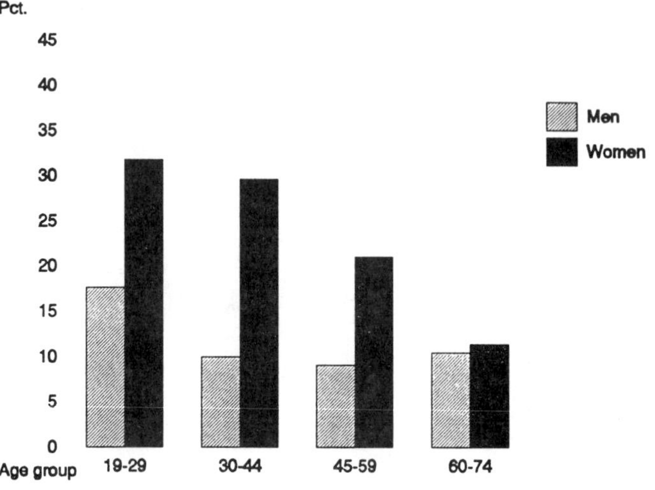

Figure 8. Belief in re-incarnation among men and women.

committed than women in white-collar jobs. Therefore the class factor has some influence. However, female workers are more religious than their male counterparts, and the same is true as for the white-collar employees. Therefore, gender has an independent impact on religiosity.

Figure 6 shows that orthodox beliefs are more accepted among women than men in all the major employment groups. The gender differences within all employment groups are significant – except for the farmers. It is worth noticing the marked difference in religious attitudes among the male and female manual work-ers. The male workers tend to score high on the atheist scale, whereas the female workers score relatively high on the scale of orthodox beliefs. The difference between the two genders can be found in ritual behaviour and belief patterns. The difference is especially remarkable, when non-institutional forms of religiosity or un-orthodox beliefs are considered. Women do not only to believe in a personal God more often than men, they also believe more often in a spirit force (see Figure 7). The difference between the gender is especially striking regarding belief in re-incarnation. It is especially strong among young and middle-aged women, though not nearly as widespread among young men (see Figure 8). This seems to indicate that women tend to be more open to religious and spiritual views than men.

The sociological consideration focuses upon the question about whether the socially defined gender roles may have religious implications. It is banal to mention that women are socialized to ensure the reproductive functions. The focus group for the women is the family, whereas men focus upon the collective of colleagues. The functionalists and feminists agree that this basic function also holds some implications for the value system. Girls are thus socialized to give special value to emotions, and to caring. McGuire's debate on religion and gender focuses on the specific subject on how religion legitimated the supremacy of the men and the control of sexuality and reproduction (McGuire 1992). It is hinted here that sexual and reproductive aspects of female life may accentuate a specific religious orientation, which goes against the male-defined mainstream religion. The substantiation of this hypothesis comes from historical and anthropological evidence rather than from modern empirical studies.

It is very probable that girls are still socialized to give special recognition to expressive rather than instrumental values, to particularistic views rather than universalistic ones, to intuition rather than logic, to life-forces rather than technical forces. It seems that religion is redefined under secularization. A religious institution is supposed to represent the Truth. It is, however, not credible to most modern Scandinavians if this Truth is expressed as a comprehensive, dogmatic world view. Therefore, the religious discourse turns to the general issues of human existence. The argument is not based upon intellectual, dogmatic statements but more on emotion and intuition. Such a change may help to explain why modern religion has more appeal to some women and less to most men. Furthermore, the ethical themes presented by religions today concern human obligations at the private or global level. They seldom take up societal debates about the economic or political problems. The themes also seem to be more directed towards the discourses of women. It seems that there may be a trend towards a redefinition of religion which is more female-oriented.[11]

The sociological approach to gender differences focuses on the patterns of socialization. The EVS-data demonstrate that women have been subject to religious socialization in their childhood more often than men. 36 % of the men were brought up religiously at home against 40 % of the women. This difference is not large, though it is significant at a 5 % level. It seems that women are socialized into religious values from their childhood to a larger extent than men. The religiosity of women should be related to the fact that women are traditional carriers of caring functions.

Conclusion

Only a minority of the Scandinavians demonstrate a strong commitment to the churches. The members of the minority churches are more committed than the average members of the state-supported churches. The most committed are often old and often women. The religiosity of the elder can be affiliated with a primary religious socialization. Women are generally a bit more religious-minded than men. This may be related to an interest in matters of life, which has for generations formed a part of the female gender role.

For the typical Scandinavian, religious questions have a low degree of saliency. A majority express belief in some vague dogma, like God – as a spirit force – and a soul, though not much more. The weakened position of religious views cannot be explained by a strong conviction in a rationalistic or ideological alternative. Many Scandinavians demonstrate an ability to compartmentalize religious, political and scientific views. Contrasting religious and ideological or scientific views are only be found among minorities, such as those with a high education and the skilled workers. The general impression is therefore that Scandinavia forms an extreme case of secularization in the sense that religious attitudes are of low intensity, religious beliefs are rather vague, religious behaviour is infrequent, and religious authorities have little practical influence on the opinions and ethics of most Scandinavians.

The findings reconfirm the importance of class, education, age and gender behind the patterns of religious attitudes. However, it is stressed that these background variables do not give us an explanation of the attitudes by themselves. They must be linked to common social psychological processes. Therefore, the study

[11] Male–female should not be understood here as biological concepts, but as cultural ideal-types.

stresses the importance of religious socialization and the formation of plausibility structures, which may reconfirm the world views in moments of crisis. The skilled workers, the women in the service-sector, the older farmers are related to specific plausibility structures. Here, the members form particular networks, which may discuss the meaning of life in a specific way. The apparent privatization of modern religiosity must therefore be corrected. No man or woman is an island, not even modern people. However, a large part of the discussions about the matters of existence takes place in loosely organized groups, with only vague religious foundations. In this way, the discussion reverts to the points made by Berger and Luckmann about the importance of plausibility structures, and the point made by Martin about the importance of religious cultures, when regarding the processes of secularization. This conclusion stresses the necessity of supplementing survey studies, as the EVS material, with in-depth interviews and field-work studies.

Literature

Bellah, R. & P. Hammond, 1980
Varieties of Civil Religion. New York.

Berger, P., 1967
The Sacred Canopy. New York: Doubleday.

Dobbelaere, K., 1981
"Secularization: A Multidimensional Concept". *Current Sociology*, vol. 29, 2.

Durkheim, É., 1985 (1912)
Les formes élémentaires de la vie religieuse. Paris: Quadrige.

Ester, P., L. Halman & R. de Moor, 1993
The Individualizing Society, Tilburg: Tilburg University Press.

Gundelach, P. & O. Riis, 1992
Danskernes Værdier. Copenhagen: Forlaget Sociologi.

Gustafsson, G., 1991
Tro, samfund och samhälle.Örebro: Libris.

Harding, S. *et al.*, 1986
Contrasting Values in Western Europe London: Macmillan.

Hertel, B. R., 1988
"Gender, Religious Identity and Work Force Participation". *Journal for the Scientific Study of Religion*.

The Journal of Oriental Studies, 1987
Feature: "Beyond the Dichotomy of Secularity and Religion". Vol. 26, 1, 1987.

Lenski, G., 1953
"Social Correlates of Religious Interest". *American Sociological Review*, 18.

Luckmann, T., 1967
The Invisible Religion. New York: MacMillan.

Luckmann, T., 1985
"Teorier om religion og sosial endring". In E. Karlsaune & O. Ingebriktesen (eds.), *Samfunn, menneske og religion*. Trondheim: Tapir.

Martin, D., 1969
The Religious and the Secular. London.

Martin, D., 1978
A General Theory of Secularization. Oxford: Blackwell.

McGuire, M., 1992
Religion — The Social Context. Belmont: Wadsworth.

Riis, O., 1992
"Religion". In H. Andersen (ed.), *Sociologi*. Copenhagen: Reitzel.

Riis, O., 1992
"Secularization in Scandinavia". Paper for the Nordic Conference for the Sociology of Religion, Skálholt, Iceland.

Secularization and Religion, 1987
Acts of the 19th CISR Conference, 1987.

Tschannen, O., 1991
"The Secularization Paradigm: A Systematization". *Journal for the Scientific Study of Religion*, 30 (4).

Ulbrich, H. & M. Wallace, 1984
"Women's Workforce Status and Church Attendance". *Journal for the Scientific Study of Religion*, 23.

de Vaus, D. A. & I. McAllister, 1987
"Gender Differences in Religion". *American Sociological Review*, 52.

SUSAN SUNDBACK

Nation and Gender Reflected in Scandinavian Religiousness

1. Introduction

Comparisons between the five Scandinavian countries on the basis of the 1990 European Values Study (EVS) show a surprisingly constant variation in the level of religiosity. Variables that measure individual attitudes on Church and religion show clear national divergences, a fact which may question the idea of a common Scandinavian culture.[1] The focus of this paper is not on inter-Scandinavian difference, but rather on the connection between the national profile of religiousness and the fact that women in all five countries appear as more religious than men. Thus, the religiousness level of *both* sexes in *all* national samples reflects the total or aggregated rating. Therefore, Icelandic men appear as clearly more positive towards religion than Swedish women while Icelandic women emerge as the most – and Swedish men as the least – religious categories in all of Scandinavia.

Such empirical findings logically lead to the proposition that Sweden is (was?) the most and Iceland the least patriarchal Scandinavian society. But such a hypo-thesis must be tested on comparative data regarding social structures and institutions, whereas data from individuals are insufficient. Two other comparative arguments, which fit the EVS-data, will be advanced in this paper: a) the aggregate data on the distribution of Christian and Church religiosity must be explained with reference to the symbolic value the Lutheran Church religion upholds in the nation-specific cultures and in collective (national) consciousness, and b) the national differences in religiousness reflect the gender relations in each country, i.e. the status given to women and traditional female values.

The first hypothesis assumes that the historical threats towards national identity has greatly varied between the five countries. Christianity has historically been a central ideological element uniting Scandinavia with Europe, but the national Lutheran Churches have simultaneously been building blocks on which the consciousness of a separate national identity has rested. Within the family of countries with traditional Lutheran state-churches, the highest legitimation given to the specific nation state rested on the idea of national forms of Christianity. In this

[1] I use the term "Scandinavian" as a synonym to Nordic to indicate that these countries – not only Norway, Sweden and Denmark, but also Iceland and Finland – belong to the same cultural sphere. (See also Martin 1978.)

respect the secularization process has not only reduced the authority of the Church but also of the nation state.

The assumption underlying the second hypothesis is that the cultural impact of religion in secularized societies is dependent on the relative balance between stereotyped "masculinity" and "femininity". While the institutional forms for religion have changed little, gender relations and the position of women and men in society belong to one aspect of Scandinavian culture which, due to the demise of traditional collective lifestyles, has undergone dynamic change. The gender structure surrounding the individual is a basic social fact, which directly – but often unconsciously – influences his/her search for identity. The respondents in any survey normally have a certain amount of self-knowledge, a social identity which defines them both biologically and culturally. The biological differentiation is however smaller than the cultural; few persons are defined as neither man nor woman, while the variation between the "masculinity" or "femininity" of men and women is indefinitely graded. Some of the respondents also have a conscious religious identity, but many of them do not. The social identity must in any case be seen as basic to the personality.

The existing gender relations are thus a more direct expression of recent national history than the aggregated religious profile which appears in surveys. Gender culture has gained increased cultural/social significance during the era of secularization, social differentiation and the declining signicance of the nation state. Sexual "liberation" is part of the modern theme of individual fulfillment and the stress on subjectivism.

I thank the participants in the XI Nordic conference in the sociology of religion held in Iceland, August, 1992, for many helpful comments on an earlier draft of this paper. Ole Riis and Thorleif Pettersson have in a constructive manner discussed with me the final version.

2. Theoretical Frame

Religion and National Identity

At the end of the 20th century we can witness the vigorous role played by religion as a marker of national or ethnic identity in a part of Europe where for decades no efforts were spared to extinguish all kinds of religiosity. The ethnic wars that have broken out in the former Communist empire have generally held a religious component. Ethnic groups often refer to themselves as Orthodox, Catholics or Muslims, by this implying more of a collective identity, rooted in history, than to the impact of Christian or Muslim principles in the everyday-life of the group.

Before the emancipation of national/ethnic identities in the former socialist societies David Martin (1978) recognized the importance of (oppressed) national identity and religion in his analysis of the different Scandinavian secularization patterns. The conceptual and historical affinity between on the one hand religion – Christianity and other great world religions – and modern nationalism as "imagined communities" has also been developed by Benedict Anderson (1983, 17–40).

The main results of the comparisons below, showing least religiousness among Danes/Swedes and most among Icelanders/Finns, with the Norwegians as a intermediate case, is readily interpreted in accordance with Martin's theory. Sweden has for many centuries been the most secure nation surrounded by friendly neighbours. Likewise Denmark was threatened only during the Second World War during the Nazi occupation. The other Scandinavian countries had to struggle for their independence in the 19th and 20th centuries, Norway somewhat less so than Iceland. The Norwegian and Icelandic movements for independence did not concern the status of the traditional religion, since Denmark and Sweden were Lutheran countries as well. The Finnish case has been different due to the geopolitical fact which dictates that Finland be a neighbour of Russia. Throughout Finnish history, relations between Finland and Russia have been coloured by different national developments of the relations between Church and State, thus underlining Finland's identity as part of the Western Lutheran branch of Christianity.

The differences in national experiences and collective history are not recorded in the EVS data, but have been internalized diversely by the individuals who answered the standardized questions. Danes, Icelanders, Finns, Norwegians and Swedes are – often unconsciously – voices for opinions on religion, Christianity and Lutheranism, which reveal the biography of their national collectivity.[2]

More about Finland

Since the Scandinavian countries with the exception of Finland are presented elsewhere in this book, it has been considered necessary here to present the Finnish background in a somewhat more detailed form than for the other countries. Finland is the best Scandinavian illustration of the intimate relations between the concepts nation and religion.

It is a historical fact that Finland in the Middle Ages was linked to Western Europe through the Christianization process, although missionaries from the Eastern Church also left early marks on the culture. For many centuries until 1809

[2] The EVS data share all the methodological problems inherent in survey-data. They are problematic for sociological analysis in the sole reliance on data from individuals and the tendency to ignore the varying social pressures to which individuals are subjected.

Finland was an important part of Sweden. The country was for a little more than a hundred years an autonomous region within (Orthodox) Russia. The advent of independence was followed by a civil war in 1918, in which the defeated Socialists failed to "free" Finland from Church and religion. In 1939–1944 two wars were fought with the (atheist) Soviet superpower.

Finland's recent history has compared to the rest of Scandinavia been violent. The civil war of 1918 is an exception to the Scandinavian pattern where class-divisions never grew so deep as to threaten the binding unity, which rested on the idea of a united nation (*folk*) across class-divisions and other social barriers (Dahl 1986, 105). The defeat of the "Reds" and the victory of the "Whites" in 1918 has made the idea of national unity a more problematic issue than in the other Scandinavian countries during the 20th century. The radical left continued to play an important political role until the 1980s although the Communist party was illegal in the period between the two World Wars. The years following the Second World War, when Finland as the rest of the world had to accept the immense military power of the Soviet Union, was a period of Communist mobilization, which recalled the memory of the unfulfilled revolution of 1918. In the parliamentary election of 1958 the Communist share of the votes was as large as for the two other leading parties, the Social Democrats (moderate left) and the Agrarian party (centre) (SYF 1958, 320). The Communist party was forced to remain in the opposition until the late 1960s, thus barred from real political power. When the radical left finally was invited to take government responsibility, this was the path toward normalization of Finnish Communism and consequent loss of popular support.

The implications of the long vigorous Communist movement on the role of religion in the Finnish national identity has been that the "beneficent circle" between Church and politics which Martin (1978, 5–34) describes as typical for Scandinavia, does not unconditionally fit for Finland. Although the general pattern has been that the non-Communist parties in the main have supported the presence of the Church in society, there has also been a "vicious circle" in the connection between radical leftism, political protest, secularism and distancing from the Church. The Finns have therefore during the 20th century largely been polarized in their attitude towards Church and Christianity to a much larger extent than in the rest of Scandinavia. There is no doubt that the comparatively high rate of withdrawals from the Finnish Lutheran Church must be explained mainly with reference to the role played by Communism in Finnish politics and cultural life (Sundback 1991).

A similar example of the non-Scandinavian type of Finnish situation, is the Christian nationalism which dominated the political scene between the World Wars. The right-wing radicalism was to a large extent directed against the threat of world-Communism. These traumatic events in recent Finnish history explain why Finnish opinions towards the Church still tend to follow the left–right political division line.

Religion and Gender

Sociology has produced innumerable studies which have supported the idea that women are more religious than men. The underlying assumption has been that gender influences religiosity. From a feminist perspective this conclusion has been questioned by twisting the argument: religion influences gender. The feminist view has been critical of religion as well as of "male science" (for example McGuire 1987).

The two research traditions often appear as contradictory, but the conflict may in fact be a reflection of the poverty of methods and an inadequate understanding of the nature of religion as an element of general culture. Thompson (1991, 381) criticizes research in this field for a common tendency to reduce religion to a one-dimensional concept or to limit the method to bivariate analysis. Women have not always been found to be more religious than men when religion has been treated multidimensionally. The expected difference has often been found in measures on religious participation while not in belief. The effect of genders usually diminishes radically when multivariate techniques are used.

Thompson provides some explanations for the firm conviction, which is not only typical of the man in the street, that women really are more religious than men. He distinguishes two major reasons why the idea is supported by sociology. The first is related to the different structural location in society of women and men. Men are associated with production and public power, women with reproduction and private identity. The interpretation of these facts is often conducted according to deprivation theory. The other explanation stresses gender socialization and argues that girls more than boys are taught to be religious. Religiousness as an expression for care and community feeling is defined as an element of femininity. The conceptual affinity between religiousness and femininity has often been explained by a common experience of "otherness" in a world ruled by men, whose priorities lie in power and rational mastering of the world. The separate cultural norms for men and women further, according to this line of reasoning, induces men to avoid religion in order to stress their masculinity.

Thompson is however not convinced of the explanatory value of gender: "it is quite possible that the sex difference in religiosity is not 'real' but can be explained by the differential proportions of women and men with a 'feminine' world-view". "Being religious" is a consonant experience for any individual or group with a "feminine" orientation. He concludes that both men and women can have this outlook and that the "gender orientation" of the people affects religiosity more than being female or male (Thompson 1991, 382). The hypothesis was in a concrete test verified on a general level; the religiousness of women and men was predictable on the basis of "degree of feminine outlook". The proof was stronger on issues like self-assessed religious feeling and devotionalism, than on belief and behaviour. The results imply that the structural and socialization explanations of differences between men and women remain effective; a strong feminine orientation was typical of a majority of the women (69 %) and a minority of the men (39 %) (Thompson 1991, 386–389).

The Thompson discussion is relevant for the interpretation of national patterns in Nordic religiosity. The general social position of women and men is of the same kind as in the rest of the Western world. Explanations of gender differences cannot overlook structural variables or role socialization in Scandinavia. The idea of a specific blend of masculinity and femininity for a certain collective culture (nation) comes naturally out of the comparison between the five Nordic countries where the national level of religiosity invariably affects both sexes but always with preserved gender differences.

3. Material and Method

The EVS data were collected in many European countries, USA and Canada. The same base questionnaire was used in all participating countries. The Nordic data were put to my disposal by the Norwegian Social Science Data Service in Bergen.[3] As Loek Halman (1992, 24) has noticed, comparative data may always reflect differences in sampling techniques. No analysis of the scope of this problem in the EVS studies has yet been done. It is clear that some questions have had different wordings (translations from the original EVS questionnaire) in the national surveys. This problem does however not seem to be very large in a Scandinavian comparison. Finnish, although not of Germanic origin, is for historical reasons conceptually close to the Scandinavian languages.[4]

The data on religion are considered valid for intra-Scandinavian comparison since the countries have a similar religious history. Still today, many decades after the breakthrough for full religious freedom, a great majority of the populations are registered Lutherans. The religio-cultural dissolution since the advent of modernity has, no doubt, increased the differentiation within the countries as well as between them. The pattern of modernization and secularization has not been identical, although broad similarities exist. The Finnish development from an agrarian to an industrial and service society was in a Scandinavian perspective

[3] The empirical data used in this study originate from the European Values Study (EVS). The secretariat of the Steering Committee of the European Values Group (EVG) is based at Tilburg University, The Netherlands. The data were put to my disposal by the Norwegian Social Science Data Service (*Norsk samfunnsvitenskapelig datatjeneste*, NSD) in Bergen where I visited in June 1992. For this I especially want to thank Björn Henrichsen, Atle Alvheim and Jostein Ryssevik. All data are in an anonymous form. All interpretations made on the basis of the data are the sole responsibility of the author.

[4] The paper should therefore be appended with the trivial warning that my interpretations are directly dependent on the reliability and validity of each Nordic national survey.

delayed. Not before the 1960s did Finland reach a level of development comparable to the other Scandinavian countries (Allardt 1987; Alestalo & Kuhnle 1984).

The fact that each national sample has been collected separately, and that the original EVS questionnaire was translated into the native languages, created a risk for differences in methods and wordings. Contacts between the five research leaders did not prevent the Finnish Gallup Institute carrying through the project in an unorthodox way – replacing personal interviews with computer interviews, thus introducing bias into the data. Men and young were more motivated to reply than women and old persons. The official data processed by Finnish Gallup have been weighted to increase their degree of representativity, while the data available in Bergen reflect the real distributions.

The Finnish material will none the less be used in this paper – the purpose is a complete Nordic comparison. Unless indicated otherwise, the weighted set of data will be referred to. The inherent tendency in the Finnish data due to a low response rate among women and elderly, is *not* biased in favour of the general hypothesis that religion is more important to the Finns than to Swedes, Danes and Norwegians. In other words: the Finns seem to be more attached to religion than most other Scandinavians despite the fact that young men have been most eager to answer the computerized questionnaire! This fact qualifies the use of the "different" Finnish material. It is further justified since the purpose is to look at comparative trends than at exact distributions on variables.

The comparisons are twofold: a) of the total samples and b) with comparisons for the two sexes within each national category. The items which are to be compared concern attitude towards Church, Christianity and religion. Not all variables on religion are picked; only those which seem to discriminate the respondents on the national level and between the sexes. The standard EVS items are referred to as Q-plus-number, for example Q355A for the question "Do you believe in God". The sample sizes and the total N of all tables are: Denmark 1 030, Iceland 702, Norway 1 239, Sweden 1 047 and Finland 588.

4. The National Religious Profiles

Subjective and Social Religiousness

The main finding of the comparison is, viewing the *subjective* dimension of religiousness, which includes Christian and general religious belief, and the personal relevance of religion, a relatively consistent pattern where the degree of religiousness increases in the following order: *Swedes, Danes, Norwegians, Finns, Icelanders*. The intermediate Norwegian position seems to be dependent on polarization of attitudes towards religion among Norwegians, an interpretation which has been supported in other research. A relatively strong support for traditional Lutheran pietism is matched by a recent anti-clerical movement (*Humanetisk forbund*) among intellectuals of a kind not found in the other Nordic countries (Lundby 1985, 182–186; 1988; Knudsen 1992, 23). The Norwegian polarization around Christianity does not have a right–leftist political dimension, nor is it connected to the idea of the nation in the way found in Finland.

The EVS questions also touch on a *social* dimension of religiosity, which may be qualitatively separate from the first mentioned subjective religiosity. The social dimension emanates from questions on the evaluations of the (Lutheran) Church as an institution in society. The distributions of answers reveal a different range of order from low to high religiousness than in the case of the respondents' evaluation of the subjective meaning of religion: *Danes, Swedes, Icelanders, Norwegians, Finns*. The importance of the social dimension of Christianity is clearly observable in the answers by the Finns and is obviously not negligible in the Norwegian attitude. The Swedes, who are least inclined to see religion as subjectively important, have compared with the Danes a more positive view on the social role of the Church.

The status of the Church is clearly less central in the EVS study than questions on individual belief, but the social items are more relevant than the subjective items to a contextual and cultural analysis of each national religious profile. The national order on the social religiousness dimension follows the real variation of institutional autonomy of the (national) Lutheran Churches in the relations to "their" states; the widest independence is enjoyed by the Finnish Church, followed by Norway, Iceland and Sweden. The strictest state church system exists in Denmark. The social position obtained by each Lutheran Church is the outcome of history and politics. Contrary to the common view that modernization produces the same kind of processes in different countries, differentiation more than convergence seems to characterize the State–Church arrangements that have evolved in the Scandinavian states during the 20th century (Gustafsson 1985, 240–242).

Items measuring Church support for *collective norms* (Q345A–Q354J) are a clear test of the idea of social religiousness. The distributions clearly indicated the expected variation among nationalities. The Finns were most in favour of Church influence on social life, Swedes expressed more Church loyalty than Danes. A majority of the Finns approved of Church involvement in nine of the ten items. Such majorities appeared on six items among Norwegians, five among Icelanders and Swedes and only two among the Danes.[5]

The social dimension of religiosity is neither conceptually nor empirically totally separate from the subjective dimension; on both dimensions Swedes and

[5] In all samples a majority approved of church opinion on the *Third World* and *euthanasia*. The support was almost as strong for church opinion and *racial discrimination*, *disarmament* and *ecological/environmental problems*; only among the Danes was the support shared by less than fifty percent. The church opinion was welcomed only by a majority of the Norwegians and the Finns regarding *abortion*, only by the Finns when asked about *infidelity*, *homosexuality* and *unemployment*.

Table 1. The relative personal importance of "religion" and "politics" (percentages of answers "very" and in parenthesis cumulatively "very" + "quite").

	Low		Religiousness		.... High
	Sweden	Denmark	Norway	Finland	Iceland
Religion (Q121)	10 (27)	8 (31)	15 (40)	16 (45)	24 (56)
Politics (Q120)	11 (45)	8 (43)	9 (50)	3 (28)	9 (26)

Danes reach the bottom line on religiosity, the relatively high Finnish evaluation of "their" Church is probably one of the factors explaining the comparatively high level of religiosity among the Finns.[6]

Individual Religiousness

The respondents were, in order to catch the subjective dimension, asked to evaluate the *personal relevance* of social areas such as family, friends, work, leisure. All these were by all Scandinavians held to be of higher value than politics and religion as such. There is a qualitative difference between the asked areas of personal fulfillment, politics and religion. The latter may to a majority of respondents seem to concern society more than one's routinized everyday-life. The national variation regarding personal significance of religion follows the expected pattern for subjective religiousness. It should be observed that there is a tendency for relevance of religion to be negatively correlated with personal relevance of politics.

The order of national variations was also supported by answers that religion was "not at all important" by less than 20 % of the Icelanders and Finns, by 21 % of the Norwegians and by about 30 % among Danes and Swedes. Politics is most important to the Swedes, clearly more positively valued than religion. The same trend, although less clearly, is present in the Danish material. The Finns were in 1989–1990 clearly pessimistic about the future of their national politics, which has also been proved in other surveys (EVA 1991).

Almost the same national tendency appeared in the distribution of answers on a direct question regarding human existence: "How often do you think of the meaning of life?" (Q322). This issue appeared as clearly most central to Finns. Otherwise the comparison followed the expected pattern with the Swedes as little

[6] There are in fact two national churches in Finland. The Orthodox minority is less than 60 000, in numbers overrun by the Protestant free churches. The relatively favoured position of the Orthodox religion is due to the Russian influence in the 19th century.

Table 2. Scandinavians' belief in God, the soul, sin and heaven.* (Percentage of "yes"-answers exceeding 50% in at least one national sample.)

	Religiousness				
	Low .... High				
	Sweden	Denmark	Norway	Finland	Iceland
God (Q355)	38	59	58	65	79
Soul (Q357)	51	41	45	59	82
Sin (Q361)	27	22	39	53	64
Heaven (Q360)	27	17	39	44	51

* The EVS questionnaire dealt with more belief items than are shown below. For the present purpose only those four items out of nine (Q355–Q363) are picked, which are affirmed in at least 50 % of the responses in at least one sample. All questions about belief (Q355–Q363) produced a great portion of "don't know" answers; for the four items in the table often 10–15%.

occupied by such thoughts. The twin-item about a meaning to death (Q323) did not differentiate well between the nations, but again the Swedes were least occupied by this question.[7] As a whole all Scandinavian peoples found life meaningful, but the meaning was neither limited to the Christian view, nor to pragmatic naturalism (Q324–Q330). Asked specifically whether the meaning of life was dependent on God's existence (Q324) the shares of agreements were recorded as follows: Finns 31, Icelanders 27, Norwegians 25, Danes 18 and Swedes 13 percent. The affirmative answer can be interpreted as clearly God-centred and representing a Christian standpoint. The Finns appear on this item as more Christian than others.

The rationale for evaluating Icelanders as more religious than Finns rests on the comparison of other items, especially answers affirming traditional Christian dogmas and beliefs. The same set of data shows that Swedish disbelief is particularly centred on the image of a personal God; Swedes seem in fact more than Danes to believe in the soul, sin and heaven. The soul seems, somewhat surprisingly, plausible both to Swedes with little belief in God *and* to the Icelanders who widely profess belief in God. The explanation could be that the Christian concept "soul" has been tranformed into a desacralized psychological concept. The distribution on the item "sin", which brings in a moral and practical quality to belief, supports the view that religion – on a personal and everyday basis – matters most for Icelanders and Finns.

[7] Q322, meaning to life; answers "often" and in parenthesis "often + sometimes". Maximum Finns 41(84)w, minimum Swedes 24(86).

Q323, meaning to death: answers "often" and in parenthesis "often + sometimes". Maximum Finns 18(64)w, minimum Swedes 12(55).

Church practice declined drastically in all Scandinavian countries already before the mid-20th century (Gustafsson 1985). Religiousness has developed into a subjective, inwardly directed phenomenon with few public attributes. The Scandinavian respondents to this EVS survey tended to restrict the role of the Church to sublime, personal, "spiritual needs" (Q343C). Acceptance of the religious legitimacy of the Church thus does not imply ritual activity or Church involvement. A clear majority in all five nations also denies Church authority in problems of personal morality (Q341A). The breakdown of Church teaching is even more prevalent when the most intimate kind of morality, such as family problems, is in focus (Q342B).

The crisis of traditional Christian ideals in the socialization of Scandinavian children is evident (Q453A–Q463K). The data give the impression that Scandinavians in general do not want to direct their children's life in any detail. The ideals that were made famous through Weber's writing on the Protestant ethic are actively advocated only by the Icelanders. A clear majority in all countries mentions "good manners", "responsibility", "tolerance and respect for others" while only among Icelanders do a majority also choose "hard work", "thrift, saving money and things", "determination and perseverance", "unselfishness", "obediance" and "religious faith". Religious faith (Q461I) is mentioned by 50 percent of Icelanders, less than 15 percent by Finns and Norwegians and less than 10 percent by Danes and Swedes. (The popularity of some of the items varied so much that it casts doubts on the soundness of method. Reason for cautious interpretation of these results is also given by the fact that every alternative ideal was most often chosen by the Icelanders.)

In spite of the relative legitimacy of the Scandinavian Churches in delivering ethical norms for *social* life, most Scandinavians – asked about the personal relevancy of "religion" – place religion in an individual and "spiritual" sphere separate from life-styles and routine behaviour. This result shows the changing cultural meaning of the concept "religion" away from its social and historical (Christian) background into a meaning close to psychological theories of individual development. The Church is viewed as an institution which belongs to "others" and collective life more than to the private sphere. The span between the Finnish and the Danish evaluation of the Church in collective morality reflects a variation in the degree of collective conviction that social life must contain a shared morality.

5. Individual Identity, Religion and Gender

Religiousness

This section will focus on the variation between the sexes. Variables which in some sense illustrate the changing conditions for religiousness are picked. It has been

Table 3. Gender differences on items describing traditional Christian religiosity (percentage of affirmative answers; total, women/men).

	Religiousness: Low …									… High
	Sweden		Denmark		Norway		Finland		Iceland	
	T	W/M	T	W/M	T	W/M	T	W/M	T	W/M
Q335 Religious upbringing	*30*	32/28	*42*	48/37	*45*	45/44	*58*	60/56	*75*	82/65
Q340 Religious person	*28*	35/23	*68*	77/59*	*45*	53/38	*54*	59/49	*74*	83/65
Q367 Comfort/strength from religion	*23*	29/19	*25*	34/18	*29*	36/23	*43*	44/41	*70*	81/68
Q355A Belief in God	*38*	43/33	*59*	67/51	*58*	67/50	*64*	74/57	*79*	87/71

* The somewhat unexpectedly high frequency of Danes who define themselves as religious persons may be an artefact, since the Danish questionnaire held another formulation of the question. Instead of "religious" the Danes answered whether they were "believing persons" or not.

considered meaningful to differentiate between traditional and new forms of religion, since especially traditional religion has been accused of patriarchalism. Only two items were however found to describe new religiosity with a non-Christian reference, which in fact decreases the possibilities of drawing conclusions on the base of Table 4.

The correlation of religious upbringing (Q335) with the respondents' evaluation of their own relation to religion (Q340) is in all samples very significant ($p < .001$) when tested with the chi-square method.[8] The relationship works positively *and* negatively; a high level of religious socialization in childhood predicts a high level of adult religiosity while a low level of religion in childhood is a good predictor of low religiosity in adulthood. The expected national order is only disturbed by the Danish data, but this may be an effect of the Danish version of the question whether the personal self is viewed as religious (Q340, see note to Table 3). It should be remembered that a statistical relation between socialization and adult

[8] The "religious upbringing" variable was dichotomous (yes/no), while three categories were included on the "religious person" variable (yes/no/atheist), 2 df, the expected values for all cells fill the criteria usually set for this test. Chi-square values for Iceland (N 686) 37,64, Norway (N 1 159) 223,84, Finland unweighted data (N 500) 74,47, Denmark (N 954) 65,16 and Sweden (N 935) 131,51.

Table 4. Gender differences on items describing new forms of religiousness (percentage of positive answers; total, women/men)*

	Religiousness Low .... Sweden		Denmark		Norway		Finland		Iceland .... High	
	T	W/M	T	W/M	T	W/M	T	W/M	T	W/M
Q364B Belief in spirit or power	*44*	51/37	*32*	35/30	*35*	37/34	*46*	49/42	*32*	33/31
Q363I Belief in re-incarnation	*17*	23/11	*15*	18/11	*13*	15/10	*24*	21/27	*32*	35/30

* The rate of "don't know" answers were generally high on belief items, sometimes almost 20%. The table is not representative of opinions in the national populations. The evading answer was especially popular regarding belief in reincarnation and it was usually more common among women than men. The unexpected gender difference among Finnish respondents may be explained with an unusual high rate of "don't know" answers (28%), which was even higher among Finnish women (33%).

level of religiosity has been found on the aggregate data level and that the variation may be less obvious in individual cases.

The interdependence of religiosity in childhood and adulthood indicates that the whole pattern of national profiles in the EVS data could be dependent on this one variable (Q335); only a majority of Icelanders and Finns (both sexes) had been raised with religion. In all nationalities women saw their own childhood as more religious than men, but the gap between women and men correlated positively with the national level of positive answers to this item. Almost half of the Norwegian and Danish respondents had been brought up with religion, but less than a third of the Swedes.

Further analysis of the religious socialization variable along age, shows that *not even the oldest Swedish respondents* were socialized into religion as children. This is a clear contrast to the Icelandic data which shows that half of the youngest respondents had been brought up with religion. A majority of Danes and Norwegians over 50 years, but a minority of those under 50, had experienced religious upbringing. This age level was at 40 years among the Finns.

Tables 3 and 4 show that national culture differentiates more in opinions to traditional Christian religiosity than to diffuse forms of new religiosity. National differences are almost negligible in Table 4 regarding belief in an abstract transcendental power (Q364B) other than God (Q355A). The high level of positive Icelandic answers on both items in Table 4, in addition to the high level of religiosity in Table 3, may seem surprising, but can be explained with reference to

Icelandic spiritualism which for long has existed side by side with Christianity (Pétursson 1985, 134). The religiously "trained" Icelanders are not unfamiliar with many of the elements typical of the "new religions".

Finns and Swedes tend more than Western Scandinavians to see God as an abstract spirit or power. The tendency is especially stressed by the Swedish women. (Could this, as well as belief in reincarnation, be a female protest in the one Scandinavian society which least seems to approve of religion?)

The gender difference in religiousness should, according to the theory presented above, not be explained biologically as revealing conflicting interests between men and women. The explanation should instead centre on bipolar cultural concepts like masculinity–femininity, instrumentality–expressivity or hard–soft values. The conventional definition of "gender" focuses on the social construction of role expectations attributed to the two sexes (Abbot & Wallace 1990, 8).[9] The cultural roots of gender explain why some men may appear "feminine" and women may share attitudes conventionally seen as typical for men. The conventionality of social life – a central element in the identity moulding power of traditions and customs – does on the other hand explain why women in general tend to uphold soft/expressive values and men tend to value hard goals and instrumentality.

If femininity–masculinity is a characteristic which can be applied to national culture as well as to individuals, we should then expect to find the same national and gender variation, as we have found in religion, in other existentially important items.

Hard and Soft Values

Table 5 gives some verification of the hypothesis that femininity is related to soft values and hard values with a masculine set of attitudes. The respondents were asked to choose between different goals for the national development ten years ahead. Of the four priorities – high economic growth, strong defence, local democracy, environment protection – the two first should be classified as "hard" and the two last mentioned as "soft" values. The two major choices were in all five countries "economic growth" and "local democracy". The national difference between the two populations that have been seen to represent the most religious or "soft" cultures is unexpected; Icelanders stress economy while Finns prefer economic expansion remarkably little. The Finns strongly want to advance local democracy as a national goal. But the national ranking of Table 5 five cannot as such falsify the theoretical proposition tested: 1) the two goals should not be seen as

[9] The discussion on "sex roles" was frequent during the dominance of the functionalist theory in sociology, which focused on the family as a basic social institution (Jallinoja 1990, 12–16). The concept "gender" was introduced after the functionalist era and is much more focussed on the relation between the individual and his/her biological sex (Giddens 1989, 156–201), which however does not mean that the family has ceased to be an important socializing agent.

Table 5. National and gender differences in preference of national goals (percentage of total N and of women/men)

	Religiousness									
	Low									.... High
Sweden	Denmark		Norway		Finland		Iceland			
	T	W/M	T	W/M	T	W/M	T	W/M	T	W/M
Q530										
Economic growth	*48*	42/53	*45*	38/53	*46*	43/49	27	23/31	*52*	45/57
Local democracy	*31*	35/27	*38*	44/32	*47*	49/45	*51*	58/44	*38*	44/33
Other answers	*21*	23/19	*12*	12/12	*12*	14/11	*21*	18/24	*10*	10/10

mutually exclusive although the respondents could pick only one (the same alternatives could also be picked as a second national goal, Q531); 2) the experienced need for economic development versus increased democracy is dependent on the objective state, or the base lines of these two sectors in each country; 3) both alternatives may semantically have divergent meanings in each national culture.

The table supports the view that men more than women choose the "hard" alternative and *vice versa*. "Economic growth" is a more central national goal for men while "local democracy" as a "soft" human relations item was more often chosen by women than men. The Danish, Norwegian and Finnish women preferred local democracy to economic growth. The Swedish women, on the other hand, generally gave economy highest priority, although they more than Swedish men also supported democracy.[10]

If a positive national identification, separable from nationalism, can be seen as a soft value, related to religiosity, then we should expect the gender pattern and the national ranking order identified above to appear in questions on national pride.

The wording of the question in Table 6, "How proud are you to be Icelandic etc ...?", may catch the spontaneous emotions, previously often named "love" for one's country, more than conscious and ideological nationalism. But the question may have been experienced as ambiguous and may have been judged differently by men

[10] Detailed analysis shows that people who choose "economic growth" need not be less "religious" – on any variable – than those who choose "democratic development". This problem is related to the fact that "religiousness" is a multi-dimensional concept. My own analysis shows for instance that men tend to value religion for its social and ethical consequences more than women who tend to value religion from the experiental point of view. This is a problematic in its own right. The main argument of the paper, that gender more than religious conviction has been basic to this differentiation, is however supported by the fact that women choose democracy and men choose economy.

Table 6. National pride among the Scandinavians (percentage of total N and of women/men)

	Religiousness Low									High
	Sweden		Denmark		Norway		Finland		Iceland	
	T	W/M	T	W/M	T	W/M	T	W/M	T	W/M
Q650										
Very proud	*38*	40/37	*41*	44/38	*44*	46/42	*39*	38/41	*50*	56/50
Quite proud	*40*	41/40	*43*	40/46	*37*	39/36	*42*	41/42	*40*	39/42
Not proud	*22*	9/23	*11*	9/13	*18*	16/21	*19*	20/16	*6*	6/7

and women. The distribution of answers to this question shows that women in all of Scandinavia, except for Finland, tend to have more "national pride" than men. Western Scandinavians, especially Icelanders, are prouder over their nationality than Finns and Swedes. The low pride level among Finns may be an additional indicator of the general pessimistic mood among Finnish respondents, but other interpretations related to the collective memory of the violent national history during this century cannot be excluded. It is possible that any item which touches on nationalism in Finland induces emotions that are ideologically and politically stereotyped. The question may have evoked answers related to the world-view, values and political outlook of the respondent. The answers of national pride should be viewed as containing ideological elements, but not necessary a full-fledged nationalist orientation. The feeling of national pride does not necessarily relate to the manifest or concrete national society. It is, for instance, possible that the expression of national pride is less related to the country as a geographical entity and more to the individual adjustment to his/her local society or to a region. The general level of national pride may in fact point to the prevalence of regional conflicts or to the strains between centre and periphery of the national state.

The next item (Q648) was constructed to measure a less conscious sense of the nation as a geographical home. This item asking which of the geographical groups the individual first of all belonged to, is less connected with ideologies of the nation state and more with subjective identity.

Table 7 reveals that the country/nation as a specifically geographical term is clearly most identity shaping for Icelanders and Finns. A large majority of the Norwegians see their local society as their most important geographical context. Swedes and Danes tend to stress their belonging with the local and regional territory more than to the country as a whole. The gender differences are small, but it should be noticed that Icelandic women more than men identify with the

Table 7. Self declared geographical first belonging* (percentage of total N and of women/men)

	Religiousness: Low ...									... High
	Sweden		Denmark		Norway		Finland		Iceland	
	T	W/M	T	W/M	T	W/M	T	W/M	T	W/M
Q648										
Locality/town	*56*	37/43	*52*	52/51	*68*	70/67	*33*	36/30	*40*	37/43
Region	*12*	10/14	*22*	23/21	*13*	12/13	*13*	13/13	*6*	23/21
Country	*24*	26/23	*22*	21/22	*14*	13/15	*41*	41/41	*48*	50/46

* "Europe" and a loose category of other answers were also recorded. The total distribution of these were among Icelanders 1+5, Finns 4+7, Norwegians 1+3, Danes 2+1, Swedes 3+1. The respondents were also asked to give their second preference of geographical belonging in Q649.

whole country and that the unexpected male tendency in high Finnish pride of Table 6 does not appear in Table 7. The Finns identify with "Finland" geographically more than ideologically. The ideological problems inherent in the national self-identification of the Finns must be explained with reference to the social cleavages which accompanied the relatively late modernization of the Finnish society.

Conclusions

The proposition put at the beginning, that "soft" values are more prevalent among women and "hard" values are typical of men, has been confirmed on a number of different items. Religion as a central "soft" value in this study has clearly discriminated among the sexes and the nations. Women differ from men not only by being more religious but also by appreciating the national collectivity which they identify with. Scandinavian women want to develop democratic human relations in their country more than men, who stress economic growth. The Swedish women make an interesting case in that they are inclined less to choose democracy and more to choose economy than other Scandinavian women. They are also less religious, when this concept is given a traditional content. On the other hand, Swedish women express a strong tendency for a diffuse and private religious feeling.

The hypothesis that the relative degree of "religiousness" in each sample should be explained with reference to the symbolic role of nation/country in each national culture has further been supported by the data. The five Nordic populations differ on a cultural dimension stretching between "soft" and "hard" values in an order that corresponds to the general total (national) level of conventional religiousness.

Other concepts used to describe the cultural qualities related to gender relations have been femininity–masculinity and expressivity–instrumentality. The order of the national samples in relative religiousness has been interpreted as a reflection of a hidden cultural dimension related to the real gender structure of each society. A national culture where "femininity" is highly valued is such a milieu where not only religion, but soft human-relations values and expressivity is legitimate. A "masculine" culture is on the other hand such that legitimates rationalism instead of religion, "hard" economy and technology instead of "soft" human relation values and instrumentalism instead of expressivity.

The ranking order from low to high on the dimensions femininity and religiousness is in the aggregated EVS data: *Sweden, Denmark, Norway, Finland, Iceland.* But in what meaningful way could it be proved that Sweden is the most "masculine" and Iceland the most "feminine" Scandinavian country?

6. Looking For an Explanation, or Why Are the Swedes So Non-Religious?

Individual answers and opinions, such as gathered in the EVS study, cannot explain why the society of the individual is structured the way it is. This chapter will turn around the perspective on the relation between individual and religious/national culture starting from the fact that every individual is born into an existing society. The individual has been in focus above, now the view is turned on the society, which has authority to shape the individual and to limit his/her freedom to mould his/her conceptual universe. The explanation of the observed national differences cannot be reached with questionnaire data. There must be reasonable historical and contextual interpretations of collective phenomena.

The starting point must be the onset of modernization and secularization.

During this stage Scandinavian culture has been differentiated more than ever before. A central change is the desacralization of the public world-view which meant that the social "world" was no longer seen as an expression of the eternal order given by God, rather as an arena for conflicting class interests. This turn was brought about when the power to define the meaning of social life was shifted from religion to politics; from the Lutheran Church to the political parties. But the political field has never been as homogeneous as the old religious system. The centralized and homogenizing Christian ideology was followed by competing and sometimes antagonistic political ideologies. Politics was from the beginning fragmented.

There was only one party which could reach a position which enabled it to exert an ideological influence almost as strong as Lutheranism had done during the preceding centuries. The Social Democratic ideology has been important in all of Scandinavia, but the power of the moderate left has been uncomparably strongest in Sweden and weakest in Iceland. Among the Scandinavians almost 45 percent of the voters at times favoured it especially after the First World War until the 1970s. The share of votes for the moderate has since the Second World War been proof of the party's political power according to the following rising order: *Iceland, Finland, Denmark, Norway, Sweden* (Lindström 1989, 99). The Social Democratic dimension is almost exactly inverse to the religiousness dimension, which differentiates between the national cultures. The only exception to the order of religiousness is that Norway with regard to Social Democratic power stands closer to Sweden than Denmark does. The party has in Sweden, Norway and Denmark enjoyed support among the populations which, for shorter or longer periods, has enabled it to rule the country on its own mandate. The Social Democratic influence has been much more limited in Finland and Iceland.

The role of the Social Democratic parties in the modernization of the Lutheran north is crucial. Nowhere else did the party for such a long time keep such a strong grip over the electorate. The wide appeal for the moderate left was to no little extent dependent on its ideological message, the "scientific worldview" cleansed of religious "irrationalism". The vision of a "new man" and a "new world" was to build on the large industrial working class.

The Social Democratic ideology was from the end of the 19th century – during the phase of political mobilization – clearly negative towards all forms of Christianity and Church influence in society. Some decades later, after institutionalization and government power, the official anti-clerical ideology was restricted although not forgotten. But it is obvious that a leftist ideology easily clashes with a traditional or fundamentalist Christian world-view. This is a fact which the open Lutheran national Churches have to adjust to in order not to alienate a large part of their membership. The moderate left has tended to view the Church as an institution which they must change in accordance with their own more pragmatic and political ideals. The Scandinavian Social Democratic parties have after 1945 in general not stressed separation between Church and State as a central political goal (Gustafsson 1985, 240–242).

It is true that the success of Social Democracy in itself was dependent on institutional, cultural and political factors which varied. Nevertheless the Social Democratic establishment in Sweden was unique even in Scandinavian terms. The"Scandinavian model" for the welfare society developed in Sweden and was widely accepted in the neighbouring countries, especially Norway and Finland. The carrying principles, such as egalitarianism and cooperation, were implemented in politics, economy and social politics (von Beyme 1992, 197). These ideas were not as such foreign to the older Lutheran society, but the secularization of culture was implemented by the simple leaving out of a divine referent, replacing it with philosophical materialism.

The final argument of this paper which could support the interpretation that the Nordic national variation in religiousness is dependent on the distribution of femininity–masculinity, soft–hard values, rests on the assumption that Social Democracy can be seen as a hard, masculine set of values. One can find many arguments against this judgement, for example typical values of the moderate left such as democracy and solidarity. But the thrust of the argumentation reaches out for the materialist philosophical foundation of Social Democracy and the progress oriented rationality behind the "Swedish model" which today seems to be losing popular support.

It would be a simplification to say that the rational and non-metaphysical culture in Sweden was determined only by Social Democracy.[11] Ulf Lindström has pointed to the fact that the gradual and originally slow Swedish development from authoritarian to democratic society (this process was usually more rapid and/or much more traumatic in the other four countries) never changed the strong historic Swedish administrative tradition. State power resting on civil servants and the bureaucracy, legalism led by practical considerations, remained intact. The political culture of Sweden is, more than of Denmark and Norway, characterized by a high regard for pragmatism and distrust for utopianism (Lindström 1989, 93, 106).

The "Scandinavian/Swedish model" has by non-Scandinavians sometimes been defined as a soft kind of totalitarianism and Scandinavian culture has been seen as dull and predictable. Discussing Sweden in this context, Klaus von Beyme (1992, 204) has pointed to the influence on Swedish intellectual endeavour of the anti-metaphysical philosophy or value-nihilism, which developed at Uppsala University in the beginning of the century around Axel Hägerström. For many decades after the Second World War, the intellectual and cultural climate in Sweden was forcibly moulded by rationalist pragmatism in philosophy as well as politics. The Social Democratic party with a leading political role and the dominant philosophical "Uppsala School" both defined religion in general and the Christian/Lutheran past as dead tradition without a sense for modern Sweden. Many Swedish Social Democratic key figures along with a great part of the academic establishment were trained in the philosophy which saw value statements as more or less meaningless and regarded not only religion but also "utopian" political ideologies as nonsense. "Real" knowledge was to be attained only about questions which could be investigated with the help of modern empiricist scientific methods. The restricted view on

[11] This is also the case for the alleged wide secularization (von Beyme 1992, 204) in the Nordic Lutheran cultures.

"real" knowledge did not inhibit authoritative, male, representatives of this nihilist philosophy from declaring that religion and Swedish Christianity was dead.[12]

Both have today lost their hegemony, but their influence is visible in Swedish attitudes. The stamp is especially clear in items of religion/religiousness but not limited to this. The argument of this paper says that there is also a restrictedness towards femininity – when we define this by traditional female role behaviours such as expressivity and "soft values" related to caring about the the well-being of the family members. As goes for the other Scandinavian countries, it is maintained that the relative impact of Social Democracy is crucial, but cannot alone explain the national cultures of the 1990s. In no other Scandinavian culture seem the major secularizing forces so easy to identify as in Sweden.

Literature

Abbott, Pamela & Claire Wallace, 1990
An Introduction to Sociology. Feminist Perspectives. London, New York.

Alestalo, Matti & Stein Kuhnle, 1984
The Scandinavian Route. University of Helsinki Research Group for Comparative Sociology, 31. Helsinki.

Allardt, Erik, 1987
Samhället Finland. Omvandlingar och traditioner. Helsinki.

Anderson, Benedict, 1983
Imagined Communities. London, New York.

von Beyme, Klaus, 1992
"Den Nordiska samhällsmodellens betydelse". Pp. 188–21 in: S. Karlsson (ed.), *Frihetens källa. Nordens betydelse för Europa*. Stockholm.

Dahl, Hans Fredrik, 1986
"Those Equal Folk". Pp. 97–111 in: S. R. Graubard (ed.), *Norden – The Passion for Equality*. Oslo.

EVA, 1991
Suomi etsii itseään. Raportti Suomalaisten asenteista 1991. Helsinki: Elinkeinoelämän valtuus- kunta/Näringslivets delegation.

Giddens, Anthony, 1989
Sociology. Oxford.

[12] See for instance Staffan Källström (1986) and Johan Lundborg (1991). Källström mentions many cultural personalities, who were influenced by Hägerström's philosophy; among these only one woman, the poet Karin Boye. Lundborg's book is about the highly influential professor, author and editor in chief 1946–1960 of *Dagens Nyheter*, Herbert Tingsten. Tingsten declared that political ideology as well as religion was metaphysical nonsense.

Gustafsson, Göran, 1985
"Utvecklingslinjer på det religiösa området i de nordiska länderna – en jämförelse". Pp. 238–265 in: Göran Gustafsson (ed.), *Religiös förändring i Norden 1930–1980*. Malmö.
Halman, Loek, 1992
"Value Shift and Generations in Western Europe, Scandinavia and Northern America". Paper presented at the XI Nordic Conference for the Sociology of Religion in Iceland 1992.
Jallinoja, Riitta, 1990
Introduktion till familjesociologi. Helsinki.
Knudsen, Jon P., 1992
"Holder 'bibelbeltet' stand?". *Tidskrift for kirke, religion, samfunn*, 1992:1.
Källström, Staffan, 1986
Den gode nihilisten. Stockholm.
Lindström, Ulf, 1989
"Politik i Norden 1889–1989: Ett socialdemokratiskt århundrade?" Pp. 91–107 in: *Norden förr och nu. Ett sekel i statistisk belysning*. Köpenhamn.
Lundborg, Johan, 1991
Ideologiernas och religionens död. En analys av Herbert Tingstens ideologi- och religionskritik. Nora.
Lundby, Knut, 1985
"Norge". Pp. 154–195 in: Göran Gustafsson (ed.), *Religiös förändring i Norden 1930–1980*. Malmö.
Lundby, Knut, 1988
"Closed Circles. An Essay on Culture and Pietism in Norway". *Social Compass* 35/1, 57–66.
McGuire, Meredith, 1987
Religion: The Social Context. Belmont.
Sundback, Susan, 1991
Utträdet ur Finlands lutherska kyrka. Kyrkomedlemskapet under religionsfrihet och sekularisering. Åbo.
SYF, 1958
Statistical Yearbook for Finland. Helsinki.
Thompson, Edward H. Jr., 1991
"Beneath the Status Characteristics: Gender Variations in Religiousness". SSSR 30:4, 381–394.

PÉTUR PÉTURSSON and FRIDRIK H JONSSON

Religion and Family Values: Attitudes of Modern Icelanders in a Comparative Perspective

The focus of this article is on religious values and attitudes that characterize Icelanders' outlook on life and how these values relate to values in other areas such as family life and child rearing. A common definition of values is a class of enduring beliefs concerning modes of conduct and states of existence that transcend specific objects and situations (Rokeach 1973). It can be taken for granted that values that characterize life in a modern society are a mixture of the values that dominated life for recent decades and values that have been handed down through the centuries. The aim is to describe the values that characterize Icelanders' view on life and assess to what extent they are unique and to what extent they are common to other Nordic countries. From one point of view one would expect the values to be similar. For example there have been close connections between Iceland and other Nordic countries through the centuries. Most of the original Icelandic settlers came from Norway and brought with them the traditions and customs of that country. Another important factor is that from 1262 to this century, Iceland was ruled by either by Denmark or Norway. Such close ties between countries, especially when the ruling country has a greater population and a more energetic and varied cultural life, should result in similarity of culture and of values. This should be especially evident in such fundamental areas of life as religion and child rearing, because as Durkheim pointed out they are cardinal to the stability and maintenance of a nation's cultural life.

In spite of the compelling arguments for regarding Icelanders as having values similar to the other Nordic countries, other evidence points in the opposite direction, the first point being that modernization started much later in Iceland than in other Nordic countries. At the turn of the century Iceland was a conservative and backward peasant society at the periphery of the Danish state. But then the mechanization of the fishing industry had started, economic progress swiftly followed and by World War II, Iceland had become a modern industrial country. This late but rapid transition from peasant society to a modern industrial country should be reflected in the values of its inhabitants. This modernization should result in modern values but because the transition occurred in such a short period

Table 1. Percentage of respondents who believe in each of the religious issues.

	Iceland	Denmark	Finland	Norway	Sweden
God	85	64	76	65	45
Life after death	81	34	60	45	38
A soul	88	47	73	54	58
The Devil	19	10	31	24	12
Hell	12	8	27	19	8
Heaven	57	19	55	44	31
Sin	70	24	66	44	31
Resurrection of the dead	51	23	49	32	21
Re-incarnation	40	17	34	15	20

of time, one would also expect to find instances of traditional values that are not found in other Nordic countries.

The Religious Belief System

Religious beliefs can be measured in a number of ways, but a simple way is to look at the variety of issues that people believe in. In the 1990 EVSSG study of values the respondents were asked to indicate their belief in the issues displayed in Table 1. If classical Christian tradition is taken as a basic premiss there are certain patterns of beliefs that one would expect to find in the answers.

As Table 1 shows, Icelanders are highly religious compared to other Nordic countries. The figures show that Icelanders have a much greater range of religious beliefs. A detailed analysis of the responses reveals to a greater extent a classical Christian value pattern in Iceland than in the other Nordic countries. A higher proportion of Icelanders believe in God, in life after death, in the soul, in heaven, in sin and in the resurrection of the dead than in any other Nordic country. This indicates that Iceland is still a traditional Christian society. However, this is not a justifiable conclusion. According to classical Christian tradition a belief in God goes hand in hand with a belief in the Devil, and a belief in heaven should be associated with a belief in hell. This is where the traditional image cracks. As far as belief in the Devil and in hell goes, Icelanders are quite compatible with the other Nordic countries. The crack in the traditional image is evident when the percentages who believe in hell and Devil are subtracted from those who believe in God and heaven (see Table 2).

Table 2. Difference in percentages between belief in God and heaven vs. belief in the Devil and hell.

	Iceland	Denmark	Finland	Norway	Sweden
Belief in God	85	64	76	65	45
Belief in the Devil	19	10	31	24	12
Difference	66	54	45	41	33
Belief in heaven	57	19	55	44	31
Belief in hell	12	8	27	19	8
Difference	45	11	28	25	23

In all the countries there is a greater belief in the existence of the more "desirable aspects" of Christian dogma, but what is striking is the difference between the belief in the desirable and undesirable entities. As shown above Icelanders adhere to some of the basic tenets of the traditional belief system, but nevertheless they take the liberty of leaving out the belief in the existence of "the downside" of the sacred canopy, that is the Devil and hell. This suggests that Icelanders' view of religion is not a traditional belief system but rather an optimistic blend of traditional and modern beliefs.

Before taking this conclusion about the religious belief of Icelanders further, it has to be established that the belief in God is a genuine belief and not a simple cognitive exercise. The answers to the question: "How important is God in your life?" suggest that Icelanders' belief in God has a relevance for their daily life (see Table 3).

The pattern in Table 3 clearly supports the conclusion that Icelanders' belief in God is genuine. This belief is not a simple intellectual exercise but a belief that one would expect to have some relevance for daily existence. Further support for this conclusion is in the answers to the question: "Do you find you get comfort and strength from religion or not?". 75 % of Icelanders said they did, whereas the answers of the other Nordic countries ranged between 27 and 49 %.

It is often assumed that religious beliefs are strongly related to urbanization. People in rural areas are said to be more religious than urban dwellers. Urbanization in Iceland has been rapid and half of the population is concentrated in Reykjavik. Only about 8 % of the population live in rural areas and the farming is heavily mechanized. Because urbanization took place relatively recently in Iceland and was very rapid once it started, it is interesting to look at the relationship

Table 3. "How important is God in your life?": A distribution of the percentage on each point on the scale.

	Iceland	Denmark	Finland	Norway	Sweden
1. Not important at all	7	26	13	25	36
2.	6	14	9	11	11
3.	9	12	6	11	10
4.	5	8	4	7	7
5.	15	15	17	13	11
6.	11	7	10	6	7
7.	12	5	12	4	5
8.	11	5	10	5	4
9.	7	3	8	3	2
10. Very important	17	6	12	16	8
Total	100	100	100	100	100
Mean	6.1	3.9	5.6	4.6	3.8

Table 4. Mean number of issues believed in by residence.

	Mean	Std Dev	Cases
Greater urban areas	4.40	2.36	418
Smaller urban areas	4.68	2.35	177
Rural areas	4.78	2.16	107
Total	4.53	2.33	70

between religion and place of residence. In Table 4 the area around Reykjavik and Akureyri is classified as a greater urban area, a town outside the Reykjavik-Akureyri area with more than 1 000 inhabitants is classified as a small urban area and the rest as rural.

The differences between rural and urban populace as shown in Table 4 are not statistically significant. The rural population does not differ from the urban population in their scope of religious beliefs as measured by the issues included in Table 1 and this contradicts the theory that it is in rural areas that traditional values are maintained because of the localization effect (see e.g. Roof 1978). This conclusion is supported by a study done in 1987 on the religious life of Icelanders (Björnsson & Pétursson 1990). This indicates that the rural areas have become modernized and consequently that the world view of people living in rural areas does not differ much from that of people living in metropolitan areas. This should not be surprising keeping in mind the considerable mobility of people from rural to urban areas and some mobility in the opposite direction.

The above discussion shows that a majority of Icelanders have not rejected God but the question still remains how this belief is integrated with other important areas of life. This raises our main research question: Does the strong belief in God among Icelanders legitimate a traditional emphasis on the highly valued institutions of family life and marriage?

Family Values: Are Modern Icelanders Traditionalists?

If religion is important to Icelanders one would expect it to have some relevance to other central aspects of life. For example, the traditional Christian beliefs of Icelanders should be reflected in their values regarding the family. One could theorize that religion is to a greater extent connected to family life in Iceland than in other Nordic countries. If that is the case a higher percentage of Icelanders should answer the question: "Were you brought up religiously at home?" in the affirmative.

Table 5 reveals that a much higher percentage of Icelanders were brought up religiously at home than in the other Nordic countries. This supports the hypothesis that religion has stronger links with family life in Iceland than in the other Nordic countries. But what about other aspects of family life? Do they reveal a difference between Icelanders and the other Nordic countries?

The EVSSG study shows that Icelanders as well as other Nordic countries place a high value on the family and on marriage. This can be seen from the question: "How important is the family?". Between 84 and 91 % of the respondents rate the family as very important. The same pattern is also found in the responses to the statement: "The marriage is an outdated institution". Between 82 and 94 % of the respondents opposed the statement. Incidentally, Icelanders ranked highest on both issues.

The high agreement among the Nordic people of the value of family life and the importance of marriage does not extend to the ideal family size. Icelanders take 3.1 children to be ideal in a family whereas the other Nordic countries think that 2.6 or 2.7 children are ideal. This difference is also reflected in the birth-rate and the index for population trends in these countries. The birth-rate in Iceland follows a traditional pattern, a pattern that is closer to the Third World than to industrialized societies.

The data presented so far indicate that Icelanders' beliefs regarding the family fall within a very traditional value system, but there are interesting and important indicators that contradict that conclusion. If one looks at their attitudes towards divorce one finds that Icelanders have the same modern view on that issue as

Table 5. Percentage of respondents who were/were not brought up religiously at home.

	Iceland	Denmark	Finland	Norway	Sweden
Yes	76	43	51	46	31
No	24	57	49	54	69
Total	100	100	100	100	100

Swedes and Danes, with Norwegians being the most conservative. This shows that even if marriage is highly regarded, the well-being of the partners as individuals has a priority over the institution of marriage. This emphasis on the individual is also evident when it comes to the position of the individual vis-à-vis the family. Traditionally the mother is the centre of the family even if the husband may be the head. The individualism hinted at above seems to have displaced the mother's position in the conventional family. More than 80 % of Icelanders believe it is acceptable for a woman to plan being a single parent. The right of the individual to choose his or her own destiny is put above all institutional arrangements. The uniqueness of Icelanders on this issue becomes evident when they are compared to the other Nordic countries.

The pattern of answers in Norway and Sweden is striking. Their attitudes to this issue are far more traditional than Icelanders. The attitude of Icelanders indicates that today the institution of family and marriage has become differentiated from the traditional religious value system. One could think that the positive attitudes towards having children indicate a traditional family pattern but in the case of Icelanders this is not the case. Children are valued because they contribute to individual well-being and happiness but not because they belong to a traditional family pattern.

In recent years there has been a high increase in the divorce rate in Iceland (*Yearbook* 1991, 67). This further supports the hypothesis that the needs and desires of the individual are primary and the traditional family institution secondary. However, this does not mean that the family and marriage as institutions are refused as value references. On the contrary they are highly valued, but on the premisses of the needs and the well-being of the individual. Icelanders are strongly opposed to the statement that marriage is an outdated institution even if they are permissive in regard to divorce. Most likely the respect for the right of the woman to choose to have a child, indicates the permissiveness or the tolerance of Icelandic society.

Table 6. Percentage of respondents approving/disapproving to a woman's wish to have a child without having a stable relationship with a man.

	Iceland	Denmark	Finland	Norway	Sweden
Approve	84	67	56	27	25
Disapprove	7	20	20	48	47
Depends	9	13	24	25	28
Total	100	100	100	100	100

It was demonstrated above that religion, especially the belief in God, is very important for Icelanders, but the data on attitudes towards family life show that religion and the family are not closely linked in modern Iceland. Our hypothesis is that modernization in Iceland is concomitant with ascending individualism. This idea is not new and is closely related to the hypothesis that egalitarian values and individualism were important values in the ancient Viking culture (Tomasson 1980, 51). What is new is that individualism is associated with permissiveness and tolerance which to a great extent was absent in Icelanders' world view during past centuries.

Be that as it may, we think that the explanation for the uniqueness of the constellation of Icelanders' attitudes towards religion and family values is traceable to the way in which modernization and the secularization process have shaped the Icelandic world view.

Socio-Economic Development in Iceland

What characterizes the family and social stratification in Iceland is the absence of nobility and a hereditary class system. Until this century the administration was headed by Danish officials and higher offices were either occupied by Danes or Icelanders highly dependant on the Danish authorities.

The trade was in the hands of the Danish trading companies and the monopoly trade in the 17th century meant that the initiative in economical matters was restricted to Danish interests. It was not until in the 20th century that an Icelandic bourgeoisie was formed on the basis of trading and fishing.

Even though there are economic differences in Iceland the population is remarkably homogeneous in cultural matters, which among other things is expressed in the absence of dialects in Icelandic. The Icelandic people have been quite aware of its historical and cultural identity as a separate nation. The political mobilization for increased national autonomy which resulted in the creation of the Icelandic Republic in 1944 furthered the cultural homogeneity of the nation. Culture was regarded as something that all Icelanders should take part in and have access to. This was the ideology behind the educational reforms in the early part of this century. Education has secured a high social mobility rate (Edelstein & Björnsson) and was the prerequisite to the great receptivity of Icelanders to modern life and influences from outside both in economic and cultural matters.

The Role of the Church and Religion

Since the Reformation, the church in Iceland has exclusively been led by national clergymen and this has meant that the church language was Icelandic. Another important factor is that the Evangelical Lutheran National Church[1] did not function as a conservative drawback on social changes, and traces of anticlericalism are hardly be found in social and political life. Thus the process of social change did not mean a confrontation of traditional social groups and the proponents of modern society. Referring to David Martin (1978), in this respect modernization in Iceland can be described as a *beneficent circle* of social and religious changes (Pétursson 1983).

This absence of confrontation is the likeliest explanation of the formal religious homogeneity of Icelanders as measured by the nominal membership to the Evangelical Lutheran Church. 94 % of the Icelanders belong to the National (State) Church. Nevertheless there has been a considerably diversity and even conflict within the church over religious and theological issues. Biblical criticism and liberal theology gained a stronghold among the clergy and the teachers at the Theological Seminary[2] in the beginning of this century. At the same time spiritualism and theosophy was introduced to a very receptive populace and their influence can still be found in the 1984 EVSSG survey where 41 % of Icelanders said they had come into contact with a dead person and in the number of respondents who profess to belief in the soul, life after death and re-incarnation (see Table 1) in the 1990 EVSSG survey.

The YMCA and YWCA and the missionary societies founded in the first decade of this century have been characterized by biblical fundamentalism and "conservative" theology. Thus different views have been found within the national church and church leaders have in practice accepted this diversity. In this century most of the clergy have emphasised the value of tolerance in religious matters which made this religious diversity possible within the national church. A majority

[1] According to the National Register 94 % of the Icelandic population belong to the national church, 4 % to the two Evangelical Lutheran Free Church Congregations, 1 % is Catholic, 2 % outside any confession.

[2] Since 1911 the Department of Theology of the University of Iceland.

of laymen have also emphasized tolerance and liberalism in dogmatic matters. This has contributed to the absence of anticlerical attitudes among the population even among people that are not practising Christians. It is not unusual for non-practising members of the national church to consider themselves good Christians even if they do not feel obliged to follow the church in doctrinal matters.

This harmony in religious matters has been gained at the expense of public conflicts over doctrinal issues which in turn has resulted in the public not being knowledgeable about the doctrinal issues debated within the church. This has made doctrinal matters irrelevant for laymen who subscribe to the ethical and sentimental ethos of the Christian faith and put into this faith whatever they feel is appropriate. From this situation the so-called private religion has derived.[3] The typical view of a modern Icelander is that his own conscience is just as fitting a judge in religious matters as the church. This may be so without him or her necessarily becoming anti-church or anticlerical.[4] This religion is most often anonymous, unreflected and composed of values and attitudes that may be contradictory seen from a rational point of view. Much of this private religiosity has some form of "folk religion attributes". Belief in supernatural phenomena and extrasensory experiences, that has been legitimated by the spiritualist movement in Iceland, characterizes the belief of the population of Iceland.

Privatization of Religion and Family Life

The 1984 EVSSG survey showed a high number of Icelanders having experienced being close to the spirit of a deceased person (see e.g. Haraldsson & Houtkooper 1991). The high belief in God as a universal spirit or some force of nature and in reincarnation in Iceland has been demonstrated in both the 1984 and the 1990 EVSSG study. This points to the influence of theosophical ideas adhered to by prominent people since the beginning of this century and preached by varieties of groups recently under the headings of the New Age.

Even if they do not rely on the church in doctrinal matters, 68 % of Icelanders say they trust the church. But that trust seems to be rather unspecified and diffuse, because when asked about the relevance of the church in specific issues, such as family matters and social problems, the support is lower as can be seen in Table 7.

In every Nordic country the church is seen to be most relevant to the spiritual needs of the population and least relevant to the social problems facing the country today. On the basis of this answer it cannot be concluded that the church is generally seen to be giving adequate answers to the problems facing the popula-

[3] For the evidence on this in Iceland see Björnsson & Pétursson 1990.

[4] Thomas Luckmann (1971) analyses the social processes behind this development in the Western countries.

Table 7. Percentage of respondents who think that the church is giving adequate answers to specific problems.

	Iceland	Denmark	Finland	Norway	Sweden
The moral problems and needs of individuals	37	20	25	41	19
The problems of family life	40	13	27	29	14
People's spiritual needs	58	49	51	55	51
The social problems facing our country today	24	8	12	19	12

tion. It is only in regard to people's spiritual needs that a majority of respondents think the church is giving adequate answers. However, if all the issues are taken together, it can be concluded that of the Nordic countries the church has the greatest relevance in Iceland.

The relevance of the church to Icelanders is even greater when it comes to the special occasions in the life of the individual and the family. A survey in 1986 showed that 97 % of the grown-up population was confirmed according to the ritual of the Lutheran Church which means that all of them have been baptized. The study showed that there was no decline among the youngest age group (18–25) included in the survey (Björnsson & Pétursson 1990). For the last two decades 85 % of the weddings are religious ceremonies even if the alternative of a civil ceremony is open to all (*Statistical Abstract* 1991, 45). All funerals are conducted from churches. Among the clergy there is sometimes a talk of the national church as a service institution for the people, which does not want to have anything to do with the church except when it is needed as a solemn framework for family life on special occasions.

Even if Icelanders are highly religious as measured by the scope of their religious beliefs and the emotional importance or quality of these beliefs, they are least likely of the Nordic peoples to go to church on Sunday. Only 9 % of Icelanders go to church once a month or more often, compared to 11 % of Danes, 11 % of Finns, 10 % of Swedes and 22 % of Norwegians. Churchgoing is a collective and institutional form of religious engagement and it does not appeal to Ice- landers.

One could put it forward as an interesting hypothesis that the same lack of enthusiasm for the institutional aspects of family can be found in modern Iceland. The family is there for individual needs, for comfort and support, but the individual is less there for the family.

Table 8. Percentage of respondents agreeing with the respective statements about parent–child relations.

	Iceland	Denmark	Finland	Norway	Sweden
Regardless of what the qualities and faults of one's parents are, one must always respect them	61	47	40	45	51
Parents' duty is to do their best for their children even at the expense of their own well-being	50	52	49	73	63
Parents have a life of their own and should not be asked to sacrifice their own well-being for the sake of their children	23	39	24	10	15

Keeping in mind the highly valued institutions of the church and family in Iceland, at the same time as we observe a thorough-going individualism and processes of privatization and modernization of every day life, it is interesting to dig further into the structure of the values relevant to parent–child relations and to values concerning the upbringing of children.

Privatization and the Socialization of the Young

Icelanders emphasize the importance of children's unconditional respect for their parents but not to the same degree that they believe that the parents should put the interests of the child unconditionally before their own (see Table 8). Compared to the other Nordic countries, Icelanders are highest on the former issue but together with Finland they rank lowest on the latter. As to the right of parents to their own life without having to offer their best for the children, they rank in the middle, Denmark ranking higher but Norway and Sweden ranking lower. Once again the autonomous and free individual is the ideal of the value system. Unconditional respect and sacrifice are religious and traditional value labels which one would think that a more modern outlook on individual freedom and autonomy would disagree with.

It is generally accepted by psychologists and pedagogists of religion that one of the strongest dimensions of religion is the affective one. Religious sentiments and experiences are in a variety of ways integrated with the parent–child relationship.

Table 9. The qualities that children should be encouraged to learn at home broken down by age and strength of belief in God.

	Strength of belief			Age			
	Weak	Medium	Strong	Under 40	41-60	Over 60	Total
Good manners	0.81	0.93	0.93*	0.89	0.89	0.96*	0.90
Independence	0.92	0.91	0.87	0.91	0.89	0.83	0.89
Hard work	0.71	0.73	0.85*	0.75	0.80	0.86	0.78
Feeling of responsibility	0.92	0.97	0.94	0.95	0.93	0.95	0.94
Imagination	0.55	0.47	0.49	0.53	0.45	0.47	0.50
Tolerance and respect	0.90	0.97	0.94*	0.93	0.94	0.95	0.93
Thrift	0.58	0.63	0.78*	0.62	0.72	0.91*	0.69
Determination	0.73	0.77	0.75	0.73	0.74	0.85*	0.75
Religious faith	0.18	0.38	0.75*	0.40	0.57	0.81*	0.50
Unselfishness	0.70	0.76	0.78	0.76	0.73	0.77	0.75
Obedience	0.54	0.69	0.75*	0.69	0.62	0.75*	0.68

* The relationship is statistically significant.

This is especially apparent in our Christian culture where the emphasis is on care for the weak and those depending on others. Even among those who do not accept or adhere to the doctrinal aspects of Christianity the Christian ethic is still held in high regard. Most likely this ethical value may be expressed in people's attitudes towards children and perhaps it would affect the qualities they judge to be preferable in children. In this light it is interesting to see if there is a difference between the Nordic countries in what qualities should be encouraged in children.

In all the Nordic countries there is a general agreement that the four most important qualities to be encouraged in children are: Responsibility, tolerance, good manners and independence. Responsibility is seen by all but the Swedes as being the most important. Tolerance is overall in second place, ranking number two in Denmark and Iceland and number one in Sweden but number three in Finland and number four in Norway.

But are the ideas on children's upbringing related to religion? Table 9 relates the qualities Icelanders find preferable in children to the strength of belief in God and the age of the respondents.

Keeping in mind the traditionalistic religious pattern, where religion was related to submission and social control, one could expect importance of belief in God to be positively related to responsibility and good manners. One could agree,

Table 10. The qualities that children should be encouraged to learn at home broken down by belief in God* and individualism and controlled for the effects of age.

	Weak belief in God		Strong belief in God		
	Individualism		Individualism		
	Weak	Strong	Weak	Strong	Total
Good manners	0.92	0.83	0.92	0.94	0.90
Independence	0.85	0.96	0.80	0.94	0.89
Hard work	0.76	0.69	0.85	0.85	0.78
Feeling of responsibility	0.93	0.95	0.93	0.95	0.94
Imagination	0.40	0.60	0.40	0.57	0.50
Tolerance and respect	0.93	0.94	0.94	0.94	0.93
Thrift	0.62	0.60	0.75	0.81	0.69
Determination	0.75	0.78	0.68	0.84	0.75
Religious faith	0.28	0.28	0.73	0.75	0.50
Unselfishness	0.70	0.75	0.74	0.84	0.76
Obedience	0.68	0.56	0.74	0.77	0.68

* The respondents are split into two groups on the basis of median score. A score of six and less is classified as weak belief and the rest as strong belief.

given this theory, that religion was negatively related to independence and perhaps also negatively related to tolerance. The results only partly fit this hypothesis. Religion is not related to responsibility – which means that almost everybody regards responsibility as a highly important quality irrespective of whether they believe in God. Religious legitimation is therefore "no longer" necessary to indoctrinate the young with the value of responsibility. The relationship between religion and the emphasis on tolerance also contradicts the "traditionalist theory". The correlation between the emphasis on good manners and the importance of belief in God is the only relation among the four qualities mentioned that could be said to confirm the traditionalist pattern.

Among the other qualities mentioned the positive correlation between religion and the emphasis on hard work is an interesting one. This relationship and the relation between religion and obedience and religion and thrift are in line with the traditionalist theory.

Judging from these results it seems as if the traditionalist value system with its religious legitimation of good manners, hard work, thrift and tolerance still exists in the repertoire of the value systems in question but that it plays a relatively marginal role. The traditional pattern is not dominant in the upbringing of children. This is supported by the fact that some central themes in children's upbringing such as the emphasis on independence, responsibility and imagination are not correlated with strength of belief.

We have maintained above that the main characteristic of Icelanders' approach towards religion and family values is individualistic. To further explore that hypothesis, Table 10 shows the relationship between strength of belief in God and strength of individualism[5] with the qualities that should be aimed for in child rearing.

The results in Table 10 show that those strong individualists who are weak on belief in God differ from other weak believers when it comes to good manners, hard work and obedience. They rank lower on these issues than other groups. The reason might be that the first mentioned qualities are considered contradictory or a hindrance of individualism as understood by the people answering the question or that the individualism in question is itself composed of values that to some extent are functional equivalents of or compensations for these values.

Belief in God does not affect the emphasis on imagination but individualism on the other hand does. Individualism is positively related to emphasis on unselfishness, determination and thrift but only among those who put relatively more emphasis on their belief in God.

Somewhat unexpected results are that neither belief in God nor individualism affect emphasis on independence or tolerance. But perhaps the most striking result is that individualism is not related to religious upbringing of children. This would indicate that religion to a considerable degree is itself impregnated by individualism to the effect that it is expressed as private religion.

Conclusion

In this paper it has been shown that Icelanders are on every indicator, except church attendance, more religious than inhabitants of other Nordic countries. Their religious beliefs are a curious mixture of traditional values and individualism. They believe in the benevolent aspects of Christian religion such as God and heaven but not in unpleasant aspects such as the Devil and hell. This streak of individualism translates itself to other aspects of life such as attitudes towards the family and the upbringing of children.

[5] Individualism is measured by an additive z-score index based on six questions in the EVSSG-survey. For a more detailed description of the scale see Petterson (1992).

References

Björnsson, B. & P. Pétursson, 1990

Trúarlíf Íslendinga. Studia Theologica Islandia 3. Reykjvavík: Háskóli Íslands.

Haraldsson, E. & J. Houtkooper, 1991

"Psychic Experiences in the Multinational Human Values Study: Who Reports Them?". *The Journal of the American Society for Psychical Research*, *85*, 145–165.

Luckmann, T., 1971.

The Invisible Religion. New York: Macmillan.

Martin, D., 1978

A General Theory of Secularization. Oxford: Basil Blackwell.

Petterson, T., 1992

"Culture Shift and Generational Population Replacement: Individualization, Secularization, and Moral Value Change in Contemporary Scandinavia". Paper presented at the XI Nordic Conference on the Sociology of Religion, Skálholt, Iceland.

Pétursson, P., 1983

Church and Social Change: A Study of the Secularization Process 1830–1930. Helsingborg: Plus Ultra.

Roof, W. C., 1978

Commitment and Community: Religious Plausibility in a Liberal Protestant Church. New York: Elsevier.

"Social Security in the Nordic Countries", 1990

in: *Statistical Reports of the Nordic Countries*. Copenhagen.

Statistical Abstract of Iceland 1991.

Reykjavík: The Statistical Bureau of Iceland.

Tomasson, R., 1980

Iceland the First New Society. Icelandic Review, Reykjavík.

Yearbook of Nordic Statistics 1991.

JØRGEN STRAARUP

Effects of Religious Individualism on Values of Life and Death in Scandinavia

1. Life and Death, "Holy" Issues

Questions about life and death are at the core of value systems, be they religious or not. In matters where human consideration pertains to whether a life should be preserved at any cost, or other factors should be allowed to enter into the picture, as well as matters where an individual's right to end his or her own life is at stake, the problems of life and death are at the centre of those systems that hold together individuals' attitudes and values. By stating this we have also stated that there is more than one level of individuals' motivations and orientations. First, a system level that holds together different individual actions and attitudes, and, second, a less systematic level where those attitudes, actions or values, which might be said to have been inspired by the system, are carried through. Typically, the system level is implied from the coherence of the less systematic level, which is where observations are made (see Ajzen & Fishbein 1975).

Not only are values of life and death central to religious value systems. Coming into life as well as leaving life have even been considered *holy processes*, i.e. something set apart from human decision and managed by God (see Eliade 1957; Durkheim 1912/1965, 51–57). Tampering with conception may in this respect be seen as interference with a divine decision of whether a life should be called into being or not. In the other end of the life line, suicide and euthanasia may be seen as other instances of taking the decision out of God's hands and claiming it for oneself, ending life at another time than that willed by God.

For countries in general and the Scandinavian countries in particular these values have entered national norm structures and legislation. The countries do not accept capital punishment (except in war). In order to get her final qualification, a physician has to solemnly promise to preserve life at all costs. Murder is the most serious crime within the penal code. When the roots of Scandinavian laws are being described and celebrated, for instance before major alterations, the heritage from religious, in this case Christian, ethics is underlined.

This should not, however, lead one to the idea that a religious distinction underlies modern Scandinavian law. Modern society, in general, does not accept the divide between holy and profane business, limiting oneself for its own part to the profane and leaving the holy to God. Since the time of the Enlightenment the notions of God and of the holy have gradually disappeared from Scandinavian law. The areas thus vacated have been taken over by the state. Nowadays society (through the state) decides over issues formerly left to God. Life and death have become issues of state control. In a number of ways the holy character of life and death has become secularized. Actively, society prevents life from coming into being (coerced sterilization), destroys growing life (abortion), demands life (military service), takes life (war). Passively, society can be said to end life by *not* taking precautions (traffic, environment, technical failure, etc.).

In a number of instances, modern Scandinavian society takes life into its hands, acting like God. This is not being done lightheartedly or easily. On the contrary, the instances of handling life and death are mostly accompanied by severe and elaborate procedures in which the rationality of that kind of societal action is thoroughly discussed before actually carried out.

2. The Problem

An institutional loss of power on behalf of the churches of the Scandinavian countries is accompanied by a decline in religious participation and belief. Parts of the religious development, however, are better characterized as "qualitative" than "quantitative" change. There seems to be a shift from confessional beliefs to more open religious beliefs.

Traditional religious belief (in the Scandinavian Lutheran setting) has been a comparatively safe bulwark against drastic change in values concerning life and death. Do new, more open-ended religious beliefs carry a value structure with the same kind of prohibition against humans touching and tampering with what in traditional belief systems is considered God's holy domain?

The overall description of individual value changes in Europe by Halman (1992) and Halman & Ester (1992), i.e. under the headings of secularization and individualization, seems to be an adequate point of departure for a description of one of its parts, Scandinavia. In terms of values this means that one may expect a decreasing adherence to the teachings and beliefs of the official church (secularization), and that individuals see themselves as less tied up with values of official religion; what is considered good, true and just depends increasingly on individual judgment and validation, decreasingly on institutional regulation (individualization).

The concepts of secularization and individualization may on the individual level be seen as aspects of one another: secularization is a component of individualization and vice versa. This is, however, too simplified a description. Linked as the concepts may be at the structural level it seems useful to use them additively in investigations at the individual level. Secularization may lead to certain effects in itself, individualization may lead to other, and the effects may be added.

In certain areas of value systems there might be an interaction effect as well. Some of the connotations of individualism may become actualized in certain areas where human values direct their holders what to do. Radicalism in moral and social questions may become triggered by a combination of secularization and individualism. An analysis of this interaction effect is the aim of this article. The basic question can thus be formulated as: Does religious individualization lead to more liberalism in matters of life and death than does non-belief?

3. Religious Orientation

Individualization of belief is part of secularization. Individuals who choose for themselves what to believe in, adhering less to what organized, traditional religion teaches, display religious individualization. Another way of becoming secularized is to denounce all kinds of religious beliefs, to become a non-believer or an atheist. In order to assess the importance of individualization within the scheme of secularization, a typology of different kinds of religious belief is needed. Using the typology with data on Scandinavians' values of life and death, one may be able to identify and describe the connection between the general concepts.

The EVSSG study included a group of questions about people's beliefs. The respondent was asked whether she or he believed in God, the Devil, sin, life after death, etc. The questions fall into two categories, the first about traditional beliefs, the second about beliefs which may be incorporated into a traditional belief system such as Christianity, but which, on the other hand, may also be interpreted freely outside any traditional belief system.[1]

The first category is *traditional religiousness*. Here the questions asked are about belief in God, the Devil, Hell, Heaven, sin, and resurrection. All these items have in common a link to traditional Christian teachings.

The second category is a less specific, less confessional form of belief, a *general religiousness*, where belief in life after death, a soul, and re-incarnation are being asked for. The items in this second category may be understood as parts of a Christian belief and value system (except re-incarnation), but they may also be seen as parts of a value system without Christian anchorage. It is in this respect that the notion of a general religiousness becomes useful, namely as an indicator of a kind of religiousness that does not fit into traditional (Christian) schemes only, but in a lot of other schemes as well.

Typology for Religious Orientation

The technical construction of the typology were guided by the following directions. Each respondent's positive answers to the five (1981) or six (1990) questions about

[1] See Halman & Vloet (1992) for an alternative analysis of the same belief data.

Number of traditional beliefs	Number of general beliefs			
	0	1	2	3
0	*Non-believing*			
1			*General orientation*	
2				
3 — 6		*Traditional orientation*		

Figure 1. Construction of typology for religious orientation.

traditional belief ("do you believe in God, the Devil, Hell, Heaven, sin, resurrection") were counted, as well as her/his answers to the questions about general religiousness ("do you believe in life after death, a soul, re-incarnation"). These counts were used for classifying respondents. Respondents giving...

... three positive answers about general religiousness and less than three positive answers about traditional belief; or

... two positive answers about general religiousness and less than two positive answers about traditional belief; or

... one positive answer about general religiousness and no positive answers about traditional belief,

were classified as *oriented towards general religiousness*.

Respondents answering in the affirmative to none of the belief statements were classified as *non-believing*, and all others were classified as *oriented towards traditional religiousness*. Figure 1 illustrates the operationalization.

Using the Typology

Before putting the typology to the test, some inquiries into its connotations are appropriate. The relations between respondents with traditional and general religious orientation as well as non-believing respondents from 1981 to 1990 do not follow the same patterns in Scandinavia as a whole and in the three countries. Table 1 presents the developments. For Scandinavia as a whole the development seems to be a shift from a traditionally to a generally oriented religiousness, whereas the proportion of non-believing is steady from 1981 to 1990. Looking closer at the three countries, a number of differences appear. Sweden resembles Scandinavia (of which it, because of the size of its population, is a dominating part). The non-believing part of the population is the same in 1981 and in 1990, and the major shift has been from "traditional" to "general", cf. Hamberg (1989). In Denmark it is instead the traditionally oriented who have had a constant proportion in 1981 and 1990. The shift towards a general orientation has been from the non-believing and one may here talk about a "return" to religiousness (from

Table 1. Religious orientation in Scandinavia 1981 and 1990, percentages.

	Denmark		Norway		Sweden		Scandinavia	
Religious orientation	1981	1990	1981	1990	1981	1990	1981	1990
Traditionally oriented	52.0	52.5	68.8	59.3	53.8	42.7	56.7	49.4
Generally oriented	13.0	19.1	9.5	11.6	15.1	25.9	13.2	20.6
Non-believing	34.9	28.4	21.7	29.1	31.1	31.4	30.1	30.0

non-believing to general orientation). In Norway, finally, there has been a shift away from traditional orientation followed by an increase, mainly among the non-believing, but also among the generally oriented.

4. Life and Death

Along with information about Scandinavians' beliefs, data on their values about life and death are necessary, i.e. problems involving human control over things that were earlier considered reserved for gods to handle. The EVSSG study included questions about two kinds of life and death questions, not allowing life into existence (abortion), and putting an end to continued existence (killing). Both are issues where life's "holiness" is being focused since the control over life is held by society or the individual.

The questions about abortion present some situations where the respondent states her/his approval or disapproval of abortion under those circumstances. Crudely speaking one can distinguish between abortions where health considerations are dealt with ("physical" indication) and abortions where non-physical considerations are put forward ("social" indications). Jelen (1984, 223f) has shown that answers to questions about conditions for approved abortion tend to focus around two groupings, which in his case are labelled "elective" and "traumatic". His material is the 1977 NORC General Social Survey (see Davis & Smith 1990), i.e. the U.S.A., and the tool he uses to arrive at that conclusion is factor analysis. His group of "elective" conditions is similar to the group called "social" indications here, and his group of "traumatic" conditions is similar to the group called "physical" indications here. Among Jelen's traumatic conditions one finds rape, which is not present among the European Value Data.

Abortion may be seen as an aspect of beginning life and as an aspect of ending life. Modern medical technology continues with accelerating pace to problematize the drawing of a clear line between "not-yet-life" and life. With the development of a technique allowing surrogate mothers hardly any abortion escapes the characterization of "ending life", of killing. To say the least, a distinction based on number of weeks indicating whether a life of its own has begun or not, has become very problematic for decisions of whether or not to allow abortion. It is becoming increasingly clear that not allowing life into being through birth is also an aspect of ending life, of killing. Therefore it can be included in a list of instances where the ending of life is discussed. The other aspects of ending life include self defence, euthanasia, suicide, and political assassination.

Religious Orientation, Life's Beginning and Life's End

Individualism in questions of faith, in this context conceptualized as general religious orientation, can, when it comes to moral issues, be expected to function as a step of departure from traditional faith. A person who has chosen not to believe in traditional elements of religion can *on the one hand* not be expected to find meaningful all of the moral and social teaching of that traditional religion whose beliefs she no longer shares. The proportions of respondents with traditional social and moral values may be expected to become smaller as the proportion of general believers becomes bigger.

On the other hand, since the general believer does believe in some of the elements proposed during the interview, she may be expected to retain some of the social and moral teaching of the traditional churches. The proportion of general believers adhering to the social and moral views characteristic of the traditional believers, ought to be bigger than the proportion of non-believers.

There is, however, another possibility. Individualism in questions of belief may be seen as something other than a step of departure from traditional religious orientation. Individualism might add something qualitative to secularization. It might be that individualism in belief, as expressed by a general religious orientation, accelerates the distancing of oneself from traditional social and moral values, abandoning the positions of organized religion, adapting for oneself a set of values of a personal choice.

Considering two kinds of moral reasoning about life's beginning and life's end, that of abortion and that of different kinds of ending life, two different hypotheses may be tested. According to the *first* hypothesis the general religionists might be expected to establish a level of accepting the taking of life somewhere between the levels of the traditional believers and the non-believers. A general religious orientation would in this case be seen as a step on the road from a traditional to a non-believing position, both religiously and morally.

The *second* hypothesis would claim that the individualism of the general believers is adding something different to values, an element of choice which gives the individual a right to decide for herself on what grounds moral reasoning should take place. In comparison with non-believing, general believers should be expected to depart more from the views of the traditional believers.

Table 2. Approval of abortion for two physical and two social indications, by religious orientation, 1981 and 1990 percentages.

	1981			1990		
Approve of abortion ...	Tradition-alists	Gene-ralists	Non-believing	Tradition-alists	Gene-ralists	Non-believing
... where mother's health is at risk	97.2	97.1	98.3	97.4	97.4	98.3
... where the child is likely to be born physically handicapped	84.3	88.6	89.5	74.9	79.0	85.8
... where a married couple don't want to have any more children	49.1	67.3	73.1	45.3	60.4	65.5
... where the woman is not married	37.5	53.6	58.4	38.8	51.4	57.4

According to the first hypothesis the non-believing are expected to exhibit the most radical values, according to the second the general believers are expected to be the most radical group, "radical" in this respect meaning departing from the values of the traditional believers.

Now, let us turn to Scandinavians' approval or disapproval of abortions. In Table 2, the levels of approval of abortions of the traditional, general and non-believing religious orientation are shown.

When analyzing Table 2 one notes that with physical indications, non-believing Scandinavians tend to approve of abortion most, traditionally oriented least. The same description is valid concerning the view of abortion with social indications. In almost all aspects of abortion the level of approval of the generally religiously oriented falls between the levels of the traditionally oriented and the non-believing, respectively. What we see here is an aspect of the first of the proposed hypotheses. The individualism in terms of beliefs does not add a qualitative new aspect to the moral reasoning of the generally oriented. The general religious orientation functions as a stepping-stone on the road from (or to) a traditional religious orientation.

The differences between the religious orientations are less spectacular than the differences between 1981 and 1990. During the nine years there has been a clear shift of level of approval of abortion. The Scandinavians of 1990 are more strict on abortion issues than the Scandinavians of 1981. Excepted from this general observation is abortion where the mother's health is at risk. With that indication there has been no shift. The most obvious change is abortion where the child is likely to be born physically handicapped. Towards that kind of abortions Scandinavians have become more strict during the nine year period.[2]

Even in the case of social indication Scandinavians have become more strict. A diminishing majority feels that family planning for married couples should be accepted as grounds for abortion. Reasons for this strictness are probably to be found in the generally stricter attitude to sexuality witnessed by Pettersson (1992) and Gundelach & Riis (1992). An increasing proportion of Scandinavians think that abortion should not be used by married couples as an instrument for family planning.

Scandinavians' views on the last instance of social indication, where the mother is not married, have not changed during the 1980s.

In sum, there are two kinds of abortions with unchanged levels of approval: where the mother's health is at risk, and where the mother is not married. In both instances the condition of the mother is at the centre of attention. If the mother can not live her life with the same quality, either physically or socially, after giving birth to her child, unchanged proportions of Scandinavians approve of abortion. When the child is likely to be born handicapped or when a married couple do not want more children, the support for abortion has diminished. In either case, religious orientation has not meant a difference. The levels of approval of abortion have been relatively constant from 1981 to 1990. The kind of religious individualism expressed in the category of general religious orientation does not seem to have had any influence when it comes to approval of abortion on four kinds of physical and social indications.

Changing topic from abortion to different kinds of ending life, of killing, the impact of religious traditionalism, generalism, and non-belief is displayed in Table 3. Justification for different kinds of ending life seems to illustrate the second hypothesis suggested above, according to which religious individualism (i.e. general religious orientation) would radicalize the moral and social values of Scandinavians, so that generalists would be more liberal in moral issues than both traditionalists and non-believers.

The first row of Table 3 displays the level of approval of abortion. Although the question was put in a context where ending life was discussed the answers were to considerable degree similar in their structure to the questions about abortion

[2]Perhaps this shift in abortion attitudes can be seen as a new evaluation of physical handicap. The Scandinavian states have imposed a set of rules on local business and government making it possible for physically handicapped to participate in everyday life. The enactment of these rules has been enhanced during the test period. Hand in hand with the rules an increasing consciousness has characterized the public, that physically handicapped human beings can live their lives with decent quality of life, and that therefore the possibility of having a handicapped child should not deter parents from giving birth to it. Even if the child turns out to be physically handicapped it should be allowed to exist.

Table 3. Frequency for justification for ending life, by religious orientation, 1981 and 1990 percentages (the larger mean, the more often).

	1981			1990		
How often there is a possible justification for ...	Tradition-alists	Gene-ralists	Non-believing	Tradition-alists	Gene-ralists	Non-believing
... abortion	4.94^{bc}	6.32^{a}	6.62^{a}	4.59^{bc}	5.75^{a}	5.78^{a}
... killing in self defense	4.43^{bc}	5.85^{ac}	5.39^{ab}	4.47^{bc}	5.53^{ac}	5.17^{ab}
... euthanasia	3.86^{bc}	5.45^{a}	5.40^{a}	4.30^{bc}	5.89^{a}	5.64^{a}
... suicide	2.42^{bc}	3.67^{a}	3.48^{a}	2.63^{bc}	3.72^{ac}	3.36^{ab}
... political assassination	1.23^{c}	1.31	1.36^{a}	1.17^{bc}	1.36^{a}	1.30

[a] – significantly different ($p < .05$, Tukey *b*) from traditionalists' mean, same row, same year.

[b] – significantly different ($p < .05$, Tukey *b*) from generalists' mean, same row, same year.

[c] – significantly different ($p < .05$, Tukey *b*) from non-believers' mean, same row, same year.

reported in Table 2. The level of justification frequency of the generalists is between that of traditionalists and non-believing.

The three following rows display a new pattern. The levels of approval of killing in self defence, of euthanasia, and of suicide are higher among the Scandinavians with a general religious orientation than for any of the other religious orientations. In these instances religious individualism adds an extra quality to the individualism marked by being a non-believer. This must be interpreted in terms of what killing in self defence, euthanasia and suicide means. One might argue that in each case there is a component of choice in the three forms of ending life. To kill in self defence is a choice of one's own life as more important than that of an aggressor. To practice euthanasia is to claim that the individual has a right to choose her moment of death, that this right exists for oneself as well as for one's friend, and that it is morally correct to help her carry out that choice. To kill oneself is to claim that the individual has a right to choose her moment of death, on her own moral grounds. The individual has a right to choose for herself on the basis of her own moral rules, not moral rules set up by other people or religious systems.

When controlling for *gender* the differences between on the one hand traditionalists and the other hand generalists or non-believers remain significant in both years. Generalists as well as non-believers justify active ending of life more often than traditionalists. The interactive effect in justification of killing in self defence proves significant only among women (both years). Women with a general religious orientation are more liberal when it comes to killing in self defence than non-believing women. The individualism embedded in the general religious orientation radicalizes women's view on killing in self defence. The interactive effect when it comes to justification of suicide disappears, when separate analyses are performed for men and women.

When controlling for *age*, dividing respondents into two subgroups, before and after their 45th birthday, at least two specifications become clear. The basic pattern, according to which Scandinavians with a traditional religious orientation are more strict than either of the other orientations, still holds in the subgroups "45 years or more" and "less than 45 years". Among the younger respondents questioned in 1981 those with a general religious orientation are more liberal towards ending life than non-believers in the case of killing in self defence and suicide, but that finding is not replicated among those questioned in 1990. The interactive effect discovered earlier concerning killing in self defence is thus restricted to the younger Scandinavians, whereas the older general religionists are not more radical in their justification than the non-believing. When it comes to values of suicide a significant difference between generalists and non-believers appears, but only among the younger respondents.

Between 1981 and 1990 there has been a limited overall development. The more strict views on abortion already discussed appear in this context as well. Abortion is justified less often in 1990 than in 1981. For euthanasia a clear liberalization is taking place; it can be justified more often in 1990 than in 1981. Behind this result one must recognize the significance of the public debate on euthanasia during the 1980s as well as the progress of medical science, which also facilitates the possibility to "help a friend" when this kind of help is needed.

In a few instances, religious individualism in the form of general religious orientation gives extra strength to liberal moral values, whereas in other instances, that radicalization of moral values is lacking. The areas where the radicalization is present are in areas where individual choice is crucial, i.e. choosing one's own life over that of an aggressor, choosing the right to have a friend kill oneself, and choosing the right to kill oneself. In instances where this element of choice is not equally pronounced, religious individualism does not add to liberalization of values.

5. Discussion

The results reported here are fragile, the differences small. This means that more work needs to be done before they can be considered validated. They indicate that individualization interacts with secularization in creating a radical liberalism in matters where the individual's right to choose for herself is focused upon. A general religious orientation (religious individualism) is associated with justification of killing in self defence and suicide more closely than a religious orientation of non-belief. Limited controls for gender and age show that, in most cases, the possibility of stating that those with a general orientation are more liberal than the non-believers disappears in the controls. Some significant differences remain, on the other hand, which I take as a hint that there is a fair chance that the tendencies I point to actually are to be found in more specific investigations.

If the findings prove valid there are some conclusions to be discussed. What other social and moral issues have characteristics similar to those aspects of killing, i.e. where the possibility for personal choice is accentuated, that show an interactive effect in this study? Human sexuality is probably such an area. Where a traditional religious orientation evolves into a general religious orientation the same radical liberalization is to be expected.

For other areas of social and moral reasoning the model of a general religious orientation as a stepping-stone between traditionalism and non-belief seems probable. For such topics as politics one would hardly expect a radicalization following from religious individualism.

For centuries, the Scandinavian states have claimed that the value base on which legislation and social and moral norms are built is Christianity. One of the latest examples of this claim is Swedish. Just before Christmas 1993 committees within the Swedish parliament, *Riksdagen*, discuss whether or not a new school bill in preparation should state that the values of the state are based on a Christian heritage. Provided that the results can be replicated in more specific studies this analysis points to a mechanism which is, or is going to be, central to the breaking down of that very heritage. When individualization enters into the religious orientation, a radical liberalization of social and moral values takes place, radical in the sense that it supercedes the liberalization brought about by non-belief.

The traditional religious orientation has been and is still a safeguard against rapid change in morality and values. That orientation lies behind the attempts at regulating by political decision the value base of state and society. With a widespread general religious orientation and a concomitant liberalization it becomes more and more difficult to state, i.e. that the question of when to start and end life is to be answered in a context where that question is considered "holy". If – when – a general religious orientation unlinks values of life and death from the nation's ideological past it becomes impossible to claim that this very past is actually the moral base of society.

Thus the individualization of religion adds to the individualization of other societal issues making it increasingly difficult to talk about shared value structures among Scandinavians.

References

Ajzen, Icek & Martin Fishbein, 1975

Belief, Attitude, Intention and Behavior. An Introduction to Theory and Research. Reading, Mass.: Addison-Wesley.

Durkheim, Émile, 1912/1965

The Elementary Forms of the Religious Life (Joseph Ward Swain transl.). New York: Free Press.

Davis, James Allan & Tom W Smith, 1990

General social surveys 1972–1990 [machine-readable data file] /Principal Investigator, James A. Davis; Director and Co-Principal Investigator, Tom W. Smith. NORC ed.. University of Connecticut, Storrs: The Roper Center for Public Opinion Research.

Eliade, Mircea, 1957

Das Heilige und das Profane. Hamburg: Rowohlt.

Gundelach, Peter & Ole Riis, 1992

Danskernes værdier. Copenhagen: Forlaget Sociologi.

Halman, Loek, 1992

"Value Shift and Generations in Western Europe, Scandinavia and North America". Paper presented at the IX Nordic Conference for the Sociology of Religion, Skálholt, Iceland, August 17–20, 1992.

Halman, Loek & Peter Ester, 1992

"Developments in Religious and Moral Values in Western Europe". Paper presented at the First European Conference of Sociology, Vienna, Austria, August 26–29, 1992.

Halman, Loek & Astrid Vloet, 1992

Measuring and Comparing Values in 16 Countries of the Western World in 1990 and 1981. Tilburg: IVA, Tilburg University.

Hamberg, Eva M., 1989

"Kristen på mitt eget sätt": En analys av material från projektet Livsåskådningar i Sverige. Religion och Samhälle, 48–49 (1989:10–11). Stockholm: Religionssociologiska Institutet.

Jelen, Ted G., 1984

"Respect for Life, Sexual Morality, and Opposition to Abortion". *Review of Religious Research*, 25, 220–31.

Pettersson, Thorleif, 1992

"Välfärd, värderingsförändringar och folkrörelseengagemang", Pp. 33–99 in: Sigbert Axelson & Thorleif Pettersson (eds), *Mot denna framtid: Folkrörelser och folk om framtiden.* Stockholm: Carlssons.

EVA M HAMBERG

Secularization and Value Change in Sweden

The European value surveys have shown Sweden to be one of the most secularized countries in Western Europe, in the sense that very low percentages of the population adhere to the Christian faith or attend public worship. According to the EVSSG survey of 1990, only 15 percent of the adult Swedish population (aged 16–74 years) believe in the existence of a personal God, 27 percent believe in heaven, and 19 percent in the resurrection of the dead. Only 4 percent attend divine services weekly, while another 6 percent do so monthly. In addition, comparison of these figures with those of the EVSSG survey of 1981, shows that both church attendance and belief in God has decreased during the 1980s.

While adherence to traditional Christian beliefs has reached very low levels, these beliefs seem to have been partly replaced by less orthodox and rather vague beliefs in the existence of a transcendent power, not understood as a personal God, and in reincarnation, developments that can be traced in other, less secularized, European countries as well. Thus, an increasing diversity in religious beliefs, i.e. decreasing orthodoxy, appears to be a general result of individualization and secularization. While, e.g., belief in a personal God has decreased in Sweden during the past decade, a corresponding increase can be seen in the share of the population who believe in a transcendent power other than a personal God: in 1981, 20 percent of the Swedes believed in a personal God and 37 percent affirmed belief in "some kind of spirit or life force"; in 1990, the corresponding shares were 15 and 44 percent, respectively.

Evidence of widely spread but vague beliefs in a transcendent power has been found not only in the EVSSG studies but in another nationwide survey as well. In 1986, a survey of world-views and value systems among the Swedish population was undertaken at Uppsala University. The present paper is based mainly on the results of this survey.[1] For the sake of convenience, I will refer to this survey as "the

[1] A random sample of 600 persons, born in 1917–1968, was drawn from the Swedish population registers. The number who agreed to participate – 399 persons – was lower than expected, the main reason probably being that a research project of a vaguely similar kind was at the time given much negative publicity in the mass media. The respondents were visited by interviewers from the Swedish Central Bureau of Statistics, who had been given special training for this task. About two dozen persons were interviewed by the present author. The interviews usually took about an hour. In addition to the interview, respondents were asked to answer a questionnaire.

Uppsala study", but it should be borne in mind that it did, in fact, cover the whole country.

For several reasons, the results from the Uppsala study can be seen as a valuable complement to those of the Swedish EVSSG surveys of 1981 and 1990. A number of questions were common to the three surveys, but as the Uppsala survey also contains information not available in the EVSSG surveys it can be used not only to shed additional light on some of the results obtained in those surveys, but also to gain information of a kind not available from the EVSSG studies.

In contrast to the EVSSG surveys, the Uppsala survey contained not only questions with standardized responses, but also a considerable number of "open" questions, which the respondents were asked to answer in their own words. For this reason the picture which emerges from this material differs in some important respects from that which can be otained from the EVSSG surveys.

The difference in results obtained by the use of questions with open as opposed to standardized responses may be illustrated by the fact that in the Uppsala study, health was mentioned as the most important value in life by a large share of the respondents (see below). In the EVSSG surveys on the other hand, where health was not explicitly mentioned as a response alternative, nothing indicates the dominant role of this value. Thus, an analysis of value priorities among the Swedish population would lack important information if it were based on the EVSSG surveys alone.

Due to the use of questions with open responses, the Uppsala survey in many cases provides a more detailed picture than the EVSSG surveys. For instance, the material reflects the great variability in religious beliefs in a way which would not have been been possible if only questions with standardized responses had been used. Another case where the Uppsala study gives a more detailed picture concerns the views of human beings versus animals (see below). While the EVSSG survey of 1990 showed that a majority of the Swedes regard animals and human beings as being equally valuable, the Uppsala survey enables us to gain a deeper insight into the respondents' thoughts about the relationship between human beings and animals.

Thus interviews using questions with open responses may contribute information of a kind which cannot be obtained from surveys using questions with standardized responses only. For this reason the present study, while making use of the Swedish EVSSG surveys of 1981 and 1990, is based mainly on material from the Uppsala survey.

Commitment as a Link between Religious Beliefs and Religious Practice

Like the EVSSG material, the Uppsala study of world-views and value systems gives a picture of Sweden as a very secularized country, in the sense that traditional church-oriented religion plays a very minor role in the lives of most Swedes. While adherence to the basic tenets of the Christian faith is low, the decline of traditional religion is even more evident in the very low prevalence of such traditional religious practices as prayer, church attendance or Bible reading.

It may be argued, that under certain circumstances the frequency of religious practice may be regarded as a measure of the personal commitment with which an individual adheres to a religious faith. In other words, personal commitment would be understood as a link between two dimensions of religiosity, i.e. religious belief and religious practice (Hamberg, 1990).[2] If regular prayer and/or regular participation in public worship are seen as indirect measures of the degree of personal commitment with which the belief in God or a transcendent power was held, the results of the Uppsala study indicate that only a minority of those who acknowledged such a belief adhered to it with a personal commitment strong enough to express itself in more or less regular religious activities. While 36 percent of the respondents expressed belief in God or a transcendent power, only 16 percent of the respondents used to pray weekly, and only 9 percent attended church at least once a month. In other words, while belief in God or a transcendent power was not very prevalent from a West European point of view, regular prayer and, especially, regular participation in public worship was even less common.[3]

Both the Uppsala study and the EVSSG surveys show that the prevalence of religious beliefs and religious practice differs between age groups. This accords with what has been found in many other studies, not only in Sweden, but in other

[2] It is clear, of course, that religious practice cannot always be regarded as an indicator of personal commitment to a religious faith. Rather, the connection between religious beliefs and religious practice is socially and culturally determined. It can be expected to vary, e.g. between different historical epochs, between different geographical regions, and between different social groups in a society. It may also be expected to vary between different religious groups, depending on the degree of social control they exercise over their members.

Only when e.g. church attendance is no longer part of a social and cultural pattern to which individuals are expected to conform, can it reasonably be seen as indicating a personal commitment to the Christian faith. In the present Swedish situation, where only a few percent of the population attend divine services weekly, this would seem to be the case. Although even in this context, participation in public worship cannot be assumed *always* to indicate commitment to traditional Christian beliefs, it seems reasonable to assume that it normally does so.

[3] Even less common than prayer or participation in public worship, however, is Bible reading. According to a nationwide survey carried out in 1984–1985, only 5 percent of the population read the Bible every week, while another 3 percent read the Bible monthly (Pettersson, 1986).

countries as well: adherence to traditional religious beliefs and practices tends to be more common in the higher age groups than in the lower (see e.g. Harding *et al.*, 1986). The reasons for the existence of this pattern and, in particular, the question of the relative importance of life-cycle effects, cohort effects, and period effects have been debated among scholars (see e.g. Hamberg, 1991).

Differences between age groups were larger with regard to religious practice than with regard to belief in God or a transcendent power.[4] This might be taken to indicate that members of the younger age group, to the extent that they still adhered to this belief, tended to do so with a lower degree of personal commitment. In addition, however, it is conceivable that the *kind* of divine power the respondents believed in may have differed between age groups: if young respondents were less prone to believe in a personal God, this might account for their being less inclined to pray or take part in worship. In other words, the differences in religious practice may be related not only to differences in personal commitment, but also to differing degrees of orthodoxy in religious beliefs.

It has sometimes been stated, *inter alia* in the Swedish mass media, that the share of the population who pray is larger than the share who believe in God.[5] In a certain sense, the results of the Uppsala study of world-views and value systems seem to support such a statement; while roughly a third of those interviewed acknowledged belief in God or a transcendent power, only 40 percent said that they *never* prayed. Of those who did pray, however, the majority prayed only occasionally. The nature of these sporadic prayers may in some instances be elucidated by the respondents' replies to other questions as illustrated by the following quotations:

It has happened that I have prayed to God in hard pressed situations, but that doesn't mean one must believe in him. (Woman, born in 1957)

If something is about to go wrong, one may say a prayer. That is, become a Christian temporarily. (Man, born in 1961)

One may ask for help when one is scared, something to resort to in a crisis. (Woman, born in 1964)

[4] Of those born in 1917–1931, 14 percent attended divine service at least once a month; the corresponding share for those born after 1945 was 6 percent. The percentage who used to pray at least once a week was 22 among those born before 1932, and 13 among those born after 1945. Belief in God or a transcendent power was affirmed by 40 percent in the oldest group as compared to 33 percent in the youngest.

[5] This phenomenon is not unique for Sweden. See Berger 1971, 40.

In difficult situations, I look upwards and pray. Don't believe in the Bible, but think there is "Something". (Woman, born in 1950)

Answers like these indicate that people who normally do not pray may in fact do so under special circumstances – even though they do not (ordinarily) believe in the divine power to whom they address such prayers.[6]

Not only can Sweden be described as a very secularized country, in the sense that low proportions of the population acknowledge the Christian faith or participate in public worship. In addition, available evidence may be taken to indicate that an increasing share of those who still adhere to the Christian faith tend to do so with a low degree of personal commitment: instead of being internalized and filling an important function in the individuals' lives, the faith – or parts of it – tends to an increasing extent to be accepted as a "rhetorical system" only (cf. Luckmann, 1967). Moreover, it is probable that conceptions of divinity are changing, the traditional Christian belief in a personal God being superseded by a more unspecified belief in a transcendent power; indications of such a development have been found in a European context as well (Harding *et al.*, 1986; "Value Patterns in Western-Europe, The United States and Canada"). A connection between these trends may be assumed: a vague belief in a transcendent power would probably tend to be less salient to those who hold it than would belief in a personal God.

While the changes discussed here involve a decline in the prevalence both of religious beliefs and of religious activities, it seems reasonable to expect the decline to be more pronounced in regard to religious activities than in regard to religious beliefs: to the extent that belief in God becomes less important to individuals and/or is replaced by a vague belief in a transcendent power, people would be less likely to engage in religious activities. In addition, these developments may be mutually reinforcing: while declining religious commitment results in declining religious practice, a decline in religious practice may contribute to a development where traditional religious beliefs are replaced by less orthodox beliefs, which may in turn further contribute to declining practice, etc.

The Church of Sweden: Belonging Without Believing

The fact that small shares of the Swedish population attend public worship or adhere to a traditional Christian faith may seem paradoxical, considering that approximately 90 percent of the population still belong to the Lutheran state

[6] The conclusion that only a minority of the Swedes pray regularly is confirmed by the EVSSG survey of 1990. According to this survey, 49 percent of the respondents never prayed and 10 percent hardly ever did so. 15 percent said that they only prayed in a crisis. Only 10 percent used to pray often, while 15 percent sometimes prayed.

church.[7] In the Swedish context, however, membership in the state church need not be associated either with religious beliefs or with religious practice. In fact, even a large majority of those who do not regard themselves as Christian and/or who do not believe in the existence of a divine power are members of the state church. This was confirmed by the Uppsala study of world-views and value systems: of those who stated that they did *not* believe in the existence of God or a transcendent power or who chose the self-description "I am not a Christian", a great majority, in both cases more than 80 percent, were members of the Church of Sweden!

Obviously, membership in the Church of Sweden is not necessarily associated either with religious beliefs or with religious practice. Rather, it has been suggested that the high level of affiliation in the Scandinavian national churches might be connected with a form of "civil religion": membership in these churches might be seen as a way of expressing solidarity with society and its basic values (Gustafsson, 1991; Riis, 1991). This might explain why formal non-affiliation is comparatively rare in Sweden. While in an American context, the phenomenon of people who are "believers but not belongers" has been discussed (Roof & Mc Kinney, 1987:52), many Swedes might be described as "belongers but not believers", with the important qualification that in the Swedish context "belonging" may be of a formal nature only: most of the "belongers" rarely engage in religious activities (Hamberg, 1990).[8]

Most Swedes Describe Themselves as Christians – "In Their Own Personal Way"

While Sweden stands out as one of the countries in Western Europe, where the decline in traditional, church-oriented religion has been especially pronounced, it is often alleged, e.g. in the Swedish mass media, that other forms of religion have emerged, usually described by the term "private religion" and assumed to contain such elements as belief in a transcendent power or divinity and/or belief in some form of life after death.[9] In addition, the "privately religious" are sometimes

[7] This is true in spite of the fact that Sweden has received a considerable number of immigrants in recent decades, most of whom do not have a Lutheran background.

[8] Cf. Davie (1990) for a discussion of "believing without belonging" in Britain.

[9] When the term "private religion" is used in this way, it denotes a phenomenon rather similar to what has been termed "implicit religion" (see Davie, 1990).

As the term "private religion" is used in this paper, it presupposes a substantive definition of religion. However, other definitions of the term would, of course, be equally possible. With a functional, instead of a substantive, definition of religion, e.g., the term might be used to denote what Thomas Luckmann has called "invisible religion" (Luckmann, 1967, 1990). (For substantive versus functional definitions of religion, see e.g. Luckmann, 1967; Berger, 1967; Robertson, 1970.)

assumed to be characterized by a great interest in questions relating to these beliefs and by certain forms of behaviour, such as private prayer or meditation.

Contributing to the assumptions of an increasing prevalence of "private religiosity", have been results from several Swedish surveys, where a majority of the population, when asked to choose between different alternatives for a religious self-description, have chosen the description "I am a Christian in my own personal way". In the Uppsala study of world-views and value systems in Sweden, the respondents were asked, not only to choose between this and other alternatives for a religious self-description, but also to give the reasons for their choice. Thus, the respondents who chose to describe themselves as "Christian in their own personal way" could be studied, both with regard to their motive for choosing this description, and with regard to religious beliefs and religious practice.

In the Uppsala survey, respondents were asked to describe themselves with one of the following alternatives (for the Swedish wording, see Hamberg, 1989):

I am a practicing Christian
I am a Christian in my own personal way
I am not a Christian.

Nine percent of those interviewed chose to describe themselves as practicing Christians, and 26 percent as not Christian. The majority, or 63 percent, chose the alternative "I am a Christian in my own personal way". At least with respect to sex, age, and education, this group did not differ significantly from the entire group of respondents, i.e. they were represented to a roughly equal extent among men and women, in different age groups, and on different levels of education.

Religious Beliefs

Roughly a third of the "Christians in their own way" explained their choice of this self-description by stating that they held – or, more rarely, did not hold – religious beliefs of some kind.

What they believed in – or did not believe in – varied. In some cases the respondents seemed to adhere to the Christian faith; in other cases they explicitly repudiated it. More frequently, however, they referred to a rather vague belief that there may be a God, a transcendent power or "Something". The following quotations may serve as examples:

That there is something. Perhaps a God or some superior power, don't know. (Man, born in 1968)

Believe that there's something. Not exactly a God, but something else. Cannot say what. (Woman, born in 1968)

I believe in something, I don't quite know what. (Woman, born in 1922)

Believe that there's something divine or spiritual, but don't know what. (Woman, born in 1917)

In response to a direct question on belief in God or a transcendent power, 41 percent of those describing themselves as "Christian in their own personal way" replied in the affirmative, while 59 percent either repudiated this belief or were uncertain. In other words, the fact that a person described herself as a "Christian in her own personal way" did not necessarily mean that she believed in the existence of a divine power.

In some cases, respondents explained their choice of the alternative "I am a Christian in my own personal way" by stating that they believed in – or did not believe in – life after death. The survey also contained a question explicitly dealing with this issue. Of the "Christians in their own way", 23 percent affirmed belief in a life after death, while 19 percent replied in the negative; the majority, or 59 percent, were uncertain.[10]

Somewhat to our surprise, reincarnation was mentioned by quite a number of respondents. As we had expected belief in reincarnation to be comparatively rare, we did not explicitly ask about it. Nevertheless, about 10 percent of the "Christians in their own way" (about 8 percent of all respondents) spontaneously mentioned reincarnation, usually expressing belief in it. In fact, belief in reincarnation seems to be fairly widespread, even more so than these spontaneous answers would suggest. According to the EVSSG survey of 1981 (the results of which were not available to us, when our study was planned), 15 percent of the adult Swedes believed in reincarnation. In 1990, this belief was held by 17 percent. In other words, belief in reincarnation seems to be even more common than was indicated by our study, a fact which is hardly surprising, considering that this belief seems to be fairly widespread in other European countries as well (Harding *et al.*, 1986; "Value patterns in Western-Europe, the United States and Canada").

Religious Activity

Another reason for choosing the alternative "I am a Christian in my own personal way" (given by a fifth of those choosing this self-description), was that the respondents were – or, more frequently, were not – religiously active in some way or another. With few exceptions, the activities referred to were church attendance or prayer.

[10] As might be expected, belief in God and belief in life after death were related: of those who expressed belief in God or a transcendent power, 50 percent believed in life after death, while almost 70 percent of those who did not believe in God or a transcendent power stated that they did not believe in life after death.

The activity (or rather, lack of activity) most often mentioned was participation in public worship. Although some persons motivated their choice of the self-description "I am a Christian in my own personal way" by saying that they attended church occasionally, it was more common for respondents to motivate this choice by stating that they seldom or never did so. In fact, an overwhelming majority (95 percent) of the "Christians in their own way" seldom or never participated in public worship.

Thus, the majority of those who described themselves as "Christians in their own personal way" seldom attended church. This was true even of those who acknowledged belief in God or a transcendent power. In many cases respondents motivated their choice of this religious self-description by stating that although they believed in God, they were not in the habit of going to church. One possible interpretation of this might be that these respondents, although they did not participate in public worship, might devote themselves to some religious activity in private, such as private prayer or meditation. However, the material indicates that this was not the case: no kind of religious activity – either public or private – was common among those who described themselves as "Christians in their own way".

Ethical Principles

Exactly a third of the "Christians in their own way" motivated their choice of this self-description by stating that they adhered to certain ethical principles or lived in a certain way. In some cases respondents combined their adherence to such principles with belief in God or a transcendent power; in other cases they expressly repudiated such beliefs. For many of the respondents, being a "Christian in one's own personal way" apparently meant doing one's best, being honest, considerate, and ready to help others. The following quotations may serve as examples:

You should be as decent as possible in your daily life. (Man, born in 1919)

To live as I consider right, to be an honest person. (Man, born in 1920)

I do my best, don't hurt anyone, try to help. I leave people alone. Can't stand slander. (Woman, born in 1917)

In some cases the answers implied that the respondents adhered to certain ethical principles, in other cases that they lived in a certain way. My impression is that the wording in both cases tends to express the same thing: the respondents think that they ought to live according to certain principles, and they also mean that they do so. Sometimes this is stated explicitly, often it seems to be implied. In many cases the ethical standards seem to be such that they should not be too difficult to live up to; one hardly gets the impression that the high ethical standards of the Sermon on the Mount are considered binding by the respondents. Rather, *being a "Christian in one's own way" seems to imply that one should do one's best within reasonable limits*.

While in several surveys about two thirds of the population have chosen to describe themselves as "Christian in their own personal way", an important reason for choosing this description seems to be that respondents regard themselves as being kind, honest, and law-abiding persons. Thus, being a Christian seems to be associated with leading a decent life, rather than with adherence to certain religious beliefs or religious practices. Possibly the reason, or at least one of the reasons, why an overwhelmimg majority of the Swedes continue to be members in the Church of Sweden, regardless of their religious beliefs or lack of such beliefs, is that the church is seen as a symbol of moral decency. This attitude may be exemplified by the statement of a respondent who declared that he did not believe in the existence of God:

I still belong to the Church of Sweden. It may be good from a moral point of view. (Man, born in 1917)

"Christians in Their Own Way" – A Heterogeneous Group

As has been stated previously, Sweden, in an international perspective, appears as a very secularized country, in the sense that low percentages of the population adhere to the Christian faith or attend church regularly. Thus, it is hardly surprising that the Christian faith apparently did not hold a strong position among the approximately two thirds of the respondents in the Uppsala study of world-views and value systems who described themselves as "Christians in their own personal way". Few of them attended services regularly, and although the percentage who acknowledged belief in God or a transcendent power was considerably higher, the beliefs held often seemed to be vague: rather than a Christian faith, the respondents tended to express a diffuse belief in a transcendent power of some kind. In addition, the material conveys the impression that belief in a divine power, where it existed, often played a minor role in the respondents' lives.

The latter impression is supported by results from the EVSSG surveys, which contained a question on the importance of God in the respondents' lives. Answers were to be given on a ten-point scale, where 1 stood for "not at all important" and 10 for "very important". In the survey of 1990, only 8 percent of the Swedes chose the highest point on the scale, while 35 percent chose the lowest. A point on the upper half of the scale, i.e. from 6 to 10, was selected by 25 percent.[11] Thus, only a minority were prepared to accord God an important role in their lives.

[11] In 1981, 10 percent chose the highest point on the scale, and 29 percent the lowest. A point on the upper half of the scale was chosen by 29 percent.

A considerable percentage of those respondents who chose the religious self-description "I am a Christian in my own personal way" affirmed belief in a divine power, while approximately the same share expressed doubts on this point, and a smaller, but still sizable, group repudiated this belief. Thus, the group who described themselves as "Christian in their own personal way" was far from homogeneous with respect to religiosity. This self-description was chosen for a variety of reasons, not necessarily connected with religious faith or religious commitment. Widely differing religious beliefs – or the absence of such beliefs – were represented among the "Christians in their own way". Obviously, the fact that a majority of the Swedes choose this self-description cannot be interpreted as evidence of a widespread existence of forms of religion which may reasonably be termed "private" or "implicit" – at least, i.e., if the term "religion" is substantively defined.

Human Beings Versus Animals – Changing Views Related to Secularization?

Concomitant with the decline in traditional religious beliefs, other changes in values appear to have taken place. For instance, a world-view where human beings are no longer regarded as being intrinsically different from animals now seems to be fairly widespread in Sweden. In the Uppsala survey, only 38 percent of the respondents were of the opinion that human beings ought to be treated with more respect than animals, while 43 percent disagreed with this view. The remaining 19 percent were uncertain.[12]

The respondents were also asked to motivate their answers.[13] Those who held the opinion that human beings should *not* be treated differently usually considered animals to be in principle equally valuable and therefore entitled to the same respect.

The reasons for holding the opinion that human beings *should* be treated in a special way were somewhat more varied. The reason most commonly given (by approximately one fifth) was that biological factors entitle human beings to special respect. In particular, the fact that human beings are more intelligent than animals was frequently given as a reason. Other respondents referred to established custom or gave pragmatic reasons for their opinion (e.g. that we depend on animals for food), while still others were unable to motivate their opinion. Very few, however, only a few percent, motivated their opinion by referring to the special status accorded to human beings in the Christian doctrine.

[12] According to the Swedish EVSSG survey of 1990, 55 percent held the opinion that human beings and animals are equally valuable, while 40 percent accorded a higher value to human beings and the rest were uncertain.

[13] This question was "open", i.e. the respondents were asked to answer in their own words.

Thus, more than 40 percent of the respondents did *not* think that human beings should be treated with more respect than animals. Of those who held the opinion that human beings should be treated differently, the majority either gave biological or pragmatic reasons for their view or were unable to motivate their opinion. Of course, the fact that many Swedes regard animals and human beings as being equally valuable, does not mean that they actually treat animals and human beings in the same way. Only a minority are vegetarians, e.g., and it seems safe to assume that almost everyone, if having to choose between saving a human being or an animal, would opt for saving a human life. In addition, the respondents often distinguished between different types of animals.[14] Insects, e.g., were sometimes mentioned as exceptions from the rule, as illustrated by the following answer:

One ought to show respect for all living beings, except mosquitoes, spiders, and flies. (Woman, born in 1950)

Thus, while in fact human beings are, of course, treated differently from animals, this special treatment now tends to be motivated by biological or pragmatic reasons rather than being based on theological or ideological grounds of principle. Although we cannot be certain that the tendency to regard animals as being in principle on a par with human beings is a new phenomenon, it would seem plausible to assume that this may be one aspect of the secularization process. In the absence of theological reasons for ascribing a special status to human beings, some persons may find it difficult to motivate such a status on grounds of principle.[15]

In addition, the view that animals should be treated with the same respect as human beings may in some instances be connected with belief in reincarnation, as suggested by this statement by one of the respondents in the Uppsala survey:

I don't kill an insect — you never know. The bumble-bee may be mrs. Johansson. (Man, born in 1925)

If animals are regarded as possibly being deceased relatives or friends, a tendency to regard animals and human beings as meriting the same degree of respect would perhaps not be surprising! The possible connection between belief in reincarnation and the views held with regard to animals might be worth attention in future research.

[14] The same tendency was noted in a recent Swedish study based on interviews. In particular, a very high value was accorded to dogs. For instance, one respondent stated that "[I felt] it was worse when my dog died, than when my mother died" (Jeffner, 1992:16).

[15] Cf. Martin Soskice (1991) for a philosophical and theological discussion of the role of a theology of creation as a basis for the ontological status accorded to human beings.

Health as the Most Important Value in Life

Belief or disbelief in life after death may conceivably be connected with other values as well. In the Uppsala survey, we asked respondents what they regarded as most important in their lives. The value most often given, mentioned by 45 percent of the respondents, was health. About a third mentioned families or friends and about a quarter of the respondents gave answers related to their economic situation.

Thus, having a good health stands out as one of the most important values in contemporary Sweden. While we have no means of knowing the importance attached to this value some fifty or hundred years ago, it seems probable that the concern for one's health has increased in recent decades. One of the reasons for this assumption is the fact that the market for health food, magazines and other products catering to the interest in preserving or improving one's health has expanded rapidly, as has the number of health centers and institutes for physical training.

Probably several factors contribute to the interest taken in health. One factor which may be assumed to be of importance is the general Western trend towards individualization, including such themes as self-expression, self-realization and personal autonomy, which tend to bestow a sacred status upon the individual (see Luckmann, 1990). Illness and death being the ultimate threat to the individual's existence, the increasing importance accorded to self-realization and personal autonomy may well lead to a growing concern for preserving or improving one's health.

Another factor, related to individualization, may be secularization, in the sense of declining adherence to traditional religious beliefs. As belief in a personal God becomes less widespread, fewer persons will believe that life and health ultimately depends on a divine power. As a result, the number of persons who see themselves as being responsible for their health can be expected to increase. In addition, changing beliefs about life after death may well have an impact on the importance attached to health, as the declining prevalence of belief in a life hereafter can be expected to result in an increased interest in prolonging the present life. Thus, it seems probable that there is a connection between the declining adherence to traditional religious beliefs, and the fact that a large share of the Swedish population now regard health as the most important value in life.

Religious Change in a Historical Perspective

It appears beyond dispute that the proportions of the population who believe in God or participate in religious activities, such as prayer and church attendance, have declined in Sweden during this century. Of course, the decline can most easily be documented where participation in public worship is concerned. Information on the prevalence of religious beliefs is available only for comparatively recent times; thus, we may run the risk of overestimating the former prevalence of such beliefs (see e.g. Dobbelaere, 1981:31–35). An important difference is that certain forms of religious practice that in the contemporary Swedish situation may be regarded as expressions of a subjectively important religious faith, e.g. church attendance, formerly were part of a social and cultural pattern to which individuals were expected to conform. While nowadays the share of the population who attend public worship is considerably lower than the share who believe in the existence of a divine power, the reverse may have been true in times when church attendance was the prevailing social norm. Thus, it is difficult, indeed, to draw conclusions about the extent of religious change in a long time perspective. This is true both concerning the prevalence of religious beliefs and concerning the degree of personal commitment with which such beliefs have been held. However, a possible – and maybe plausible – hypothesis would be that during the past century there has been a decline, not only in the share of the population who adhere to the Christian faith, but also in the saliency of this faith to the "average" believer. In other words, Swedes in general are now less disposed to acknowledge belief in the Christian faith, and to the extent that they still do adhere to this faith, or to certain tenets thereof, they tend to do so with a lower degree of personal commitment: the faith to which they still hold on in theory occupies a less central role in their lives.[16]

It is sometimes alleged that simultaneously with the decline in traditional, church-oriented religion in Sweden, other forms of religion have emerged, e.g. what in the Swedish context has been called "private religion". It does seem probable that adherence to the Christian faith has to some extent been replaced by a rather vague belief in a transcendent power. Certain other beliefs, e.g. belief in reincarnation, also may have gained ground. Thus, the situation seems to resemble the description given by Luckmann of a modern society where the "official", institutionally specialized, form of religion is no longer routinely internalized *au sérieux*, and where, as a consequence of this, the individual systems of ultimate significance tend to be both syncretistic and vague (Luckmann, 1967:99 *et passim*). However, empirical evidence hardly indicates that it would be meaningful to describe Swedes in general as being "privately" religious, *if the term "religion" is substantively defined.* Rather the data indicate the presence of widely diffused sets of beliefs, heterogeneous and vague, that from strict, substantive criteria can hardly be understood as religion:

I believe in something, I don't quite know what.

[16] A similar situation seems to prevail in Denmark, where recent data indicate a trend towards a vague sense of religiousness, in an uncommitted way (Riis, 1991).

It is generally agreed that Sweden is one of the most secularized countries in Western Europe, in the sense that small percentages of the population adhere to the Christian faith or attend public worship. In addition, the surveys referred to here indicate that most Swedes are, at best, moderately interested in questions concerning religion (Hamberg, 1989). On the other hand, available data show that Swedes, living in the modern welfare state, are on average more happy and satisfied with their lives than are Europeans in general (Pettersson, 1988). The possibility of a connection between these facts has been suggested (Pettersson, 1993). While data from the Uppsala survey can neither confirm nor disprove the existence of such a connection, this possibility may merit further research, as suggested by the answer of one of the respondents:

> I'm not seeking in any way, I'm happy and harmonious as things are. My life does not need improving. If the situation were different, it is not quite inconceivable that I might turn to religion, if I were *not* happy, or something. (Woman, born in 1948)

It should be pointed out, however, that even if a correlation can be established between low levels of traditional religiosity and high levels of subjectively experienced satisfaction with life, this need not be interpreted as evidence of a direct causal relationship; such a correlation may well be due to underlying factors influencing both religiosity and life satisfaction. To the extent that satisfaction with life is related to material welfare, it seems more likely that *both* the increase in material welfare and life satisfaction *and* the decline in traditional religiosity should be seen as different aspects of the process of modern economic growth, which since the beginning of the industrial revolution, to varying degrees, has been transforming Western societies.

References

Berger, Peter L., 1967

The Sacred Canopy. Elements of a Sociological Theory of Religion. New York: Doubleday & Company, Inc.

Berger, Peter L., (1969) 1971

A Rumour of Angels. Modern Society and the Rediscovery of the Supernatural. Harmondsworth: Penguin Books Ltd.

Davie, Grace, 1990

"Believing without Belonging: Is This the Future of Religion in Britain?". *Social Compass*, vol. 37, nr. 4.

Dobbelaere, Karel, 1981

"Secularization: A Multi-Dimensional Concept." *Current Sociology*, 29, 2:1–216.

Gustafsson, Göran, 1991
Tro, samfund och samhälle. Sociologiska perspektiv. Örebro: Libris.
Hamberg, Eva M., 1988
Religiös tro och religiöst engagemang. En analys av material från projektet Livsåskådningar i Sverige. Religion och Samhälle 1988:6, no. 32. Stockholm: Religionssociologiska Institutet.
Hamberg, Eva M., 1989
"Kristen på mitt eget sätt". En analys av material från projektet Livsåskådningar i Sverige. Religion och Samhälle 1989:10–11, no. 48–49. Stockholm: Religionssociologiska Institutet.
Hamberg, Eva M., 1990
Studies in the Prevalence of Religious Beliefs and Religious Practice in Contemporary Sweden. Uppsala: Uppsala University.
Hamberg, Eva M., 1991
"Stability and Change in Religious Beliefs, Practice and Attitudes: A Swedish Panel Study". *Journal for the Scientific Study of Religion*, vol. 30, no. 1.
Harding, Stephen & David Phillips with Michael Fogarty, 1986
Contrasting Values in Western Europe. Unity, Diversity and Change. London: Macmillan.
Jeffner, Anders, 1992
Djur och människor. Argumentbilder och strukturer i allmänt spridda värderingssystem. Uppsala (Mimeo).
Luckmann, Thomas, 1967
The Invisible Religion. The Problem of Religion in Modern Society. New York: The Macmillan Company.
Luckmann, Thomas, 1990
"Shrinking Transcendence, Expanding Religion?". *Sociological Analysis*, vol. 50, no.2.
Martin Soskice, Janet, 1991
"Creation and Relation". *Theology*, January.
Pettersson, Thorleif, 1986
Svenska folket och Bibeln. Religion och Samhälle 1986:8, no. 8. Stockholm: Religionssociologiska Institutet.
Pettersson, Thorleif, 1988
Bakom dubbla lås. En studie av små och långsamma värderingsförändringar. Stockholm: Institutet för framtidsstudier.
Pettersson, Thorleif, 1993
"Welfare Policies, Religious Commitment and Happiness." In: L. Brown (ed.), *Religion, Personality and Mental Health*. New York: Springer-Verlag.
Riis, Ole, 1991
The EVSSG-Study as Basis for Sociological Studies of Secularization in Europe. (Mimeo)
Robertson, Roland, 1970
The Sociological Interpretation of Religion. Oxford: Basil Blackwell.

Roof, Wade Clark & William Mc Kinney, 1987
American Mainline Religion. Its Changing Shape and Future. New Brunswick: Rutgers University Press.
Value Patterns in Western-Europe, the United States and Canada, 1991
Mimeo prepared for the European Value Systems Study Group.

THORLEIF PETTERSSON

Culture Shift and Generational Population Replacement: Individualization, Secularization, and Moral Value Change in Contemporary Scandinavia

The well-known theory on cultural change presented by Ronald Inglehart (1977; 1990) assumes the economic, technological, and socio-political changes of the past decades to have transformed the culture of Western industrial society. According to Inglehart's theory, the unprecedented levels of economic development, the emergence of welfare states, the rising levels of education, and the expansion of mass communications have led to gradual changes in a wide range of basic values, e.g., values concerning politics, work, family, religion, environment, social and moral issues. These value changes are generally understood as a shift from materialist to postmaterialist values. Thus, the rise of postmaterialist values is a sign of a broad cultural change that is assumed to be reshaping contemporary Western society.

The value shift from materialism to postmaterialism is assumed to occur by intergenerational population replacement. This assumption is founded on two basic hypotheses. *The scarcity hypothesis* assumes that an individual's priorities reflect the socio-economic environment. Things scarce are given the highest subjective value. *The socialization hypothesis* assumes that the relationship between socio-economic environment and value priorities is not one of immediate adjustment. Thus, a substantive time lag is involved because to a large extent an individual's basic values reflect the conditions prevailing during one's formative pre-adult years (Inglehart 1990, 68). However, the socialization hypothesis does not suggest that value priorities are totally immutable during adultgood, but merely that they are difficult to change.

The scarcity hypothesis, partly founded on Maslow's well-known need psychology, explains why consecutive generations formed during gradually increasing levels of material welfare will establish gradually increasing levels of postmaterialist values. As the needs for physical safety and security are increasingly satisfied, the needs for belonging and self-actualization become more prominent, and the values satisfying the higher order needs will increase in importance. The socialization hypothesis explains why the value systems established during early socialization tend to remain stable. However, the scarcity hypothesis also implies short term period effects, e.g., that adult generations might change their value priorities as a response to important socio-economic changes. Such period effects reflect short-term fluctuations in the socio-economic environment that are superimposed on long-term cohort effects, reflecting the conditions prevailing during a given age group's formative preadult years (Inglehart 1990, 82). Thus, all adult generations might evidence more or less equal and short term value changes, but according to the socialization hypothesis, generational value *differences* due to different pre-adult formative experiences would remain. The assumption of stable intergenerational value differences might thus be regarded as essential to Inglehart's theory of cultural change. "Action *cannot* be interpreted as simply the result of external situations: Enduring differences in cultural learning also play an essential part in shaping what people think and do" (Inglehart 1990, 19).

It can be argued that Inglehart's theory is comparatively open concerning the scope of the value change. While materialism due to the reference to Maslowian psychology is consistent as an emphasis on physical and economic safety, the postmaterialist value pattern seems to include a wide range of differing values. Any value related to Maslow's higher order needs at the time of value formation might be regarded as a postmaterialist value. Thus, the rise of Postmaterialism seems to be "only one aspect of a still broader process of cultural change that is reshaping the religious institutions, gender roles, sexual mores, and cultural norms of Western society" (Inglehart 1990, 66). Obviously, the postmaterialist values cover a wide range of issues, maybe too wide to be analyzed as homogeneous in terms of underlying psychological motivation.

In this regard, the relationship between postmaterialism and religious values is of special interest. Since Inglehart finds links between materialism and traditional Judeo-Christian values, and since postmaterialism is distinguished by lower emphasis on traditional religious and moral norms, his theory can be viewed as a secularization theory as well. However, it should be noted that Inglehart views the linkage between the rising postmaterialism and the decline of traditional religious orientations as conditional and not as inherent. Due to their higher interest in the meaning of life, the postmaterialists are said to possess more potential interest in religion than the materialists. "If a decline of religion is taking place, it is not necessary built into the conditions of advanced industrial society. The established religions may be loosing a growing and potentially mobilizable constituency, by default" (Inglehart 1990, 211). However, this conclusion seems to be based on two different understandings of the concept of religion, one substantive and one functional. That the postmaterialists are committed to existential questions does not necessarily mean that they should be an easy constituency to all kinds of answers to such questions, e.g. answers that assume such transcendental belief systems that the established churches cannot avoid to propose.

Given the broad understanding of the postmaterialist value dimension, it is difficult to decide whether any given value domain under scrutiny is covered or not by Inglehart's theory. Theoretically, values satisfying Maslow's safety and sustenance needs at the pre-adult time of value establishment should be regarded as materialist values, while postmaterialist values by definition satisfy Maslow's higher order needs. However, the assumption that specific individual psychological needs (*inter alia* sustenace vs social needs) should be monotonously related to the formation of specific societal values might be questioned. In order to secure a safe relation between needs and values at the time of value formation, one would prefer independent measures of the two. Further studies of young peoples' needs and values are therefore needed (cf. Inglehart 1990, 160). A reanalysis done by the present author of data from a Swedish panel study of young people (Johansson & Miegel 1992) showed a significant correlation of .52 between materialistic values at the personal level and Inglehart's standard items for materialistic values at the societal level. The corresponding level for the postmaterialist values was lower ($r = .15$), but still significant. In a general sense, such results support the scarcity hypothesis and the hypothesis of a direct link between young prople's psychological need structures and their social values.

It has been suggested that the philosophical value theory underlying Inglehart's work prevent independent measures of needs and values, i.e., that Inglehart assumes a naturalistic value theory that defines values as needs (Johansson & Miegel 1992, 59f, 127). However, such a criticism seems mistaken; to maintain that young people establish a certain value structure *because* they have a certain need structure, is not to claim that values and needs by definition are identical entities. But if the latter is not suggested, it becomes the more important to assess values and needs independent of each other at the time of value formation. Only then could an empirical relation between the two be safely assessed. At any rate, it is argued here that the definition of materialist and especially postmaterialist values need clarification, n.b., if the definition is not limited to the values explicitly mentioned by Inglehart's standard item battery for materialist and postmaterialist values.

Sociological theory has since long assumed that modern society is characterized by an increasing individualism. Admittedly, the concept of individualism is often used in different meanings. From a historical analysis, Turner (1991, ch. 7) distinguishes between a) individualism as a doctrine of individual rights, b) individuality as concerned with the growth of sensibility, taste, consciousness and will, and c) individuation as a set of practices by which individuals are identified and separated by marks, numbers, signs and codes. In the European Value Study, individualism is understood as a sense of individuation of the person and a stress on the supreme value of the human being, as an emphasis on personal autonomy, as a concern for self-development as a primary value, and as a recognition of moral responsibility to others (Ester *et al.* 1993, 18). In other words, in the EVS study, individualism is seen as a combination of Turner's first and second component.

However, the open character of the postmaterialist value dimension makes it difficult to relate Inglehart's theroy to such an understanding of individualism. According to Inglehart's theoretical analyses, it is unclear whether individualism in such a sense should be regarded as a materialist or postmaterialis value. Basically, the Maslowian need for belonging is regarded as a need of the higher order (Inglehart 1990, 152). Any value satisfying this need must by definition be regarded as a postmaterialist one. As far as individualism is conceived of as something in opposition to or in tension with the value of belonging, individualism should *not* be regarded as a postmaterialist value. Accordingly, a contemporary Japanese decline in the sense of group obligation is not viewed by Inglehart as evidence of increasing postmaterialism, but as a process of individuation, reflecting the gradual decline of the individual subordination to the collectivity to which one belongs (cf. above), individualism should not be viewed as a postmaterialist value.

On the other hand, the items used to tap the postmaterialist values related to Maslow's higher order needs for belonging and esteem ask, e.g., about how important it is to have more to say in government decisions and on jobs. Such items seem to tap the dimension of submissiveness vs. personal activism and autonomy, a dimension often related to the individualistic tendency. Similarly, the postmaterialist values are by definition related to the need for self-actualization, something often regarded as an individualistic tendency. Furthermore, individualism can also be seen as manifesting itself in the gradual transformation and "de-coupling" of traditional and civic values. Thus, the decreasing willingness to legitimate moral convictions by a Christian world view, the increasing emphasis on personal development and achievement in working life, the change from a materialistic value orientation to a postmaterialistic preference in the domain of socio-political domain, can also be seen as signs of growing individualism (Halman & Ester 1991). On such grounds, it can be argued that individualism should be regarded as a postmaterialist value, at least in a general sense. It should also be noted that Inglehart describes the current political value change as a shift from state authority "toward individual autonomy" (Inglehart 1990, 11), something often thought of as a facet of individualism.

Generally, it can therefore be argued that Inglehart's theory is related to the issue of individualization, a theme frequently covered by sociological theory. In this sense, individualization should be viewed as a social process, not to be confused with the individual psychological process of individuation or individual value development. Differently put, societies might show different degrees of individualization while individuals might differ in identity development and value formation. On the other hand, individualization and individual identity formation must not be viewed as unrelated processes. Individual identity in modern and individualized society is said to be peculiarly open, peculiarly differentiated, peculiarly reflective, and peculiarly individuated (Berger *et al.* 1973). Accordingly, the degree of individualization is reflected by the distribution of individual identities.

The more “unfinished selves”, the more incompatible social roles, the more reflection on one's identity, and the more valuation of individual freedom and autonomy, and, *mutatis mutandis*, the more postmatieralists, the more individualized the society.

To summarize, it can thus be said that Inglehart's theory on cultural change assumes a gradual shift toward postmaterialism to be taking place in contemporary Western society. It can be argued that a growing individualism is an essential part of this value change. This cultural shift should mainly take place by intergenerational population replacement and should be manifested by decreasing adherence to Christian beliefs and practices, traditional social moral values, traditional family values, traditional sexual mores, etc.

Inglehart (1977; 1990) has presented extensive empirical support for parts of his theory of value change. These results will not be reviewed here. Since the present paper analyzes data from the Scandinavian part of the European Value Study, a short summary of the main value changes that according to this study have occurred in Europe and North America during the past decade is more appropriate.

From the European Value Study, it is concluded that the religious and moral values shifted in the direction of individualization. Religious values became less adhered to, civic morality decreased and permissiveness increased. These changes occured mainly by intergenerational population replacement (Ester *et al.* 1993, ch. 3). A development towards increased freedom of value choice led to a plurality of individualized value orientations in the realm of religion and morality.

In the political domain, economic and cultural individualism were increasing together with political interest, postmaterialism and protest proneness. At the same time, confidence in the institutions were on the decline. These value shifts, too, seemed to occur mainly as a consequence of a replacement of birth cohorts (Ester *et al.* 1993, ch.4)

Generally, it can thus be concluded that the European value changes of the past decade support Inglehart's theory of value change. However, the processes of culture shift in different parts of Europe should not *a priori* be regarded as homogeneous and identical. The cultural shifts might differ from region to region. A more detailed analysis of culture shifts in Denmark, Norway, and Sweden will therefore be undertaken here. Since the Scandinavian countries in certain ways are different from continental Europe (Gustafsson 1987; Listhaug 1990; Ester *et al.* 1993; cf. Halman's contribution to this volume), a separate analysis of these countries might show cultural changes other than those found in Europe at large.

Results

In this paper the Scandinavian, i.e., the Danish, Norwegian, and Swedish, data from the 1981 (1982 for Denmark) and 1990 European Value Study surveys are used. Each survey contained about 1,000 respondents representative of the adult population aged 18 to 75 years. The samples were random probability samples from general population registers.

Appendix A gives information about sample sizes and weighting procedures. For further information on the Scandinavian surveys, see Listhaug *et al.* (1983), Listhaug & Huseby (1990), Gundelach & Riis (1992), Pettersson (1988a; 1992). For general information on the EVS study, as well as a EVS bibliography, see Harding *et al.* (1988) and Ester *et al.* (1993).

In the analyses presented below, seven value dimensions are studied using the following measures:

1) *A Christian religious involvement score*, tapping regular service attendance and the subjective importance ascribed to a belief in a personal God;
2) *A Civic virtue score*, tapping attitudes towards a) claiming social benefits one is not entitled to, b) avoiding paying fares on buses and trains, c) cheating on taxes, d) buying stolen goods, e) "borrowing" a car, f) using marijuana or hash, g) keeping money found, h) lying in self-interest, i) taking bribes, j) failing to report damage one has done, and k) threatening workers who refuse to participate in a strike;
3) *A Sexual relations strictness score*, tapping attitudes towards a) married people having an extra-marital affair, b) sexual intercourse under the legal age of consent, c) homosexuality, and d) prostitution;
4) *A Bio-ethical strictness score*, tapping attitudes towards a) killing in self-defence, b) euthanasia, and c) suicide;
5) *A General permissiveness score*, tapping attitudes toward the issues mentioned for the sexual relations strictness score and the bio-ethical strictness score above;
6) *A Traditional family score*, indicating a) the view that marriage is not an outdated institution, b) the opinion that children need a home with both a father and a mother to grow up happily, and c) a dislike of a single mother who wants to have a child without having a stable relationship with a man;
7) *A General individualism score*, indicating the opinions that a) one often tries to persuade others, b) one experiences great (8 or more on 10-point rating scale) freedom of choice in one's own life, c) the opinion that a worker need not follow a superior's instructions if not convinced, d) one would find it important that jobs allow personal initiatives, e) one would find it good if individual development were to be more emphasized in the near future, and f) one finds it bad if authorities were to gain more respect in the near future.

Table 1. Value changes in the Scandinavian countries. Adjusted and non-adjusted value scores for seven value dimensions. Results from the 1981 and 1990 EVSSG-studies. For the definition of value scores, see text.

	Non-adjusted values		Adjusted values[1]	
Dimension of value change	1981	1990	1989	1990
Christian religious involvement	.04	–.08 ***	.02	–.06 **
General individualism values	–.19	.24 ***	–.18	.23 ***
Traditional family values	–.16	.19 ***	–.15	.24 ***
Civic virtues	.10	–.03 **	.05	–.02 *
General permissiveness	.07	–.05 ***	.07	–.11 ***
Sexual relations strictness	–.05	.11 ***	–.12	.15 ***
Bio-ethical strictness	-.04	–.04 **	.02	–.02 n.s.

1 Christian commitment adjusted for individualistic values
Individualistic values adjusted for Christian commitment
Other values adjusted for Christian commitment
and individualistic values

*** $p < .001$
** $p < .01$
* $p < .05$
n.s. not significant

The calculational procedures for these scores are described in Appendix A. Reasons for defining the scores in this manner can be found in several comparative analyses made by Loek Halman, chief EVS researcher at The Institute for Social Research, University of Tilburg (see Halman 1991; 1992; Halman & Ester 1991; Ester *et al.* 1993). The results for the Scandinavian value changes between 1981 and 1990 are calculated from the weighted Scandinavia EVSSG data file. Weighting procedures are described in Appendix A.

The over-all value changes for the seven value dimensions are shown in Table 1. The results show a decreasing commitment to Christian values while individualistic values and traditional family values, respectively, have gained increased support. A decreased support for civic virtues can also be noticed. At the same time, a general permissive outlook has decreased. The decreasing permissiveness seems to be the net result of two opposite tendencies; i.e. a decreasing adherence to bio-ethical strictness values together with an increasing support for stricter views on sexual relations.

The results for the adjusted value changes, obtained by multiple classification analyses (MCA analyses), show the decreasing Christian commitment and the increasing individualism to be mainly unrelated to each other. Contrary to the increased support for strict views on sexual relations and traditional family values, respectively, the decreased adherence to stricter bio-ethical values, and, to a

Table 2. **Intra- and inter-cohort differences for six value dimensions.** Factor- and z-scores from the Scandinavian EVSSG-studies of 1981 and 1990.

		Christian religious involvement		Sexual relations strictness	
Age 1981	Age 1990	1981	1990	1981	1990
	18–26		–.29		.00
18–24	27–33	–.29	–.16 *	–.54	–.01 **
25–34	34–43	–.19	–.18 n.s.	–.25	.00 ***
35–44	44–53	–.05	–.10 n.s.	–.14	.08 ***
45–54	54–63	.03	.12 n.s.	.08	.27 **
55–64	64–73	.30	.31 n.s.	.21	.49 ***
65–75		.57		.41	
All cohorts		.04	–.08 ***	–.05	.11 ***
Only cohorts aged 18–64 in 1981 and 27–73 in 1990		–.04	–.03 n.s.	–.13	.14 ***

		Bio-ethical strictness		General individualism values	
Age 1981	Age 1990	1981	1991	1981	1990
	18–26		–.29	.25	
18–24	27–33	–.25	–.17 n.s.	.02	.35 ***
25–34	34–43	–.09	–.08 n.s.	–.03	.38 ***
35–44	44–53	–.07	–.03 n.s.	–.07	.27 ***
45–54	54–63	.09	.22 n.s.	–.20	.03 ***
55–64	64–73	.26	.27 n.s.	–.37	–.10 ***
65–75		.43		–.62	
All cohorts		.04	–.04 **	–.19	.24 ***
Only cohorts aged 18–64 in 1981 and 27–73 in 1990		–.02	.02 n.s.	–.13	.21 ***

		Civic virtues		Traditional family values	
Age 1981	Age 1990	1981	1991	1981	1990
	18–26		–.65	.12	
18–24	27–33	–.56	–.24 ***	–.38	.13 **
25–34	34–43	–.14	.02 **	–.26	.12 ***
35–44	44–53	.10	.11 n.s.	–.27	.15 ***
45–54	54–63	.31	.34 n.s.	–.13	.28 ***
55–64	64–73	.37	.46 *	.05	.41 ***
65–75		.56		.13	
All cohorts		.10	–.03 ***	–.16	.19 ***
Only cohorts aged 18–64 in 1981 and 27–73 in 1990		–.03	–.12 **	–.20	.20 ***

*** $p < .001$ ** $p < .01$ * $p < .05$ n.s. not significant

certain degree, the lessened support for civic virtues, seem to be related to the growing secularism and individualism.

The results for the generational replacement hypothesis are shown in Table 2. The declining Christian commitment, the decreasing adherence to stricter bioethical values, and, to a certain extent, the decreasing civic virtue values can be accounted for by the mechanisms of generational population replacement, i.e. an intragenerational value stability together with apparent intergenerational value differences.

On the other hand, the increasing individualism, the growing traditional familism, and the growing support for stricter views on sexual relations, can*not* be accounted for by intragenerational value stability and generational population replacement. Rather, the results indicate that the latter three value changes should be accounted for by evident intragenerational value changes, i.e. period effects. For the individualistic values, the intragenerational value changes are roughly of the same magnitude for all cohorts, while for the views on sexual relations and the traditional family relations, respectively, the intra-cohort value changes are greatest for the youngest birth cohorts. Most important, for these cohorts, the intergenerational value differences evident in the 1981 data cannot be traced in the data from 1990.

Discussion

The Scandinavian value changes during the past decade are partly supportive of Inglehart's theory on cultural change and consonant with the over-all European value changes, partly theoretically unexpected and different from the general European culture shift. These similarities and differences concern both the direction of the value change and the role played by intergenerational population replacement.

As for the direction of value change, both the European and the Scandinavian value systems are affected by a growing individualism, a decreasing commitment to Christian values, and a lessened support for civic virtues. In both Europe and Scandinavia the lessened support for the civic virtues was found to be at least partly related to the growing individualism and the decreasing commitment to Christian values. Both in Europe at large and in Scandinavia, a growing individualism and secularism thus seems to be followed by a lessened support for traditional social values, i.e. civic virtues. In these respects, the Scandinavian value changes mirror the over-all European changes.

The European moral value changes found by the EVS study are most often analyzed in terms of two general moral orientations, a civic virtue dimension and a general permissiveness dimension, respectively (see e.g. Halman & Ester 1992). As mentioned, both the Scandinavian and the European value changes for the civic virtue values were similar. As for the permissiveness moral value dimension, most European countries showed an increasing permissiveness. The Scandinavian results showed a value change in the opposite direction. Thus, contrary to the European case, the Scandinavian value changes also witnessed an increased support for traditional family values and stricter views on sexual relations, respectively. Such changes were not found by the over-all European analyses.

The unexpected Scandinavian decreasing permissiveness has to do with the definition and measurement of this value dimension. According to detailed studies of the factorial structure of the EVS questionnaire moral value items, both bio-ethical moral values (e.g. suicide, euthanasia) and values concerning sexual relations (e.g. homosexuality, prostitution) are included in the general permissiveness value dimension. The general permissiveness value dimension thus covers both bio-ethical issues and sexual relations. However, a closer look at the Scandinavian data reveal two interesting patterns. It can be shown that the covariation between the views on sexual relations and the bio-ethical issues, respectively, is significantly lower in 1990 than in 1981 (correlation coefficients .54 and .43; Fischer's $z = 5.03$, $p < .001$). At least for Scandinavia, it can therefore be concluded that the evaluations of bio-ethical and sexual relations issues, respectively, have become less dependent of each other during the past decade. Furthermore, the analysis of the Scandinavian data has shown that the values for bio-ethical and sexual relations changed in opposite directions and by different mechanisms (for the latter, see below). The bio-ethical values became more permissive while the views on sexual relations became less permissive. Corresponding detailed analyses for the various European countries are so far lacking. However, from the present analyses it can be concluded that the Scandinavian trend towards increasing bio-ethical permissiveness is comparable to the European trend towards increasing general permissiveness, while the Scandinavian trend towards stricter views on sexual relations is contrary to the general European development.

The decreased commitment to Christian values and the increased support for traditional family values and stricter views on sexual relations, suggest that the often found covariation between on the one hand a Christian commitment and on the other traditional family values and stricter views on sexual relations have weakened. Thus, the Christian value system's impact on other cultural dimensions have changed. Such structural changes will, however, not be discussed here. Suffice it to mention that such changes can be seen as a "de-couplement" of formerly associated beliefs and values, an often assumed effect of individualization.

As for the mechanisms of value change, the decreased Christian commitment, the decreased support for stricter views on bio-ethical issues, and to a certain extent, the decreased support for civic virtues, respectively, can be accounted for by intra-cohort value stability together with generational population replacement. These value changes therefore support Inglehart's theory. On the other side, the increased support for traditional family values, strict views on sexual relations, and individualistic values, respectively, cannot be accounted for by such a mechanism. For these value dimensions, the intragenerational value changes are significantly evident for all cohorts. Thus, each generation has become more in favour of individualistic values, strict views on sexual relations, and traditional family values, respectively, during the past decade. This intragenerational value change is the main explanation for the corresponding over-all value changes. The effects of generational population replacement are indeed minor. In this context, it is most important to note that the intragenerational value changes have affected the intergenerational value differences evident in the 1981 data. For the familism and sexual relations value dimensions, there were significant intergenerational differences among the four youngest birth cohorts during 1981, very possibly due to different experiences during the formative years of each cohort. Nine years later, the corresponding intergenerational value differences can*not* be established. Instead, the four youngest generations of 1990 have converged into a seemingly homogeneous value system. This finding is clearly *not* expected on the basis of Inglehart's hypothesis of stable intergenerational value differences. The unexpected finding merits further attention.

A possible explanation for the unexpected Scandinavian cultural shift towards stricter views on sexual relations and increased support for traditional family values, respectively, might assume an unusually strong period effect, capable of dissolving earlier and firmly established intergenerational value differences. In this respect, AIDS can be proposed as a reasonable explanation for such an unusually strong period effect, at least concerning the views on the sexual relations. That AIDS should affect a switch towards traditional family values is perhaps less obvious, but nevertheless possible. Increased support for traditional family relations, including e.g. sexual relations confined to husband and wife, might be instrumental for preventing infection from a deadly disease, disseminated by "free" sexual relations.

That AIDS might have an impact on norms regulating sexual behaviour is assumed by Inglehart. Unless "the spread of AIDS is halted within the near future, we would expect to find a gradual reversal of the growing tolerance towards both homosexuality and extramarital affairs that seems to have emerged in recent decades" (Inglehart 1990, 205). Increasing sense of unsecurity (fear of AIDS) is assumed to increase the need for absolute norms. However, it was not assumed that such changes would affect the intergenerational value differences, assumed by the socialization hypothesis to remain stable.

That the unexpected Scandinavian value changes are not (yet?) found in other countries might be viewed as a compelling and easy argument against AIDS' assumed impact on the norms regulating sexual behaviour. However, the Scandinavian countries being among the most liberal ones concerning sexual permissiveness, people here might be better motivated to change their views on sexual relations than people in countries with less permissive views. That the Scandinavian results are more typical for Denmark and Sweden than for Norway, by tradition less permissive than Sweden and Denmark, is quite understandable from this argument. That the unexpected value changes are most noticeable among those who showed the most permissive views in 1981 is also in line with this point of view. Further support for the hypothesis of AIDS' impact on the growing familism and the increasingly strict views on sexual relations is supplied by analyses showing that those who object to having AIDS-infected persons as neighbours, are more familistic and stricter on sexual relations than those who do not object to such neighbours, even when views on civic virtues, bio-ethical values, Christian values, age, a general tendency to object to various minorities as neighbours, and, *mutatis mutandis*, views on sexual relations or traditional family values, were controlled for ($p < .01$ in both cases). Thus, stricter views on sexual relations and adherence to traditional family values are significantly related to the fear of AIDS. The proposal of AIDS as an explanation for the unexpected Scandinavian value changes has thus gained some empirical support. However, further checks on the possible impact of AIDS on sexual and family norms, using more suitable data, are needed. So far, the hypothesis is tentative only.

Of course, it must be emphasized that the unexpected dissolvement of the 1981 intergenerational value differences is demonstrated, sofar, only by a single study, and that it remains to be seen whether repeated value surveys would yield similar results.

The results have showed the religious values of each cohort to be particularly stable during the period under study. It should be mentioned that other Swedish studies of religious values and behaviours have showed similar cohort stability for other periods as well (see e.g. Hamberg 1991). Furthermore, Swedish Church statistics from the previous century showed that "in periods of Holy Communion rates [...] no systematic age group differences occur. However, in periods of declining Communion rates [...] the younger age groups showed less frequent observances. Thus, the decline in Holy Communion observance rate might be accounted for by the younger generations' abstention from a behavioural pattern still adhered to by the older generations" (Pettersson 1988b, 23). Thus, that religious values do change by the mechanisms assumed by Inglehart's theory can be demonstrated by other data sets and for other periods of time than the EVS data from the 1980s.

Such findings suggest that Inglehart's socialization hypothesis might be especially valid for the domain of religious values. The reason might be found, *inter alia*, in the fact that "we find a more coherent structure among religious than among political values" (Inglehart 1990, 182). In more general terms, the degree of coherence among value systems might therefore be used to qualify the socialization hypothesis. This hypothesis should primarily be applicable to value domains where the level of coherence is comparatively high. From this point of view, the hypothesis that contemporary cultural change is characterized by increasing levels of value fragmentation, becomes relevant (cf. Halman & Pettersson 1994). Increasing levels of value fragmentation would suggest that the socialization hypothesis become less important. The more value systems are fragmented, the less they are coherent, the less they are likely to remain stable once they have been established.

In summary, it can be concluded that two kinds of value change have occured in Scandinavia during the past decade. A declining commitment to Christian values, a lessened support for civic virtues, and a decreasing adherence to strict bio-ethical views, support Inglehart's theory, both regarding the direction of value change and the role played by intergenerational population replacement. On the other hand, the growing individualism might be viewed as consonant with the theory regarding the direction of value change but less consonant with respect to the role of intergenerational population replacement, while the increased attachment to strict views on sexual relations and the increasing positive evaluation of traditional family values are contrary to the theory, both regarding the direction of value change and the assumption of stable intergenerational value differences.

That these unexpected Scandinavian findings are obscured when analyzing value changes in Europe at large, shows that culture shift might well be differentiated and varied, disallowing detailed propositions about identical processes of value change that should be evident throughout all advanced industrial societies. Rather, cultural shift seems to occur by different mechanisms and for different reasons in different cultural regions.

Appendix A

Data files and composition of value dimensions scores

The combined 1981 and 1990 Danish EVSSG data file contains 1,135 and 970 Ss respectively; the combined Norwegian file contains 1,003 and 1,194 Ss respectively; the combined Swedish file contains 928 and 986 Ss respectively. The additional youth sample in the 1981 survey is excluded from the analyses. In order to be comparable to the Norwegian and Swedish data files, the Danish values for 1981 are weighted according to basic demographic criteria.

The total Scandinavian EVSSG data file from 1981 and 1990 thus contains 6,216 Ss. When analyzing Scandinavia as a whole, the national files are weighted in accordance with each country's relative proportion of the total Scandinavian population. These weights are calculated from the fact that the Swedish population is 47 % of the Scandinavian population. The corresponding figures for Denmark and Norway are 29 % and 23 % respectively. Since the Swedish 1981 and 1990 data file contains 31 % of the combined Scandinavian file, the Swedish Ss are weighted by a weight factor of .47/31. The corresponding weight factors for the Danish and Norwegian Ss are .29/.34 and .23/.35 respectively.

The value dimension scores used in the analyses are defined as follows:

1) *A Christian religious involvement score* defined as an additive z-score index of regular monthly church attendance, belief in a personal God, and great importance ascribed to one's image of God (8 or above on a 10-point rating scale).
2) *A Civic virtue score*, defined as standardized factor scores from a one-factor solution of ratings on 10-point justification scales (1 = item can never be justified; 10 = item can always be justified) for a) to claim social benefits one is not entitled to, b) to avoid paying fares on buses and trains, c) to cheat on taxes, d) to buy stolen goods, e) to "borrow" a car, f) to use marijuana or hash, g) to keep money found, h) to lie in self-interest, i) to take bribery, j) to fail to report damage one has done, and k) to threaten workers who refuse to participate in a strike.
3) *A Sexual relations strictness value score*, defined as standardized factor scores from a one-factor solution of ratings on 10-point justification scales for a) married people having an extra-marital affair, b) sexual intercourse under the legal age of consent, c) homosexuality, and d) prostitution.
4) *A Bio-ethical strictness value score*, defined as standardized factor scores from a one-factor solution of ratings on 10-point justification scales for a) to kill in self-defence, b) euthanasia, and c) suicide.
5) *A General permissiveness score*, defined as standardized factor scores from a one-factor solution of the 10-point justification scores mentioned under scores 3) and 4) above.
6) *A Traditional family value score*, defined as an additive z-score index of a) the view that marriage is not an outdated institution, b) the opinion that a child needs a home with both father and mother in order to to grow up happily, and c) a dislike of a single mother who wants to have a child without having a stable relationship to a man.
7) *A General individualism value score*, defined as an additive z-score index for the opinions that a) one often tries to persuade others, b) one experiences great (8 or more on 10-point rating scale) freedom of choice in one's own life, c) workers need not follow their superiors' instructions if not convinced, d) it is important that jobs allow personal initiatives, e) it would be good if individual development would be more emphasized in the near future, and f) it would be bad if authorities would gain more respect in the near future.

For the wording of the various EVSSG questionnaire items, reference is made to IVA (1991) and Harding *et al.* 1986. The Scandinavian versions are described in Listhaug *et al.* (1983), Gundelach & Riis (1991), and Pettersson (1988).

References

Barker, D., L. Halman & A. Vloet, 1993
The European Values Study 1981–1990. Tilburg: IVA, Tilburg University.

Berger, P., B. Berger & H. Kellner, 1973
The Homeless Mind. Modernization and Consciousness. New York: Vintage Books.

Ester, P. & L. Halman, 1990
"Basic Values in Western Europe: An Empirical Exploration". Tilburg University, Department of Sociology, Working paper seriesa. Paper presented at the XII World Congress of Sociology, Madrid.

Ester, P:, L. Halman & R. de Moor, 1993
The Individualizing Society. Tilburg: Tilburg University Press.

Gundelach, P. & O. Riis, 1992
Danskernes værdier. Copenhagen: Forlaget Sociologi.

Gustafsson, G., 1987
"Religious Change in the Five Scandinavian Countries". In: *Religion and Belief Systems: Comparative Social Research* (B Thomasson), vol 10. London: Al Press.

Halman, L., 1991
Waarden in de Westerse Wereld. Diss.. Tilburg: Tilburg University Press.

Halman, L. & P. Ester, 1991
"Trends in Individualization in Western Europe, North America, and Scandinavia: Divergence or Convergence of Underlying Values". Paper presented at the symposium "Growing into the Future", Stockholm.

Halman, L. & R. de Moor, 1991
Information Bulletin EVSSG 1991. Tilburg: IVA, Tilburg University.

Halman, L. & T. Pettersson, 1994
"Individualization and Value Fragmentation: Results from the European Value Study 1981–1990". Paper presented at the XII World Congress of Sociology, Bielefeld, Germany 1994.

Halman, L. & A. Vloet, 1992
Measuring and Comparing Values in 16 Countries of the Western World. Tilburg: IVA, Tilburg University.

Hamberg, E. M., 1991
"Stability and Change in Religious Beliefs, Practice and Attitudes: A Swedish Panel Study". *Journal for the Scientific Study of Religion*, 30 (1).

Harding, S., D. Phillips & M. Fogarty, 1986
Contrasting Values in Western Europe. Unity, Diversity and Change. London: Macmillan.

Inglehart, R., 1977
The Silent Revolution: Changing Values and Political Styles among Western Publics. Princeton: Princeton University Press.

Inglehart, R., 1990
Culture Shift in Advanced Industrial Society. Princeton: Princeton University Press.

IVA, 1991

The EVSSG International Standard Codebook. Available from The Institute for Social Research, University of Tilburg, PO Box 90153, NL–5000 LE Tilburg, Netherlands.

Johansson, T. & F. Miegel, 1992

Do the Right Thing. Lifestyle and Identity in Contemporary Youth Culture. Diss., University of Lund. Stockholm: Almqvist & Wiksell International.

Listhaug, O, 1990

"Macro Values: The Nordic Countries Compared". *Acta Sociologica* 33.

Listhaug, O., A. Todal Jenssen & H. Mysen, 1983

Values in Norway: Study Description and Codebook. ISS rapport nr 11. Trondheim: University of Trondheim.

Listhaug, O. & B. Huseby, 1991

Values in Norway 1990. Study Description and Codebook. ISS rapport nr 29. Trondheim: University of Trondheim.

de Moor, R., 1992

"Value Patterns in Western Europe, the United States and Canada". Mimeo. Tilburg: Tilburg University.

Pettersson, T., 1988a

Bakom dubbla lås. En studie av små och långsamma värderingsförändringar. Stockholm: Allmänna förlaget.

Pettersson, T:, 1988b

"Swedish Church Statistics: Unique Data for Sociologia'cal Research". *Social Compass* 35 (1).

Pettersson, T., 1992

"Välfärd, värderingsförändringar och folkrörelseengagemang". S. Axelson & T. Pettersson (eds.), *Mot denna framtid*. Stockholm: Carlssons förlag.

Turner, B., 1991

Religion and Social Theory. 2nd edit. London: Sage.